THE NINE MYTHS
OF AGING

**Maximizing the Quality
of Later Life**

Douglas H. Powell

W. H. Freeman and Company
New York

Text and Cover Designer: Cambraia Magalhaes

Library of Congress Cataloging-in-Publication Data

Powell, Douglas H.
    The nine myths of aging : maximizing the quality of later life /
Douglas H. Powell.
        p.   cm.
    Includes bibliographical references and index.
    ISBN 0-7167-3104-5
    1. Aged—Psychology. 2. Aged—Health and hygiene. 3. Aging.
4. Quality of life. I. Title.
HQ1061.PG8   1998
305.16—dc21   97–51718
                                                              CIP

Printed in the United States of America
First printing 1998

To my special loved ones:

Ginny; Carolyn and Doug, Jr.; George and Lee; and most of all Michael, James, Peter, Katharine, and Alexa. The love between us gives my life meaning as husband, father, father-in-law, and, particularly, grandfather.

CONTENTS

PREFACE

This book emerged out of my research on cognitive aging. It began a decade ago. At that time I was asked to head a team of experts to develop a cognitive test that might accurately distinguish normal functioning in older adults from those beginning to manifest the first faint signs of Alzheimer's disease and other forms of cognitive impairment. Thanks to the remarkable efforts of our research team and the cooperation of dozens of medical organizations, senior centers, research programs, and nearly 2,000 volunteers, that project was completed. The story of that effort is detailed elsewhere. The pages ahead describe some of what I learned along the way about the aging process.

As a relative newcomer to the field of aging back in the mid-1980s, I was struck by the accumulated folk wisdom about older people that we were unable to verify in our studies. For example, we found a low, not a high, correlation between the physical health of community-dwelling elderly volunteers and their scores on cognitive tests. So, while completing this and other research, I began to collect these myths, half-truths, and oft-told tales, which seemed to have little empirical support in our research. Neither, I later discovered, did they find corroboration in the reports of others. One purpose of *The Nine Myths of Aging*, then, is to identify some of these myths and to articulate what I believe to be the truth about some of these issues. Since I wrote this book as a working clinician who regularly meets with community-dwelling older people concerned about whether their intellectual skills are diminishing and about what they can do to retain their mental vigor, the second purpose of this book is to offer specific suggestions to these older adults about maximizing the quality of their later years.

As I have carried out the research that is at the foundation of this book, my appreciation has grown for gerontologists, who labored in this field in relative anonymity during the third quarter of this century while generations of their colleagues focused on children and adolescents, youth, and adults in midlife. Among those to whom I feel a particular debt are James Birren and Vern Bengston, whose significant contributions began in the 1960s; K. Warner Schaie and Sherry Willis, who founded, nourished, and reaped the harvest of the Seattle Longitudinal Study and whose publications dominated the 1970s and 1980s; and, more recently, Timothy Salthouse and his Georgia Tech colleagues, as well as Paul and Margaret Baltes and their coworkers at the Max Planck Institute in Berlin, whose recent publications have much influenced my thinking.

The key points made in *The Nine Myths of Aging* are nearly always based on more than one study, carried out in more than one location, and using more than one group of subjects. Reference notes, keyed to specific page numbers, are collected at the end of the book. Their function is to amplify, qualify, or clarify many of the statements contained in the text.

This book reveals a lot about me and people I know. Part of the reason is that the personal anecdotes were intended to lighten some of the heavier going. But, also, as I began to tell these stories, I found I enjoyed it. All the anecdotes and vignettes, including some about me, have been altered slightly to make identification impossible or to create a more interesting story. To my knowledge, no story is completely accurate.

The reader will find a strong emphasis on cognitive aging, because this is the topic I know most about. There is a serious attempt, however, to include other facets of the aging process that include physical, psychological, and social aging. I also want to acknowledge up front that I am writing about the population I know best, which is largely a more advantaged, upper-middle class, well-educated group of women and men. The extent to which findings specific to these populations generalize to other groups remains to be demonstrated.

This book would not have been possible without the vision of the Board of Directors of the Controlled Risk Management Insurance Company, Ltd. (CRICO) and the Risk Management Foundation (RMF) of the Harvard teaching hospitals. It was this Board who saw the need for a cognitive screening test shortly after the passage of Public Law 99-592 in 1986. This law forbade age-based mandatory retirement as of January 1, 1994. They encouraged and funded research upon which this book is largely based. Thanks, too, to the Florida Medical Association, who permitted us to recruit physicians from their organization, and to the county medical societies of Florida, who opened their doors to allow us to test nearly a thousand physicians during the development of MicroCog. Particular appreciation is extended to Dr. James Perry, then President of the FMA; the deans of the University of Miami, University of South Florida, and University of Florida medical schools; and Dr. William Hale, the founder and director of the Florida Geriatric Research Program. The FGRP provided the largest number of "normal" (that is, nonphysician) subjects for research.

Over the three years that this book has been in preparation, a number of people have labored over the manuscript. Thanks go to them for their efforts: Michelle Bertucci, Belinda Chu, Janet Cooper, Katherine Fromm, Erin Joyce, and Maryjane Quinn. My friend, chef extraordinaire, and agent, Dick McDonough, encouraged my early efforts to find my "voice." This book has benefitted greatly from the editorial assistance provided by Ayisha Day, Susan Finnemore Brennan, Elizabeth Knoll, Georgia Lee Hadler, and Jodi Simpson, and the production work of Maura Studley, and Sheridan Sellers. And, finally, my wife, Virginia, has had the wisdom to know when to offer encouragement and support and when to be silent during those times I needed to find my way through the thicket unassisted.

INTRODUCTION

As I drove out of the service station, I heard the faint noise of something rolling down the car's trunk and fallng onto the highway. The sound was familiar. It was the distinctive rattle-rattle-clunk that a gas cap makes when you have rested it on the trunk of your car while filling up, and then drive away, having forgotten to screw it back in. "Oh, no," I thought, "Not again." I had heard that same sound several months ago at this very same gas station. I was frightened. "Well," I thought to myself, "this must mean that I really *am* losing it." In the last three years I had been through two cataract surgeries and cancer, and had an arthritic knee scoped. Did I mention my heel spurs? Obviously, my body was going. Maybe my brain was not far behind.

That night I told my wife what had happened and finished up with the conclusion that, having entered the seventh decade of my life, my mental powers were obviously slipping. Perhaps I should take that early retirement package Harvard was offering before I started to embarrass myself in public.

There are advantages to a long marriage. She smiled, "But, Doug, you have always been like this. Remember the time in 1966 when we were taking the kids to the Midwest. You forgot to put the gas cap back on in Ashtabula, Ohio." My daughter chimed in, "And how about the fact that you are always losing your glasses?" She recalled two occasions when I had frantically searched for my glasses just before leaving for work. Each time she had looked at me and said, "Daddy, your glasses are on the top of your head." My son reminded me that over the decades my aging briefcase has been returned to me from a half-dozen different places after I had left it behind.

They were right. Forgetfulness has been a quality of mine for many decades. So why was I so willing to believe that this most recent gas cap incident was proof that my mind was going? Why didn't I laugh along with the others now, as in the past, chalking it up to my usual absentmindedness? Because I had turned 60 that previous December was why. That was the birthday I had most dreaded—the end of middle age, the start of twilight time, most of the good chapters behind and the bad ones ahead. Each of us seems to have in our minds a particular birthday when we believe that the prime of life ends and old age begins. Now I recognized that I was starting to look for evidence that I was becoming an old man. It is not so surprising, then, to believe that my memory was headed South because I was elderly.

The next day I stopped by the service station and told the manager about the incident and inquired whether he had seen a green Volvo gas cap. He laughed and said he had not found that one. But he had others. In fact, he had a plastic grocery bag half-filled with gas caps from every vehicle imaginable. "Have you noticed any pattern," I inquired, "among the people who drive off without replacing the gas cap?" imagining that he would tell me they were all senior citizens. He responded "Nope. They all forget. Kids, old folks, women, men, everybody." Then he added, "They probably all had something else on their minds."

That comment reminded me that on the afternoon of my most recent gas cap incident I had been on my way home to talk to my wife about our baby grandson, who might require surgery. It also reminded me that every time I had misplaced my glasses or briefcase I had been either preoccupied, in a rush, or trying to do two things at one time—or all of the above. The forgetfulness had much less to do with the number of candles on my birthday cake than with how many thoughts were simultaneously filling my mind.

My reaction to the misplaced gas cap brought home to me how vulnerable I was, how vulnerable all of us are as we grow older, to misconceptions, half-truths, and myths about aging. We are influenced by this type of folklore because we increasingly fear the negative consequences of aging in the fourth quarter of our lives, and this apprehension makes us fair game for these myths that may contain a kernel of truth, but are exaggerated, oversimplified, and generalized to fit all.

I should have known better. For the five years prior to the gas cap incident, I had led a team that developed a test designed to distinguish high-functioning physicians and other professionals from those showing the first signs of mental decline. On the basis of tests of hundreds of older physicians and others in late life, I knew very well that age plays only a small role in how vigorous we are in the years after 55. Many of the individuals we evaluated, perhaps as many as half of those under 75 and a third of those 75+, functioned as well as most mid-life adults.

When I think about the strong mental abilities of those septuagenarians and octogenarians, I am reminded of the old-time Cleveland Indians' pitcher, Satchel Paige. Discrimination kept him out of baseball until very late in his career. When he was finally allowed to pitch, he was elderly by major league standards. To a reporter's question about how he could still pitch at 47, Paige replied, "How old would you be if you didn't know how old you were?"

Satchel Paige's oft-cited quote focuses our attention on the difference between chronological and functional age. Determining chronological age is a simple matter of counting birthdays. Far more challenging is the problem of assessing functional age, for which there are no reliable markers. There are no tree rings to count. Efforts to find biological markers of aging by measuring physical qualities, such as heart and lung function, grip strength, ear length, and dozens of other qualities have been unsuccessful.

Functional aging refers to how well we are able to do things related to our life experience. Satchel Paige could pitch well enough to strike out those in their 20s when he was chronologically in his mid-40s. So he was functionally closer to 25 than 45. Similarly, the functional age of a firefighter might be measured, not by his birth date, but in terms of how quickly he can scamper up a ladder to the third floor. Ditto for an airline captain coping with an inflight emergency. And how do you judge the functional age of your active great grandmother? Probably not by her birth certificate. Instead, you assess her functional age by her capacity to care for herself, by how well she drives, and by the degree to which she remains active in the family and in her community. Functionally she may be closer to her mid-50s than her contemporaries, some of whom may be in nursing homes.

Efforts to find psychological test scores that tell us how "old" elderly women or men might be have been no more successful. Psychologists have become quite skillful at measuring features such as attention, memory, reasoning, and spatial ability. But the correlation between these particular aptitude scores and how well someone actually functions in real life is quite small. What we find in both physical and cognitive realms is that the whole is often greater than the sum of its parts. From the seventh decade of life onward, many older people perform surprisingly well in spite of numerous specific limitations. Presently, no existing biological or psychological index can tell us infallibly what someone's functional age might be. We know it when we see it, but, as yet, we do not know how to measure it.

This deficiency brings me to the first of my two motives for writing this book: What can you and I do to remain as physically and mentally vigorous as possible in the years ahead? What good will it do us to live longer unless we can live more fully during these additional years? My own studies on cognitive aging and the work of others I have reviewed while teaching courses on the aging process have brought me pretty well up to date about some of the pathways to optimal aging. I want to share these ideas with you. And I do not mean just you who are getting along in years. This book is also intended for those in the prime of life. Many of the keenest elders I have known began their pathway to optimal aging while still in their 40s.

My second motive for writing this book is that there seems to be many half-truths, misconceptions, and myths about growing older that block the way to maximizing the quality of our later years. If we can look clearly and honestly at the aging process, we are in a better position to understand how we are likely to change as we grow older. Armed with the knowledge of which abilities fall off most rapidly with age and which do not, and being aware of direct and indirect methods we can employ to refresh certain aptitudes, we are in a position to take steps to shallow the downhill glide of some of our skills and actually reverse the decline of others.

Myths about aging need to be dispelled because they cloud the truth. While containing some degree of accuracy, these fragments of folk wisdom often have little practical usefulness; and they may even be dangerous. Take, for example, the use-it-or-lose-it myth. This is the belief that continuing to exercise our minds will enable us to retain our intellectual powers. This folklore about cognitive aging has been passionately maintained in spite of a half-century of research showing that older people use it and still lose it. Cognitive decline, like physical decline, is a normal event in everyone's life cycle.

But there is much more to be said about the subject than that we can use it and still lose it. We need to face the reality of waning intellectual powers by taking specific steps to remedy the situation, just as we have confronted arthritic joints and dimming eyesight. We must recognize that we will probably have difficulty remembering the names of the new people we meet, where we left our purse or car keys, or how to operate a new word-processing program. But, just as we benefit from orthopedic chairs and brighter lights, we also can maintain ourselves at the highest possible level mentally by learning about the normal cognitive changes that accompany growing older and about things we can do to maintain and even upgrade our skills. That's what this book is about.

My research about the aging process over the past decade has lead to the discovery of a number of other myths about growing older. I should hasten to say that these are my own personal nine myths about aging. I have continually encountered each of them over the past decade of research, even though they have little or no scientific basis.

◆ WHAT IS OPTIMAL AGING?

Optimal aging, for me, means continuing to function at the highest possible level in the context of the inevitable limitations that growing older places upon us. In other words, optimal aging is getting the best out of what is possible for as long as possible—physically, cognitively, socially, and psychologically. In the chapters ahead we will identify those actions we can take and those circumstances we can place ourselves in that raise the probability of our own personal optimal aging.

A useful way to think about how optimal aging differs from normal aging is to consider the difference between a 6-volt and a 12-volt battery. When I began driving in the 1950s, cars were equipped with 6-volt batteries. They were peppy in the beginning and slowly wore down: the starter cranked more slowly, the lights dimmed as the battery gradually lost its strength. We spoke of a "low battery," and we charged up these 6-volters. As they aged, the recharges energized them for shorter periods of time. Then, one cold morning when we pushed the starter button, the battery gasped a brief death rattle, and was gone.

Contrast the 6-volt battery's declining life cycle to what happens with today's 12-volt battery. When I tried to start my Volvo one bright spring morning not so long ago, nothing happened. The ignition did not turn over, the lights did not come on, the horn was silent. The night before I had driven home in a rainstorm and everything had worked perfectly. I called Shaun at the Texaco station down the street and he drove up to give me a jump start. When he arrived, he had a new battery in his truck. "I just want a jump start, Shaun," I said, "not a new battery." I went on to opine that something must be wrong with the alternator because no low-battery light glowed the night before when I drove home. A new battery should not be necessary. Shaun smiled, "No one in your generation understands the difference between today's 12-volt batteries and the old 6-volters you had in your cars when you started driving." He went on to give a lengthy description of just how different they were. The bottom line is that a 12-volt battery has no gradual decline in power. They were alive and vigorous last night; this morning they are gone. This model for optimal aging is one we should all embrace.

What evidence is there that optimal agers exist in large numbers? How do we know that there is anything we can do to help ourselves have a better final quarter of our lives than our parents and grandparents did? My evidence that optimal agers exist comes from research using physicians and other adult volunteers to develop MicroCog. This test measures cognitive abilities—attention, calculation, memory, reasoning, and spatial abilities. We gave it to over 1,000 physicians and almost 600 other adults aged 25 to 92 years. When my colleagues and I looked at the scores of those in the eighth decade of their lives, we found that about 48 percent of the physicians and 40 percent of the other adults had scores comparable to those of their middle-aged counterparts. Even when we set a higher standard, about 12 percent of both groups qualified. Others have found the same large proportion of high scorers among their senior subjects. For instance, Benton's research team discovered that 33 percent of octogenarians scored as well as younger adults on eleven separate tests of mental ability. There seems to be a consensus that large numbers of optimal agers are with us.

The next question is, How do they get that way? Is optimal aging simply a matter of genes, having parents and grandparents who were still sharp in later life? Or are there things that we can actually do to influence positively the trajectory of our own very personal aging? The answer is "yes" to both questions. Studies of the IQs of identical twins have found that heredity contributes 50 to 60 percent to the quality of cognitive vigor in the later years. The remainder comes from environmental influences, life experiences over which we have some control. Evidence from the laboratory, from research in the field, and from real-life experience confirms that the choices we make in midlife (and perhaps before) increases the probability of optimal aging. For example, regular moderate exercise is correlated with a stronger cardiovascular system, a more effective immune system, and better memory and reasoning skills. Did you know that health is also associated with how many good friends you have, how you handle stress, and the extent to which you have control over some aspects of your life? And older people who are open to more diverse experiences score higher on cognitive tests than those for whom one day is pretty much like the next.

Starting early has its benefits. Recognizing that cognitive decline may exist from our mid-40s onward can lead to constructive actions that can be practiced over a lifetime. For instance, hypertension has far more serious consequences intellectually for middle-aged adults than for those beyond 60. Several investigations have shown that 40-year-olds with a diastolic blood pressure above 90 mmHg score lower on a host of mental ability tests than do those with normal blood pressure. Controlling blood pressure for midlifers, as well as those of us who are getting along, should be a priority.

Even if midlife is a decade or more behind you, don't despair. We can enhance our physical and mental vigor much later in life than we might imagine. Exercise and weight training for women and men 70 to 98 produced remarkable physical improvement. An illustration of the power of these programs was strength training for 90-year-olds at the Hebrew Rehabilitation Center for the Aged in Boston. After just eight weeks of regular workouts, they increased their muscle strength by 174 percent and walking speed by 48 percent.

Exercise can be mental, too. One of the most exciting breakthroughs in the past decade has been the development of cognitive training programs. Behavioral scientists in all time zones of the United States and in Europe have reported that short periods of instruction with women and men 60+ resulted in higher test scores on subsequent cognitive tests. "How long can people continue to improve?" you ask. "There must be a limit." Gerontologists examined differences in improvement made by subjects who received five hours of training when they were 67, 74, and 81 years old. The two younger groups improved their reasoning and spatial ability to the level of their test scores fourteen years earlier. Even the octogenarians were able to make modest gains.

Most young-olds, and some old-olds, have a remarkable reserve capacity to restore themselves physically and mentally to earlier levels of functioning. All they require is opportunity, motivation, and willingness to work. It can be hard work and there are no guarantees. But doing so raises the probability of living as fully as possible in the fourth quarter of our lives.

WHAT CAN WE DO TO AGE OPTIMALLY?

On reaching his one-hundredth birthday, Eubie Blake, the famous ragtime pianist, said, "If I'd known I was gonna live this long, I'd have taken better care of myself." With increasing life expectancy, most 55-year-olds have another three decades of life ahead of them. Thus we are well advised to heed Eubie Blake's advice. Moreover, for our society to function in the new millennium, it will require the contributions of vigorous elders. So what advice would we have given a 40-year-old Eubie Blake? What advice do we have for ourselves at 55 or 75?

Scientific knowledge has already improved the health of many elders. A 1997 report by the National Academy of Sciences notes a dramatic decrease in the proportion of Americans over 65 who are unable to care for themselves because of ill health. In 1982, about 25 percent of US citizens 65+ were disabled. In 1994, the percentage was 21.3. This decrease means that 1.4 million older Americans who would have been disabled had the proportion of those in ill health remained at 25 percent are able to care for themselves today. Numerous reasons have been offered to account for these gains: less smoking, better diet, more weight loss, better control of blood pressure, increased consumption of aspirin to reduce heart attacks and strokes, estrogen supplements to reduce women's risks of cardiovascular disease and osteoporosis.

Impressive as these gains have been, they are the result of scientific research in the 1970s and 1980s. Today much more is known about other actions we can take to optimize our personal aging process. These new discoveries about optimizing the quality of our growing older lie in four domains: optimal physical aging; optimal cognitive aging; optimal social aging; and optimal psychological aging.

The chapters ahead contain quite a bit of advice. Each of the next nine chapters begins with a myth that I once believed, or at least did not dispute whenever I heard others voicing it. After presenting the myth at the beginning of each chapter, I will look at the evidence contradicting this belief and present my version of the truth about the subject. The second half of each chapter will provide specific suggestions to help us along the pathway to optimal aging. Here is a summary of the key points in the chapters that lie ahead.

Myth 1: Aging Is a Boring Subject

A surprising number of informed people who should know better believe that the topic of aging is boring—because they assume that nothing can be done to alter the quality of our later years. In fact, aging is a more interesting topic today than at any previous time in history, for several reasons: demographic (senior citizens are more numerous now than ever before and their proportion of the total population continues to grow), physical (a greater proportion of oldsters are leading healthier and more vigorous lives), legislative (mandatory age-based retirement is now prohibited by law), and economic (in the next decade the United States will need workers 65+ to continue on the job). Because American society will need the contributions of its elders in the new millennium, innovations will be required to accommodate the special needs of older individuals who continue to work.

Myth 2: All Old People Are Pretty Much the Same

The stereotype is that older women and men all look, act, and think alike. The truth is that groups of seniors have a far greater spread in physical and mental abilities than midlife adults do. While the capacities of some individuals inevitably decline with age, many individuals in their 70s, and a few beyond 80, func-

tion as well as younger counterparts. Research shows that between 40 and 50 percent of the factors contributing to optimal
aging are within our control. These factors include regular
moderate exercise, diverse intellectual interests, and frequent
contact with the younger generations. Optimal agers also avoid
self-inflicted ageism, keep anxiety under control, and practice
selection, optimization, and compensation.

Myth 3: An Unsound Body Equals an Unsound Mind

The myth is that poor physical health is often associated with
reduced mental powers. This half-truth comes from clinical
observations of injured or ill patients who exhibited lower
mental capacities. The reality is that the mental powers of
older community-dwelling adults are increasingly independent
of their medical histories. In fact, we can have a lot wrong with
us physically and still remain sharp intellectually. This statement has been verified in my own and several other centers.
However, some physical conditions *do* adversely affect intelligence, for example, cardiovascular disease and high blood pressure. Recommendations for maintaining a sound mind within
an increasingly unsound aging body include avoiding heart
problems and maintaining normal blood pressure through diet,
exercise, and appropriate medication.

Myth 4: Memory Is the First Thing to Go

Many of the jokes about getting older are about failing memory
for names and things. This myth persists despite nearly unanimous agreement in the scientific community that other mental
powers nose downward before factual memory declines. Reasoning and spatial skills, processing speed, working memory,
and dual-task attention begin to slip first. Suggestions to compensate for the predictable lessening of these powers include
setting aside plenty of time for complicated tasks, finding ways
to augment working memory, and avoiding tasks that require
you to do two things at one time. These compensating activities
are profitably begun in midlife.

Myth 5: Use It or Lose It

According to this misconception, we can continue to carry out challenging mental activities at the same level as long as we continually practice them. This myth is alive and well in spite of fifty years of research showing that we use it and still lose it as we grow older. The "it" refers to intellectual capacities. In spite of normal age-related losses, however, most of us will be able to function competently well into the fourth quarter of our life span. Actions that help us maximize our capacities in later life are valuing experience (including knowing our individual reactions to stress, valuing hard work, seeking expert assistance, and knowing the rhythm of things), working smarter (doing only one thing at a time, avoiding sudden changes in priorities, paying attention to diurnal cycles, and working through others), mobilizing environmental support to compensate for a reduced working memory (using electronic assistance and databases, accessing computerized expert systems for analyses, and devising strategies for memory retention), remaining committed, and watching out for self-inflicted ageism.

Myth 6: Old Dogs Can't Learn New Tricks

This falsehood still exists in many corners of the work world. Yet no myth has been more thoroughly disproved than this one. Scientists studying community-dwelling older people in different parts of the world and in the laboratory have produced evidence that physical and mental capabilities can be improved dramatically with practice. Brief cognitive training sessions enhance reasoning and visual spatial skills. So do indirect methods such as exercise and meditation. Ditto for the physical domain. Aerobic and anaerobic training dramatically improved muscle strength and flexibility. Opportunities for continuing growth abound for seniors willing to challenge themselves. Elderhostel and Outward Bound organizations have special programs for older women and men, as do colleges and universities. Presently oldsters are learning to use personal computers in record numbers and spend more logged-on hours each week than the average teenager does. With more people working longer, organizations will benefit from actively encouraging their older employees to continue to upgrade their skills.

Myth 7: Old People Are Isolated and Lonely

Contrary to this widely held belief, research shows that most people cope with predictable losses among close friends and family without experiencing lengthy periods of loneliness. Among those who have lost loved ones, there is a difference between being alone and being lonely. Most elders living by themselves do not report feeling lonely when they have the security of knowing that they are connected to others who care about them. Things we can do to lower the probability of a lonely old age include starting earlier to reweave social networks, seeking virtual friends on the Internet (SeniorNet specializes in older folks), choosing quality over quantity (a few compatible close friends are better than a large number of acquaintances in our late prime), recognizing that women and men have different social needs, and getting used to accepting the care of others.

Myth 8: Old People Are Depressed, and Have Every Right to Be

Although growing older inevitably brings with it losses, the overwhelming majority of seniors cope with these negative events without developing a lengthy depression. Indeed, women and men 65+ report fewer signs of depression than midlife adults do. When both younger and older volunteers were asked to rate their overall happiness, those who classified themselves as "elderly" marked themselves above average on the happiness scale just as often as younger and midlife subjects did. Suggestions for keeping our spirits up as we age are planning carefully and well in advance if we wish to continue to work, seizing opportunities to play, coping with stress effectively, enhancing immune system function, monitoring our mood state and taking action if we get depressed, and conducting a life review.

Myth 9: Wisdom Requires Being Smart and Elderly

Wise people are often portrayed as intellectually gifted and gray haired. While these characteristics are found among wise people, the qualities of wisdom set down over the past 2,500 years by thinkers in both the East and the West have little to do with eiither intelligence or old age. They are modesty, kindness, dispassion, and self-control. These are not the components of traditional IQ measures. These aspects of wisdom derive from life circumstances common to nearly all of us. Wisdom does not require getting older, but it does seem to come from suffering, a life fully lived, self-knowledge, and continuous learning. Wisdom comes more from making the journey than from reaching the destination, and it is within the reach of all of us.

Summing Up: Guidelines for Optimal Aging

Distilling the advice of previous chapters yields several suggestions for action to increase the probability of our own individual optimal aging. First, because the quality of our lives is greatly influenced by health, we need to do all we can to maintain those aspects of our health we can control. In other words, we should follow sensible guidelines for what we put into our body. We should keep our blood pressure under control, take medication when necessary, and follow a regular, moderate exercise program to enhance cardiovascular and immune system functions. (It is hard to think of something exercise is *not* good for.) Other suggestions include being open to diverse experiences, learning to use a personal computer, developing various ways to cope with the stress we will inevitably confront, paying attention to differences in the needs of women and men, recognizing that, for many, full retirement is overrated; and cultivating reserve capacities. Evidence clearly indicates that starting to follow these guidelines early improves the likelihood of a vigorous later life.

There are no guarantees here. Bad things can happen to the good and the industrious. And much remains to be discovered about the pathways to optimal aging. But what is crystal clear is that the failure to follow these guidelines almost certainly will guarantee a later life of diminished quality.

★ GLOSSARY

Some of the terminology used in this book and the scientific studies cited throughout may not be familiar to many readers. So a brief glossary of frequently used terms and often-cited research is provided below. More detailed descriptions of these terms and scientific investigations are contained in the Notes at the end of the book.

Age-associated changes Many of the downward trends in test scores described in this book are age-associated changes. That is, they are correlated only with growing older and are not, strictly speaking, the cause of the decline.

Baltimore Longitudinal Study of Aging (BOLSA) In 1958, more than 1,500 male participants ranging in age from 17 to 96 entered the study. About 700 women participated, beginning in 1978. Every two years, all participants are given a series of physical and psychological tests that take about two and one-half days to complete. This is called a longitudinal study because the 2,200 volunteers have been followed for an average of thirteen years.

Independent community-dwelling older adults Many of the statements about older adults (especially the old-old (75+) age group) apply to volunteers for gerontological research who live in the community on their own. The results of these studies do not generalize to those who did not choose to participate in these investigations, and/or were unable to do so because of ill health or confinement in a residential care facility.

Mayo Clinic Older Americans Normative Study (MOANS) Five hundred and twenty-seven volunteers ranging in age from 56 to 97 from Olmstead County, MN, who considered themselves normal and were considered cognitively normal by their personal physician, were the participants in this study. Investigators hoped to use this population to establish norms for testing that could be applied to individuals with a range of clinical problems. Extensive health and cognitive measures have been obtained on these individuals.

MicroCog   A computerized cognitive test measuring attention, memory, reasoning, calculation skills, and spatial ability.

MicroCog Study   The participants, 1,002 physicians and 581 normals ranging in age from 25 to 92, were given Micro-Cog. Test score averages were calculated for each ten-year age group. Subgroups of the participants were given other tests and questionnaires.

Old-old   The less vigorous phase of growing older. It typically refers to individuals whose age is 75+. Also called "last season" or "fourth age."

Rectangular model of optimal aging   A model of aging in which physical and intellectual powers are maintained at the highest possible level for as long as possible, with a brief rapid decline at life's end.

Reserve capacity   Unused capability indicated by an improvement in physical or intellectual facility of older adults after direct or indirect training.

Seattle Longitudinal Study   One of the first large-scale studies of the intellectual changes associated with age. The study began in 1956 with over 5,000 volunteers in the Seattle area as subjects. They have been tested about every seven years through 1991.

Variability   This term refers to how widely the scores for a particular age group are dispersed. Usually scores of older age groups have greater variability, that is, they are more widely scattered than the scores of younger cohorts are. Thus, the scores of subjects from 35 to 44 years tend to show less variability than those of subjects 65 to 74. Other terms meaning roughly the same thing are standard deviation, variance, and dispersion.

Young-old   The more vigorous phase of years beyond middle age. The term usually refers to the age range 60 to 74.

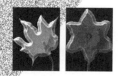

MYTH ONE:
AGING IS A BORING SUBJECT

I was trained to work with children and adolescents. The first twenty-five years of my career were devoted exclusively to young people in schools and universities. I still do this work. So it was not a complete surprise to see the looks of confusion, bordering on incredulity, when about ten years ago I told several of my colleagues that I had accepted the job of heading up a research project on cognitive aging. Several smiled and chalked up this change of direction to a midlife crisis. And one especially good friend, Jim, said straight to my face, "Why would you be interested in old people? You've spent your whole life working with youngsters. They are exciting, vigorous, growing; society welcomes them because their productive years lie ahead. Old people are worn out, sick, everything's failing; society marginalizes them because the best part of their lives are behind them. How could anyone find that interesting? Aging is such a dismal, boring subject." That smarted.

When I retorted that this research could lead to results that might enable us to find ways to improve the quality of our later years, Jim sneered, "Probably all you'll be able to come up with is bunch of bumper sticker nonsense: 'I'm not getting older, I getting better.' or 'Aging is a matter of attitude.' Everyone knows it's all downhill after the big Five-Oh! And there's nothing much you can do to change it."

Well, Jim, at the time I didn't have much to say, because we were just starting our work understanding the aging process. But now I know a lot more. For instance, I know that there are lots of things within our power to do that can positively influence the quality of our own personal aging. Jim, this book is for you—and also for the rest of you who want to learn how exciting the world of aging can be.

◼ THE REALITY

During the past decade, I headed a team of experts who have developed a new cognitive test—MicroCog—that can distinguish those well-educated older women and men who are continuing to function at a high level from those whose capacities have been compromised. Along the way, I learned a great deal about the cognitive aging process, especially in well-educated, competent individuals.

Consider, for example, the fact that better-educated individuals tend to lose their mental powers more rapidly as they age than do people with lower initial abilities. Longitudinal studies of the cognitive aging of people nearly always discover that more years of education is highly correlated with higher scores on intelligence tests in older age. That's the outcome in bold print. But the material in a smaller font often makes another crucial point. Although people with the most education have the highest test scores throughout most of their life span, the gap narrows because those with the highest marks at 60 or 70 lose relatively more of their abilities in the next decade or two.

In other words, the people with the most intelligence to begin with have the most to lose as they age.

We discovered that, whereas the majority of individuals in a group of 65- or 75-year-olds may trend downhill in some abilities, quite a large number of those 65+ continue to function on a par with individuals in their prime. We called the group that didn't decline optimal agers. The gap between their high intelligence scores and those with ordinary intelligence in the prime of life did not shrink over the next several decades. As we looked more closely at these optimal agers, we found that many of them engaged on a daily basis in kinds of activities different from those who were aging normally. We found support for our ideas about the behavior of optimal agers in the research of others worldwide—there were optimal agers everywhere, women and men who were doing things to alter the normally declining trajectory of their intelligence, as well as their physical abilities, in the last quarter of their lives. This was exciting. Definitely not boring.

CHALLENGES AND OPPORTUNITIES IN OUR AGING WORLD

Our adrenaline really started pumping when we looked beyond our own studies in the late 1980s and recognized that the entire field of aging was going to be an exceptionally important topic for the next several decades. Dramatic changes have occurred in the United States and elsewhere over the past quarter-century, changes affecting not only older people but the rest of us as well. These changes are demographic, physical, legislative, and economic. Demographically, senior citizens are more numerous today than at any time in the past, and the proportion of senior citizens in the world's population continues to grow. Physically, a substantial number of older women and men live healthier and more vigorous lives, and they will want to continue to enjoy activities from which they have previously been excluded. Legislatively, mandatory retirement on the basis of age is now illegal for most occupations. Economically, the US society in the first decade of the twenty-first century will find that it needs to employ older workers beyond what has been the normal retirement age.

Each of these changes unsettles the status quo. And, make no mistake, they present serious challenges with which each of us must deal. But they also offer substantial opportunities to extend the number of years of optimal aging into the next millennium.

Demographic Trends

Nearly everyone knows that America is graying. In the United States in 1990, there were more people 55 and over than there were teenagers. By the year 2000, one American out of seven will be over 65; twenty-five years later the proportion will be one in five. These projections probably underestimate the actual growth in the post-65 group. The 85+ group, presently numbering over three million, is the fastest growing segment of the population. Greater numbers of elders is not a uniquely American phenomenon. By the year 2025, the 65 and over population in Japan will double. The People's Republic of China, Korea, and Malaysia all anticipate a tripling.

These statistics play out in everyday life when we take a moment to notice. At the church in the small New England town where we live, it was customary for the congregation to stand during parts of the worship service. About five years ago, this line appeared at the bottom of the program: "All who are able may stand." Elsewhere, shopping malls allocate increasing numbers of parking spots for the handicapped, most of whom are elderly. On a recent flight to San Antonio, I was struck by the gaggles of wheelchairs at the arrival gates—chairs ready to receive older travelers, frail in body, but adventurous in spirit.

Politicians feel these demographic changes. The legislation that the American Association of Retired Persons (AARP) lobbies against has little chance of passing. Every politician serious about being elected to office includes stops at senior centers and retirement communities. The media have caught on as well. It is difficult today to page through a Sunday newspaper without coming across some reference to growing older. Columns for the "Senior Set" or "Over-50" proliferate. New magazines target the mature readers.

The interests of professional, academic, and business people are being drawn to older adults. On returning from summer vacation, my mail included copies of three new professional journals focusing on gerontology. Three psychiatrist friends, who trained with me to work with children and adolescents, now care exclusively for geriatric patients. In the last ten years, the most rapidly expanding divisions of the American Psychological Association have been gerontology and neuropsychology, the latter a field interested in cognitive impairments associated with aging, such as Alzheimer's disease.

Educational institutions are adjusting to the changing demographics. Degree programs training people to provide services to the elderly, for example, physical therapy and home care, are expanding. More and more colleges and universities offer courses on aging. I heard about a new one recently—exercise gerontology. The human development curriculum, which used to devote 90 percent of its time to the years between infancy and adolescence, now includes many more lectures on the phases of adulthood beyond the midlife crisis.

How quickly has American business recognized the needs of the senior market? The other night I had an insomnia attack and decided to edit some of these chapters. Tuning in to a late-night talk show, I heard, back to back, ads for an herb to improve attention and memory, and a drink to ensure that you will keep that promise you made to attend your granddaughter's wedding. A decade ago it would have been hard to imagine hearing a broadcast advertising the merits of adult diapers or a compound to shrink the prostate.

New grocery stores are being built with wider aisles to accommodate independent handicapped elders in battery-operated three-wheel scooters. Companies making light-weight portable wheelchairs, lifting chairs, and similar equipment are doing well. Much of the new construction in our town seems to be for elders: two new nursing facilities, one comprehensive retirement community, and a condominium complex built for older individuals downsizing after the children have left.

Improved Physical Health

Last year on a flight to San Antonio to talk about the myths of aging, I became aware of just how much the enthusiasm for exercise and fitness has grown among older citizens. After we leveled off, I reached into the pocket of the seat in front of me for the airline magazine. From it I learned about the exploits of Helen Klein. She is the 72-year-old grandmother who holds six dozen US and world records in ultraendurance events, such as 100-mile or 24-hour runs.

In San Antonio I picked up the phone book to look up a friend's number and happened to glance at the cover. On it were pictured a dozen remarkably fit looking women and men in track suits. All were well past retirement age. They were participants in that city's Senior Games. These events are held all over the world. That year, at the Senior Olympic Games in Osaka, Japan, there were more than 5,000 participants. The oldest was 83.

Like Helen Klein, many older people who exercise continue to compete at what, a generation ago, would have been an astonishing level of proficiency. One uncomplicated index of the proficiency of today's physically fit older athletes is comparative times for distance running. For instance, the US records for male and female 75-year-olds for ten kilometers (6.2 miles) are 43:24 and 53:40 minutes, respectively. Anyone who has ever tried running that distance will discover just how fast the times of these septuagenarian runners are. What is even more impressive is how much the performance of older athletes has improved relative to that of younger adults. Take the best US time for running ten kilometers. Among those in the age group 40 to 44, the records have dropped 3.4 percent for men and 1.0 percent for women in the past ten years. In the 70 to 74 group, the improvement has been 10.6 percent for males and 8.6 percent for females.

Little doubt exists that the physical vigor of many present-day 55-, 65-, 75-, and even 85-year-olds is superior to that of their parents and grandparents at the same age. Exercise is a priority for many. However, much of this improvement comes from an understanding of the benefits of eating more healthfully—reducing the amount of fat, cholesterol, and calories in our diets and adding more fruit, vegetables, and fiber. Adults of all ages know about the value of stopping smoking and moderating the intake of alcohol and caffeine.

For me, the contrast between those active, attractive seniors and my memories from childhood of older relatives and friends was startling. I retain vivid pictures of constant smoking, regular heavy alcohol intake (although no one considered himself anything but a "social drinker"), and daily consumption of heavy meals. Although some worked outside with their hands, most couldn't have run around the block and would have considered you insane if you suggested it. In their mid-50s, they looked and acted elderly.

Today not one of my male friends smokes, although most of us did at one time. None uses much alcohol, and most favor decaf. All retain an interest in physical activities: they run, hike the Appalachian Mountain Trail, kayak or canoe, or play golf or racquet sports. They work out at home and at a gym. I hasten to admit that I am no paragon of fitness (30 percent butterfat at the last calibration), but I try to work out regularly. When I go to Phil's Gym, he produces a workout schedule for the rowing machine geared to my age. No more do I have to follow guidelines for 40-year-olds. Now I judge myself against the chart showing how fast the average male, 60–69 (heavy), can row 2,000 meters.

Not all seniors enjoy athletic competition or getting sweaty. But better physical health in old age opens the way to activities that may have been closed to them in middle age—especially opportunities for play and spending time with friends and family. For most, full-time work limits the freedom to play, to create, to express our individuality. On the whole, organizations that employ us require us to adapt to their systems and demand that we restrain our unique qualities.

Retirement from full-time work brings with it a number of opportunities for experiencing our individual uniqueness and creativity through playful activities that were not available to us when we were working. Mark Twain's character Tom Sawyer persuades his friends to whitewash his fence by presenting the task as an activity that he pretended to enjoy, not as a chore he had been made to do. In this scenario, Mark Twain has put his finger on an important difference between work and play. Work is what we are obliged to do, he tells us, whereas play is what we are *not* obliged to do. To use our leisure time creatively, we should take on activities that we choose freely, activities that don't evoke a sense of dreary obligation—growing a garden full of roses, reading all the works of Eugene O'Neill or Virginia Wolfe, learning to waltz or tango, playing the piano or the recorder. Although these activities may require more energy than our work ever did and may be frustrating, they are play and not work because we don't have to do them every day and we don't have to be an expert.

Playful activities also are a vehicle for creating new connections with others. Among working adults, good relationships with fellow workers are rare. Many working environments have become so competitive or "cubiclelized" that friendly relationships are impossible. "I make it a policy to avoid having friends at work," one executive told me. "I hardly know anybody in my company," said a staff assistant. "My work and my social life are totally separate." But the social networks of both have grown substantially since their retirements as a result of their common interest in Habitat for Humanity. They have become members of a group called "RV gypsies" who work for Habitat for Humanity. All over 60, this particular group of men and women migrate in recreational vehicles from place to place, spending two weeks here, a month there, constructing houses for Habitat. Most are not experienced carpenters, so they receive supervision on the work site. They enjoy the pleasure that comes from putting up a wall or roofing a house. They also have a wonderful time with one another. Who wouldn't? They get to travel all over the United States, on their own schedules, and feel good about doing something useful. How many paid jobs out there provide all that enjoyment?

Legislative Changes

Recognizing that the capabilities of many older workers are the same as workers in their prime, Congress has passed a law banning age-based mandatory retirement. Initially, two exceptions were made—public safety officers and tenured faculty. As part of the new legislation, Congress directed that studies should be carried out prior to the effective date of the law to assess the potential impact of eliminating mandatory retirement for these two groups. More about that in a moment.

The passage of these laws solves one problem but exposes another. These statutes grant opportunities to those among us who deserve a fair chance to lead productive occupational lives. But the challenge is to decide what standards will be used to replace the arbitrary age limits of 55 or 60 or 65 to determine when someone is unable to do the job anymore. The obstacles on the way to replacing age-based standards for mandatory retirement are scientific and political.

Scientifically, we need adequate tests or other mechanisms to determine whether someone has the skills needed to perform in an occupation. Most experts agree that some sort of screening test is the best way to assess whether you or I measure up to the standards your or my work requires. The biggest problem with using tests is that none has yet been able to judge the performance of older workers on the job. Accurate and valid measures of occupational performance are still a decade or more away.

The saddest example of this reality was the FAA grounding of Bob Hoover, who has been called the dean of aerobatic pilots. For decades, he has enthralled air show crowds with his astonishing flying skills. When he was 71, just after completing a series of these remarkable maneuvers at an air show in Wisconsin, an FAA observer thought Hoover looked frail and might be "too old to fly." At the request of the FAA, Hoover took a series of neuropsychological tests. These "showed" that he was impaired and should not be able to fly an airplane competently. As a result, Hoover's license was suspended, even though the FAA did not disagree that Bob was still a skillful aerobatic pilot. This is a little like saying, just after he has been given the Most Valuable Player award in an all-star game, that the former Boston Celtic great, Larry Bird, is not suited to be a professional basketball player because he is too slow and can't jump.

There is another side to this issue, however. Not all those in the seventh and eighth decades of their lives are as intellectually

competent as they need to be to continue their work. I was
reminded of this recently when David, a professor of surgery at
a southeastern medical school and chief of surgery at a large
local teaching hospital, told me about an older mentor of his,
Dr. Cutler. "Cutter," as he came affectionately to be called, was
an orthopedic surgeon of great skill. In his prime, he was
revered by generations of medical students, residents, and colleagues. In fact, he was David's teacher and predecessor as chief
of surgery. But sadly, over the past year or so, Cutter was obviously becoming cognitively impaired. Crucial details of patient
histories slipped his mind. On at least two occasions, Cutter
lost track of what to do next during surgery—he needed one of
the senior attending surgeons beside him when he operated.
He could no longer teach because of a growing tendency to
lose track of the point he had been trying to make a few
moments earlier. Habitually he forgot where he had parked his
car. The last straw was when Cutter nearly operated on the
wrong knee of a patient. No one wanted to confront this venerable doctor, although it was plain that it was time for him to
stop practicing medicine. After talking to his wife and children,
who confirmed the doctor's mental decline, David decided that
on the eve of his sixty-eighth birthday, David and the other surgeons would throw a lavish retirement party for Cutter. Former
students and grateful patients, hospital administrators and politicians, friends and family, attended. Testimonials were delivered, gifts given, and tears shed. Everyone wished him well in
retirement years. The next day David found Cutter back at the
hospital, dressed in his greens, asking why there was no surgery scheduled for him.

Politically, the realities of creating and implementing a system for screening in or out older workers on the basis of scientifically valid testing is far more complex than the development
of the test itself. Just how complex these problems have become
is illustrated by the legislation affecting public service officers
and university faculty. Scientific studies recommended that
both public service officers and tenured faculty be given the
same opportunity as everyone else to continue work beyond the
normal retirement ages for their occupations. Sadly, that has
not been the end of it. At first, Congress ignored the recommen-

dations of the scientific advisory group and continued to require faculty members to retire at the usual age; then they relented and allowed professors to work as long as they desired. Congress initially included firefighters and police officers under the umbrella of other occupations prohibiting age-based mandatory retirement for one year. Intense lobbying by two influential unions representing firefighters and police officers, as well as organizations of local cities and towns, sparked a fierce debate about whether public service officers should have to retire at a specific age. As these words are being written, Congress is still arguing the pros and cons of this law. Stay tuned.

Common sense is beginning to resolve some of the problems of older individuals who want to stay on the job. For instance, older members of the Cornell physics department reached a consensus that they would voluntarily reduce their teaching loads in their 60s and retire fully at 70 to make room for younger scholars. Senior faculty elsewhere are being offered attractive early retirement packages. At the University of Pittsburgh, a plan is in the works to give professors 60 and over a lump-sum payment of two and one-half times their salary for giving up their tenured positions. Provisions may be made for future part-time teaching, office space, and secretarial support. Certainly not all of the solutions to this problem have yet been imagined. Meeting the needs of both the older employees who want to continue and employers who require the highest quality performance from their workers is a challenge that awaits solution.

Economic Needs

It is a good thing that laws now ban mandatory age-based retirement. For the American economy to continue to expand in the first quarter of the twenty-first century, its aging "baby boomers," born in the 1946–1964 era, will need to work longer than before. This prediction may seem implausible in the present economic climate, where recent college graduates have a hard time finding work and the parents of these graduates worry about keeping their own jobs as organizations downsize. Yet, the reality is that fewer young people are entering the workforce today than twenty years ago. In 1990, about 1.3 million young people aged 18 to 24 started full-time employment; in contrast, approximately 3 million persons in the same age group went to work just over a decade before. This reduction in the number of young people entering the workforce is a direct result of what has been called the "baby bust" generation. Born in the years 1965 to 1977, their birth pools were about one million smaller than baby boomers of the two prior decades. Because the baby boom generation still will be in their working prime through the first decade of the twenty-first century, and because all of the baby bust generation will have entered employment by then, the turn of the century will find the average US worker closer to 40 than 30. For these reasons, the economy will need to continue to employ those who have passed their sixty-fifth birthday.

Continuing to work beyond the normal retirement age will very likely entail making adjustments to a changing job setting. As a result, most workers probably will not be employed at 70 by the same organization that employed them at 45. There are two reasons for this scenario. The first lies in the rapidly evolving corporate and professional culture. In highly competitive, bottom line-oriented organizations, lower costs are achieved by mergers and consolidations; by moving the company from Detroit to Tampa, where labor costs are lower; by outsourcing certain functions; and by off-site manufacturing. The result is that tens of thousands of jobs have been eliminated in the United States over the past decade. Although the economy continues to create new positions, they are not the same ones that were eliminated. And many of the newly created jobs require different skills and experience.

The second reason most of us can look forward to several different jobs is that the average age of first retirement continues to decline. In the 1900s, two out of three men 65+ were working. In 1990, only 16 percent of the males and 7 percent of the females held full-time jobs at the same age. The reason for this decline is not clear, although experts point to better pension programs and increased availability of disability benefits. After a year or two, however, many current retirees return to the labor pool. In the past ten years, there has been an increase of nearly 75 percent in the proportion of retirees 55+ who have started working again.

For these reasons and others, the working lives of today's workers will be a little like professional athletes in the era of free agency. No more Joe DiMaggios in Yankee pinstripes or Bill Russells in Celtic green for their entire playing careers. No more planning to work for Big Blue or the Big Three or any other organization from start to finish.

"How depressing," you say? No more job stability or security. No more mutual commitment, "'til retirement do we part." True. But what is also true is that nowadays neither the individual employee nor the employer takes the other for granted. Both are aware of their interdependence. The employer knows the value of keeping competent workers happy. Turnover costs big bucks—about two times a worker's annual salary. For their part, employees know too that they need to remain productive and need to continue to improve their skills to retain their marketability. So the relationship between employee and employer today is far more often driven by merit than by loyalty.

As just noted, a major challenge for the worker in today's corporate climate is maintaining value through the process of continuing growth. Whatever our line of work is, we must stay abreast of new developments in our field. We must read the trade journals, attend our profession's annual meetings, and look for opportunities to learn new skills. Whereas these activities come naturally in our 30s and 40s, they are less appealing in our 50s, and sometimes we are a little embarrassed to show up for upgrading at 60 or 70, when we have more wrinkles, a bigger bald spot, or grayer hair than anyone else in the room. We must stop being self-conscious. If we are going to be players, we must continue to play. That is how we retain our marketability.

My cousin manages a company that rents professional-level employees to organizations on a temporary basis. One growth industry for him is the airplane manufacturing business. I asked him whether any of his contract aeronautical engineers were our age (in their late prime). He thought about it for a minute and replied, "No. Most of the aircraft designers are younger because there are no more slide rules and blueprints. It's all computer assisted design—CAD—now." But then, after a few thoughtful moments, he added, "But if any of those geezers wants to learn CAD, I have lots of jobs for them. As long as they can push their walker through the door, they are employable if they can design an airplane on a PC."

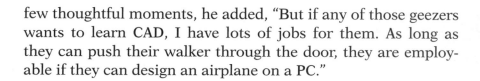 RECAPPING

A number of informed people believe aging is not an especially interesting subject because they think getting older is all about decline and loss. Moreover, they believe that there is nothing that can be done to maximize the quality of our later years. In fact, these are misconceptions. Lots can be done, through activities well within our powers, to improve the quality of our later years. Moreover, this is the best time in history to be growing older. The reasons are demographic—the United States and the rest of the world presently have larger numbers of citizens 65+ than ever before, a statistic that means they constitute a political force to be reckoned with; improved physical health—large numbers of older women and men are far more vigorous than their parents and grandparents; legislative—age-based mandatory retirement is now prohibited by law for most occupations, a fact that will enable individuals to work longer than before if they choose; and economic—today's older workers are likely to be needed by the economy to work well into the fourth quarter of their lives if they wish to do so.

These changes bring with them challenges and opportunities that include providing care, education, and services to a growing proportion of elders; finding enjoyable and useful outlets for a growing proportion of the physically and mentally vigorous senior set; developing tests and other techniques to enable us to distinguish those aging individuals who remain sound in body and mind from those whose capabilities have been compromised by the aging process; and helping older workers who want to continue employment remain marketable.

2

MYTH TWO:
ALL OLD PEOPLE ARE
PRETTY MUCH THE SAME

Remember when you saw your grandparents with their friends? Or the first time you visited an elderly relative in a retirement community? Were you struck by how much alike they looked? My grandparents used to entertain their friends who "dropped by" on Sunday afternoon, as was the custom in the small midwestern town where we lived. I recall thinking how similar they were in their weathered appearance, the clothes they wore, their stiff, sometimes painful movements, and the enjoyment of stories from the past, retold many times. My adolescent eyes found few differences among them in their appearance, their physical vigor, and their mental acuity. As a teenager, I recall thinking, "When you have seen one old geezer, you have seen them all." It did not occur to me then that there was, in fact, far more variety among these similar-appearing elders than among my group of 16-year-old friends.

No doubt what I saw and read about as a child and teenager shaped this view. Until the 1970s, the overwhelming majority of adults I read about or watched in the movies and on TV were vital, involved men and women in their prime. Much was made of the differences among them: their morality (*The Postman Always Rings Twice, Double Indemnity*), heroism (*High Noon, On the Waterfront*), individual traits (*Fountainhead, Shane*). Typical of the middle-aged adults featured in TV families were the Cleavers in *Leave It to Beaver*. When anyone over 60 was portrayed, they nearly always played secondary roles, and my impression of them ranged from negative to benign. I remember them as quirky (Walter Huston in *The Treasure of Sierra Madre*), crippled (Lionel Barrymore as Dr. Gillespie), asexual (Ethel Barrymore in anything), or dying (Barry Fitzgerald in *Going My Way*). Contrast this with the images of older people that today's teenagers are exposed to. They are treated to *Murder She Wrote, Matlock,* and the *Golden Girls* on TV, and they watch bright, competent, vigorous, and sexually active seniors in movies such as *Cocoon, Fried Green Tomatoes, Grumpy Old Men,* and *Carried Away,* which displays 60ish Dennis Hopper and Amy Irving totally nude and making love.

For most of the decades of my adult life, I didn't give any particular thought to the idea that old people were certainly not all the same. Not by academics, not by gerontological researchers, not by professionals, and not by policy makers, was there recognition of the fact that old people were definitely not the same. Until January 1, 1994, American retirement laws made it clear just how strongly held was the view that older people are all the same. Older workers could be required to retire at a particular age: 55 for police officers and firefighters; 60 for airline pilots; 62, 65, or 70 for the rest of us. The "logic" behind these laws is that, after a particular birthday, we are thought to be no longer able to do what we easily accomplished the day before. We are pensioned off, never mind that many women and men at 65 or 75, and some at 80, may be as competent as workers in their prime.

The thinking that old people are all about the same was typical of my generation of academics and practitioners. While I don't think that I ever truly subscribed to these stereotypes about older people, I have no recollection of challenging any of these images—which is strange. When I reflect on my own family, and the elders I saw around me, my beliefs should have changed. There was my mother, for example, who walked two miles to work and back most days, even when she was 72. There were her exceptionally keen friends at the retirement home where she spent the last nine years of her life. I picture her friend, Elsie, who lead a Great Books discussion group. Elsie was 96. Then there was my father, who devoted the two decades of his life following retirement to energetically buying, refurbishing, and reselling "antiques" he found at yard sales all over the state. That was when he wasn't rising at 4 AM to be on the water before the bass stopped hitting. He died at age 84 of a heart attack while trying to push his car out of highway traffic after the engine failed. At the time, I thought my parents and their high-functioning friends were unusual, statistical outliers, not representative of most older people. Now I recognize how much my mother and father and many of their friends were not unique, but in reality represented a large proportion of their age group.

What brought home to me how deeply entrenched was the myth that old people are all the same was a lunch with two producers of a prime-time TV news show. This realization occurred in the late summer of 1995, when it was beginning to be clear that Senator Robert Dole would be President Clinton's Republican opponent in the coming year. The producers had seen our research on cognitive aging and asked me to meet with them. In the middle of an elegant lunch, they got to the point. Specifically, they wondered what types of cognitive impairment could be expected of Senator Dole on the basis of his age—at that time, about 73. The producers took out their notepads expectantly. When I told them that our research showed clearly that you can predict very little about one's memory or other cognitive skills after the age of 60 because of the growing variability among older people, I heard the clicks as their ballpoints retracted and they put away their notepads. That a 70-some-year-old could be on a par mentally with someone in his prime was not the story they wanted to tell.

There are two dangers in the myth that old people are all about the same. First, this belief has served as a basis for age-based mandatory retirement. Although now prohibited by law, widespread discrimination still exists toward older workers because of the implicit assumption that one 55-, 60-, or 70-year-old is just like all the rest. Second, this myth can worm its way into our subconscious, resulting in our suddenly believing that we are too old to do something competently today that we per-formed capably yesterday. In this instance, we become the vic-tims of our own self-inflicted ageism.

★ THE REALITY

Of all the myths, the one which science has thoroughly exploded in the past decade, and the one which nearly every informed gerontologist agrees is false, is the idea that old people are all about the same. "What took you so long?" you ask. The reason is that scientists studying aging have previously concentrated their attention on those statistical analyses called "measures of cen-tral tendency"—in other words, averages or mean scores. And it won't surprise you to learn that these same researchers found that average scores declined with age. Whether they were mea-suring cardiovascular function or IQ score, the typical 45-year-old beats the ordinary 65-year-old, who outperforms the average 85-year-old. No surprises here.

What has been overlooked by focusing on mean scores by age group is what happens to the variability of the scores with each advancing decade. Variability, or standard deviation, refers to how widely scattered the scores are on whatever it is you might be measuring. Scientists have found that IQ scores for a group of 70-year-olds, for example, have a much wider range than do the scores of those who are 40. You can visualize this by holding the fingers of your left hand in front of you and pressing them tightly together. That is what the scores of the

40-year-olds look like. Now, hold your index finger parallel to the ground, but open your fingers as wide as they will go—that gives you an idea of what the spread of the scores of the group of 70-year-olds looks like. Our research team uncovered concrete evidence of the growing dispersion among older adults when we developed MicroCog. We gave the test to 1,000+ physicians ranging in age from 25 to 92. We found that the mental ability scores on MicroCog trended downward with age as we expected. But we also noticed something else. The older physicians had far greater variability than the younger ones. For example, the spread of scores from top to bottom for those 70 years old was 60 percent wider than that for those 40 years old. This increasing age-group variability tells us that old people are definitely *not* all the same. A number of older individuals continue to function as well as individuals in their prime, whereas others in their age group inevitably decline—some quite dramatically.

Evidence for the presence of elders who continue to function at high levels appears all around us. The remarkable physical skills of many septuagenarians were illustrated on June 6, 1994. On the fiftieth anniversary of the Normandy landing by Allied Forces, a battalion of today's 82nd Airborne dropped near Saint Mare Eglis. Following them came a flight of lumbering World War II C-47s from which parachuted several dozen of the original members of the 82nd Division who had landed shortly after midnight on June 6, 1944. Most were well into their 70s and looked amazingly fit in TV interviews. In even better shape than many of those World War II parachuters is Helen Klein, who was mentioned in the last chapter. She is a 72-year-old grandmother who holds six dozen US and world records in ultraendurance events such as 100-mile runs. Thinking that her physical constitution might be something quite special, she was asked to volunteer for a study at the Washington University Medical School in St. Louis. She was found to have the muscles of a woman in her 20s and the bone structure of a 30-year-old. Helen Klein is the physical equivalent of the 70-year-old physicians we tested whose cognitive skills were as strong as mid-life physicians.

On the job, we also witness evidence of high-quality abilities put to use by those close to or beyond normal retirement age. One illustration of the highest quality on the job by an older individual is the saga of Captain Alfred C. Haynes. At 3:16 PM on July 19, 1989, Captain Haynes was at the controls of United Flight 232, flying from Chicago to Los Angeles. While cruising at 37,000 feet, the DC-10 suffered a catastrophic engine failure. The engine in the airplane's tail literally blew up. Pieces of the engine ripped through the tail section, causing the loss of all three of the hydraulic flight control systems, making the aircraft nearly uncontrollable. Captain Haynes and his crew were somehow able to fly the crippled DC-10 to Municipal Airport in Sioux City, Iowa, where the plane crash-landed forty-five minutes later That the aircraft was able to be controlled at all and that there were any survivors in this highly unusual emergency were considered miracles by the aviation community, achievements attributable to Captain Haynes's extraordinary airmanship.

How did Captain Haynes cope with this emergency? The possibility of catastrophic failure of all three hydraulic control systems was considered by the designer of the DC-10 to have less than a one in a billion chance of occurring. Consequently, the emergency United Flight 232 experienced had never been planned for, let alone practiced in simulations. Nevertheless, it did occur; and suddenly Captain Haynes and his crew had no ailerons to control the roll, no rudders to coordinate turns, no elevators to control climbs and descents, no wing flaps to slow them down, no brakes, and no nose wheel for steering when down on the ground. They were left with very little to work with.

The younger crew members required Captain Haynes's years of experience right away. Fourteen seconds after the loss of hydraulic pressure, the copilot reported that he could no longer control the airplane. The aircraft was rolling to the right onto its back, into what is called a "graveyard spiral," a prelude to diving straight into the ground. Instinctively Captain Haynes shut the power off to the left engine and firewalled the right one. This maneuver stopped the roll to the right and the plane slowly stabilized. Afterward, when asked why he did this, he replied, "I do not have the foggiest idea, but it seemed to work." Captain Haynes then found that it took two pilots at the controls simply to keep the plane level. He put a third pilot in charge of controlling the throttles of the airplane. This was a vital function because the only way to turn was to decrease the power on one side while increasing it on the other: turning left was achieved by chopping the power in the left-hand engine and maxing the power in the right one. To descend, they needed to bring back the power in both engines by exactly the same amount.

The miracle was that they were able to get the airplane in the vicinity of an airport. Still, Captain Haynes lacked the precise control needed to land a jumbo jet. The normal rate of descent at touchdown is 300 feet a minute. Their rate of descent when they hit the ground exceeded 1,800 feet per minute. As they hit the ground, the tail and right wing broke off the cockpit, causing the fuselage to turn upside down. That 174 passengers and 10 crew members lived is a miracle, a credit to the instinctive reactions, quick thinking, team leadership, and remarkable skill of Captain Haynes.

At the time of the accident, Captain Haynes was 59½ years old. He had to retire six months later because airline industry regulations stated that pilots could not fly beyond the age of 60 because of the possible "decline" in mental agility associated with aging. It would be very hard to sell this idea to any of the survivors of United Flight 232.

Would other airline pilots verging on 60 have reacted as brilliantly as Captain Haynes on that hot July afternoon? Would most 40-year-olds have done as well? We can never know the answer to these questions. What we do know is that this nearly 60-year-old man piloted an aircraft as well as anyone of any age, at any time, could have flown it.

Suppose that emergency had happened a year later, when Captain Haynes was on the golf course instead of in the left seat of United Flight 232. Suppose that other occupations had mandatory age-based retirement—novelists, physicians, nuns, politicians, musicians, and artists. We would be deprived of the talents of James Michener (89) and Barbara Cartland (95), Michael DeBakey (85), Mother Theresa (86), Nelson Mandela (79), Lionel Hampton (85), who were still productive at the ages shown. Then there was Grandma Moses, who didn't even start painting until she was 78 and continued past her one-hundredth birthday.

The accomplishments of Helen Klein, of Captain Haynes, and of the others, along with research findings worldwide on the increasing age-related variability clearly show that the older we become, the less likely will anyone be able to predict what we can and cannot do physically and mentally. About all that can be safely assumed is how many candles we will have on our next birthday cake.

★ CHARACTERISTICS OF OPTIMAL AGERS

What distinguishes the optimal agers, those whose minds and bodies remain vigorous while the abilities of their contemporaries nose downhill? Is it all in the genes? Or are there things we can actually do to raise the probability of aging optimally?

One way to look at the effects of heredity on mental and physical characteristics is to examine what happens to identical twins who have lived most of their lives apart. Swedish scientists tested 80-year-old identical twins who had the same genetic makeup, but who obviously did not share the same environment for most of their lives. They found moderately strong correlations between the IQs of these octogenarian twins. They estimated that about 60 percent of the factors contributing to the similarity of cognitive ability was genetic and the rest related to environmental influences. Other reports summarizing the findings from dozens of twin studies have found that heredity accounts for 50 to 60 percent of what goes into mental ability. The genetic influence is about the same for physical characteristics such as systolic blood pressure. So it seems that somewhere between 40 and 50 percent of the factors affecting how we function are related to environment rather than to genetic makeup. What are these environmental forces?

Current research is trying to identify the environmental factors that are correlated with aging optimally. One such investigation was reported in the doctoral dissertation of Susan Anderson. She separated 40 older male physicians into high and low groups on the basis of their scores on MicroCog. Subjects in the high-scoring group were called optimal cognitive agers (OCA), and the others were labeled normal cognitive agers (NCA).

Anderson then constructed an extensive questionnaire about behavior patterns she thought might influence how well the mind worked. There were questions about physical activity (for example, exercise, energy level, sex drive), intellectual involvement (for example, taking courses, reading for challenge or pleasure), social networks (for example, primary relationships, number of friends, frequency of contact with children and grandchildren, memberships in clubs or organizations), and psychological factors (for example, mental state (depression, anxiety, and anger), means of coping with stress, and inner feelings of optimism, joy, or competence).

Nearly thirty significant findings emerged. The OCAs were more energetic and exercised moderately. They also reported higher libido. In the intellectual domain, they read challenging books and magazines, but they also read for fun. Socially, the OCAs had more frequent contact with children, grandchildren, and younger friends than the NCA physicians did. In the psychological sphere, the higher-scoring 70-year-olds regularly felt joy and competence in some portion of their lives. They also tried to create time to be with their families, had more interesting hobbies, and took frequent vacations. In contrast, the NCAs were locked into routines, did not delegate much, and engaged in a smaller number of avocational activities. They took fewer vacation days than the OCA group did. While these findings await confirmation from larger investigations of a more representative group of females as well as males, they give us several ideas about what we might do to maximize the quality of our own personal aging.

In other parts of this country and abroad, social scientists have identified other qualities that optimal agers share. Three of the most useful are avoiding self-inflicted ageism; keeping anxiety under control; and using the process of selection, optimization, and compensation.

Avoid Self-Inflicted Ageism

Ageism is the belief that we can determine what a person can and cannot do on the basis of age alone. It's been "the reason" for discrimination against older citizens. It shares much in common with sexism, racism, and anti-Semitism. Discrimination against individuals on the basis of gender, race, religion, and age has been against the law for over three decades. Prejudice remains, however; and this prejudice needs to be recognized for what it is—and overcome.

Overcoming any prejudice begins at home. In other words, avoid being both the victim and the perpetrator of ageism. You and I and the rest of the elder class may have embedded somewhere in our subconscious the very childish stereotypes of older men and women described at the beginning of this chapter. Perhaps we saw many of them as limited in what they could do because of their poor diets, obesity, and smoking and drinking habits and because of what they thought about and discussed. For some of us, these childhood images of what is appropriate behavior as we grow older condition our view of what we "should" or "should not," "can" and "cannot," do. Thus, in our hearts, we may consider it unseemly that this 70-year-old should don her spandex and work out at the gym four days a week, because we remember our mother and grandmother in a housedress every day, girdle and all. Or a 75-year-old learning how to use a computer is inconceivable to us because no one we knew while growing up ever tackled anything that complicated after midlife. That two retirees we know should leave their small southern town for a fall of Elderhostel programs in Italy rather than retiring to Florida may strike us as beyond unusual.

One way to avoid being a prisoner of these subconscious, irrational views of what is and is not appropriate behavior for seniors is to look for role models. Go where high-functioning oldsters congregate and do what they do. Look for fitness clubs that cater to elders. Consider taking short courses in the worldwide Elderhostel programs, and investigate opportunities for enrichment in the courses offered by local high schools, colleges, and universities. Be unafraid to try new things, especially those things you have always wanted to do but never had the time, energy, or money to do. Learn to paint, play duplicate bridge, downhill ski, windsurf, or access the Internet.

Recognize, too, that there will be moments in the course of our lives when self-inflicted ageism, ever lurking, jumps out at us. Especially vulnerable are those continuing to work in demanding jobs into their seventh and eighth decades. Typically, the demon of self-inflicted ageism tries to colonize our minds just at that time when we fail to accomplish something we value greatly. A good example of the insidiousness of this mental process, and how to overcome it, is demonstrated by my friend, Louise. Married for over four decades to an architect, Louise found her true vocation in her late 40s, when she began selling real estate for a large national firm in Newport Beach, CA. Within ten years, Louise became one of the top realtors in California. When she was 60, she was number one in her state. The next year, two things happened to cause her to think that she was suddenly "too old" to sell real estate anymore. Her husband sold his architectural practice to a junior partner and wanted to spend more time with her on their new sailboat. Then, Louise had a bad year in sales.

Shortly after her year closed and Louise was no longer number one, she had lunch with an old female friend. She sighed, "Maybe I am too old to sell houses anymore. When I look at the pictures of the other realtors beside mine on the page, I look like their mother." Louise wondered if she were too old to continue to do what she had done so well for so long. Her friend commiserated and pointed out that she had put together a remarkable career in real estate, and maybe it was time to let the younger people have their turn. She could spend more time with her grandchildren and sailing with her husband.

Afterward, Louise found herself becoming furious at the suggestion that she pack it in. She talked to a priest. He helped her to recognize how much she enjoyed being a realtor. She loved the competition with bigger agents in Los Angeles and San Francisco. But, most of all, she just purely enjoyed selling. She finally concluded, "I just don't want to leave while the music is still playing."

Louise then replayed the previous year to see whether there were some things that had happened in her work that might explain her less than stellar performance. She found several things that she felt might have contributed. First, she had spent a lot of time getting out her listings on computer and developing her own Web page. As she thought about it, she concluded, "I've spent too much time looking at the monitor and not enough time in face-to-face selling to potential clients." Then she examined the signs that had been put up in the yards of houses for sale and displayed her name. She redesigned the sign and made the size of her name a few points larger.

She had a further insight into why her sales had dropped. She realized that the Orange County, CA, real estate market had become overpriced. The boom of the 1980s was over, and houses were no longer selling for 20 to 50 percent more than the people had paid for them a few years earlier. So she took the initiative to educate her clients to reduce their expectations so that their houses could be priced more realistically. Two years later, Louise's picture was on the front page of the real estate section: Number One Realtor in the State of California and in the Top Ten in the Country.

What prevented Louise from sliding down the slippery slope into self-inflicted ageism? After all, she was among the elders in the real estate business in her area, and a pleasant semiretirement beckoned. Besides her gritty determination to be number one, what kept Louise going were three important thoughts. First, Louise believed that the dip in her real estate sales was caused by factors that were within her control and could be changed, not something out of her control such as her age. Second, she felt this was a temporary setback and would sort itself out with some changes in her approach, rather than thinking that another bad year was inevitable. And, third, Louise believed that she could improve her marketing strategy instead of believing that she had done all she could. That's how Louise overcame her doubts about being too old and became number one again.

Keep Anxiety Under Control

When I was in my 40s, I remember attending retirement parties of friends and thinking, "That must be really nice. No more 70-hour weeks, no more nights with on-call emergencies. No more stress and anxiety. Nothing more to worry about than whether the fish are biting. Just taking it easy and relaxing." I didn't know in those days that retirement does not automatically bring with it the cessation of stress and its attending anxieties. There is plenty to worry about, even when you're not clocking in every morning. Living to a ripe old age may well offer the opportunity to do all those things a demanding job denied or the freedom to fill each day with an itinerary of one's own choosing, including doing nothing at all. But also there is, for many, a gnawing sense of foreboding and apprehension. How much will inflation or a market correction eat into my retirement nest egg? What's the impact on my marriage going to be if I don't go to work every day? Suppose I outlive my friends and there is no one left to care about me except dutiful but distant relatives? How am I going to pass the next driver's license test with my eyesight going? Should I move into a smaller house now, or right into an old folks' community? How healthy will I be and for how long? You get the drift.

Life is no easier for those who remain employed. In addition to contemplating most of the apprehensions just noted, employed elders carry the burden of trying to keep up with the younger generations. You might think that oldsters, with years of proven competence behind them, would have every reason to be self-confident and free of anxiety. In fact, the opposite is true. The elder statespeople in most fields are often quite insecure about their abilities, especially their mental skills. This is not a "new" finding. Over a half-century ago, a psychologist reported results of his efforts to compare cognitive test scores of older and younger faculty at a large California university. The investigator reported that several faculty did not volunteer because of unmistakable signs of test-taking anxiety. They conveyed their feelings thusly: "No! I just can't go through with it!" or "I'm afraid of failure." All were older professors.

Part of the reason for the discomfort of the older professors is that they "seemed patently anxious to excel," reported the investigators. They "knew" that mental abilities declined with age and that they were at some risk of performing less well than they had in the past, even though they were accomplished in their disciplines. They did not go gently into the acceptance that their test scores might be lower. Many stipulated that they would only agree to be tested at the "most efficient time of the day."

An interesting contrast between the older and younger faculty members emerged with respect to errors. The younger professors, when confronted by their failure, blamed the test items for being "irrelevant" or "silly" and quickly forgot about the experience. The older professors, however, took their mistakes hard. Sixteen of the senior professors apologized to the examiners for their "terrible showing" on the test. None of the 30-year-olds did. Two especially determined older faculty members reported getting out of bed in the middle of the night to solve a problem that had baffled them the previous day.

A number of older successful seniors worry excessively about revealing that they can no longer be the smartest "student" in the class. Without this appellation, they feel diminished, less capable, less worthwhile, even though they still may be at the top of their powers as a professor, physician, scientist, or executive. Furthermore, every day brings with it the potential for meetings, classes, and formal or informal contacts with quick, clever youngsters, contacts in which there is the danger that the professor may be exposed as being a little slower, a little more forgetful, a little less knowledgeable than he or she was before, evidence that he or she is surely "losing it."

So it should not come as a surprise to most individuals in their late prime that studies of community-dwelling elderly consistently find that anxiety is a frequently and strongly felt emotion. Consequently, we need to be prepared for coping with anxiety as efficiently as possible in our maturity. As any teenager will tell you, anxiety is not the special province of the old. Students have plenty to worry about, and so do their parents. Suffering is no stranger to them. How we manage anxiety in our youth and in our prime is likely to follow us into our later years. So think about effective ways of keeping these inner tensions under control in the first and second quarters of your life.

Experts in anxiety management describe two ways of lowering tensions associated with stress—problem-focused coping and emotion-focused coping. As you might imagine, problem-focused coping actions confront a problem directly. This approach can involve taking direct action to alleviate inner tension by reducing the stress itself. For example, if your former workaholic husband has retired and is now spending all his time and energy around the house telling you how to reorganize your spices, you can directly deal with the situation by saying, "stay out of my kitchen," thus removing the source of stress.

Emotion-focused coping actions reduce anxiety by soothing inner tensions rather than by confronting and eliminating the source of stress directly. Doing nothing to remove the source of the tension, they simply reduce our overall level of anxiety. They're valuable when we have to play the cards that were dealt. This might mean living with loneliness or a bad family situation, coping with declining health, poverty, or a nasty job. Under these conditions, we turn to things that calm our nerves, revive our spirits, and help us through the night.

One method of keeping our anxieties under control is by putting unpleasant feelings out of our minds. Some call these psychological self-protective responses "ego defenses." We suppress or repress these thoughts to maintain a stable mood. Among Harvard graduates now in their 70s who had been followed since just before World War II, those in the best health also had the highest rankings on their ability to soothe their anxieties while still remaining aware of the stresses in their lives. For example, the healthiest among them used suppression rather than repression to calm their nerves. Suppression involves consciously putting difficulties out of our mind while recognizing what we are doing and making plans to confront a problem later when we can deal with it. Repression involves shutting disquieting thoughts out of our minds with no plans to deal with them later. That often creates more problems than it solves.

A second type of emotion-focused coping response is to seek relief through medication, exercise, prayer, and other activities that divert our attention from stress. Many find chemical relief. In fact, more than any other country, citizens of the United States count on drugs to reduce emotional upset. Antianxiety and antidepression medications outsell other prescriptions. Coming up fast are potions for sleep. Various self-medications help us manage the ravages of stress. Without coffee in the morning, cigarettes throughout the day, and a few drinks later on, many believe they would not be able to hold themselves together.

Some people count on other physical ways to soothe jangled nerves. Take exercise—"I need to work out every day," a 74-year-old friend of mine said as he was coping with a terminally ill spouse, "Without it, I'd go mad." Other relief comes in the form of religion or prayer. The Bible tells us that suffering is a part of our lives. Many of us are comforted by feeling part of a religious community, by hearing the words of the ancients who have suffered and endured, and by singing those old hymns, which fill our hearts with joy or bring peace.

The secular world has its comforts, too. Many have had their suffering reduced by meditation, yoga, relaxation training, and other psychological techniques. All these techniques have a well-documented record of soothing tensions. Some of us seek other activities of a nonmedical, nonreligious, nonpsychological nature—distractions that provide respite and give pleasure. These activities can be as diverse as reading a good book or watching a TV show, walking in the woods or on the beach, having tea with a friend, playing cards or chess, golfing, sailing, going over a collection of stamps or coins, or shopping. Temporary as the relief these activities give may be, they also provide a welcome time out from our problems. Life, after all, is lived in the short run.

What have we left out in thinking of ways to soothe our tensions? We have forgotten to list the value of talking to loved ones about our problems. This third kind of emotion-focused coping includes talking to someone who can listen, be sympathetic, and perhaps be helpful. It's not necessary for them to give us advice about how to solve the problem creating the stress. It's enough that they are there for us.

Investigators in the Midwest and on both coasts have all found that the quality of our lives is positively influenced by how many people we can count on when we are under stress. For instance, middle-aged midwesterners who had more friends, relatives, or coworkers that they could talk to about their daily hassles were found to have fewer physical symptoms and were slightly happier than those with smaller social networks. A report from Pittsburgh found that resistance to colds was correlated with the size of the circle of friends. Having more friends was associated with better health. Among the Harvard graduates, those in the best physical and psychological health were those who also had closer ties to families and friends.

It turns out that the emotional support these networks provide is even more important to our physical and mental health than activities that directly assist us. It's not necessary that a loved one do anything in particular as long as they are available emotionally. This finding reminds me of the truth of the phrase, "Don't just do something, stand there."

This is not to say that having someone encourage us to stay on a proper diet following coronary problems or to exercise regularly, or drive us to the physician is not valuable. It certainly is. It's just that being there for us is of equal or even greater value.

Studies of well-adjusted older volunteers also find that these women and men regularly use a mix of problem-focused and emotion-focused responses to stress. Volunteers from three Eastern cities used both types of responses. They used problem-focused coping mechanisms slightly more often than emotion-focused responses. For instance, a man worried about his periodic cardiac arrhythmia talks to his physician and learns all he can about the causes of these rapid heartbeats and what he can do to reduce their frequency. A woman in her 70s, still working part time, feels marginalized by her new younger boss. She confronts him directly and finds that he had assumed that she was about to retire. When she tells him she has no plans to leave, he welcomes her back into the inner circle.

Differences do exist between how younger and older adults cope with stress. For instance, in California, 70-year-olds dealing with stress were more likely to seek emotional support and less likely to confront unpleasant events directly than those in their 40s. Midlifers were far more willing to tackle a problem head-on and were slightly more reluctant to share their troubles with others. Differences exist, too, in how individuals react to stress. Some elders seem to thrive on mild to moderate difficulties in their lives. Their moods and health actually improve instead of worsening with a dose of tension in their lives.

Anxiety, then, is not an emotion we leave behind in middle age. Plenty of hassles and more serious stresses lurk in the fourth quarter of our lives. So it is worthwhile to examine periodically the problem-focused and emotion-focused anxiety management tactics we use. Are we allowing our son and daughter-in-law to depend on us to babysit when we would rather take that course at the community college? Should we think about a confrontation to clear the air? Are we toughing out our worries about our spouse's cancer when talking to a friend would surely help? Continued monitoring of how we are coping with stress helps us avoid putting up with any more than we have to as we grow older.

Practice Selection, Optimization, and Compensation

My personal favorite method of optimal aging is called selection, optimization, and compensation. This strategy was developed by psychologists at the Max Planck Institute in Berlin. As we might assume from the title, the essential ingredients in this method of coping with getting older can be broken down into three steps. First is selection. As we age, there is an advantage in narrowing the range of our activities, concentrating our energies on those that are most important to us and giving up those that are less central. Those activities that continue to have priority are usually selected because of our skills, motivations, and opportunities. In our prime, we jogged, backpacked, played tennis, and golf. By the time we reach our mid-70s, it's just golf, which provides enough exercise and good companionship. We can practice the same type of selection on the job. An ophthalmologist in Boston whom it has been my good fortune to know told me he gave up retinal surgery twenty years earlier but continues to consult with other practitioners, sees tricky cases, and works in his laboratory nearly every day. He is 84.

The next ingredient is optimization. This approach means doing everything we can to maximize our performance at those things that we choose to do. It might entail something as simple as scheduling our most challenging tasks for times of the day when we are at our best. An example is visiting with the grand-children in the morning when we are sharper and more ener-getic. Or, if a professor is a morning person, she may want to teach her difficult statistics class before noon, when she is at her diurnal peak. The small, less-taxing research seminar is put off to the afternoon. Optimization requires more preparation. The older professor also recognizes that she needs to be more thoroughly prepared for her lectures at 68 than she was at 40. So she constructs handouts with detailed examples of how par-ticular statistical problems are to be solved.

Compensation is doing everything we can to bolster fading abilities. Glasses and hearing aids compensate for impaired sight and hearing. For those continuing to participate in athlet-ics, compensation may mean using orthotics, braces, and pain medication for creaky joints so that we can continue to play those games we love. For the widow needing to drive alone from Chicago to visit her children in northern Wisconsin, her compensation might entail getting help from AAA in the form of a TripTix showing the best route to her destination. If the initial phase of the trip is especially complex—say, getting from her apartment through the city to the interstate high-way—she might want to make several practice runs until she is comfortable. When she leaves the interstate near the small town where her daughter and grandchildren live, she may plan to stop and obtain final directions at a service center, verifying her planned route.

An illustration of selection, optimization, and compensation is the later career of Arthur Rubenstein, the famous pianist. In his 70s and 80s, with age taking its inevitable toll on his physi-cal abilities, he wanted to continue his career as a soloist. He used the process this way. Rubenstein played fewer pieces in his recitals. He selected those he most enjoyed and could play best. Then he optimized his capabilities by practicing much more than he had in his prime. But the aging process slows up how fast we can make our fingers move, no matter how hard we practice. How would he compensate for this physical slowing when some passages require the pianist to play very rapidly? He compensated by playing the slower passages even more slowly, so that when he played the up-tempo movements the contrast made it seem as though the allegro was moving at a fast pace.

I don't play the piano, but I do play tennis. Years ago, I had a lesson in selection, optimization, and compensation before I knew what it was. It was the day I played with Colonel Jarvis in San Antonio. I was out by myself on a hot, late Sunday morning, practicing my serves when a tall, spare, elderly gentleman approached. He inquired whether I would like to hit with him. At that time, I was 26 years old, physically quite fit, and a competent tennis player. After we rallied for awhile, Colonel Jarvis asked if I would like to play a set. I said, "Sure," thinking to myself, "I'll take it easy on this old guy. Can't have him dropping dead of a heart attack in the middle of the rally." No event could be further from the reality of what transpired. Colonel Jarvis had flawless strokes, was never out of position, and never ran unnecessarily for a ball he could not reach. He baffled me with an exquisite selection of spins, chops, lobs, and the occasional wicked cross-court backhand. The first set was no contest. The second set wasn't that close either, as Colonel Jarvis consistently returned my best shots, rattling me into unforced errors.

After our game, I invited Colonel Jarvis back to our apartment for a cool lemonade. I asked him how he had managed to play so well. Although he didn't use the precise terms, Colonel Jarvis described his judicious selection: He never ran for a ball he could not easily return, and he never tried to do too much with the shots other than keeping the ball in play. Then he told he how he used optimization: Recognizing his declining powers, he took regular lessons from the coach at one of the local universities, focusing on his cross-court backhand. To keep sharp, he regularly worked out with the college's varsity players. And I can see today how he employed compensation: His wicked cross-court backhand seemed a great deal faster when it was preceded by slow lobs and chops. When I asked him his age, he told me: "I will be 77 at my next birthday," and smiled.

Since then, I have been beaten regularly by someone many years my senior. And the story is always the same. They have selected tennis as the game they wish to play seriously, focusing their energies on that one sport. They have optimized their performance by staying in good physical shape, practicing consistently, and getting expert coaching. They play regularly, almost always with younger individuals. And they compensate for the lack of power by mixing up their shots. You see a lot of chops and spins and lobs; then, just as you are getting ready for those, they smash a backhand by you.

I have learned from the Colonel Jarvis's of the world. Now, in the seventh decade of my own life, I find myself practicing hard, getting lessons, and playing with younger people. Thus, I lie in wait, ready to play tennis with my son and son-in-law, and daughter and daughter-in-law, and grandchildren, too. I hope to pass along to them the same lessons about optimal aging that Colonel Jarvis taught me on that hot Sunday morning.

★ RECAPPING

The myth that old people are pretty much the same has been a common stereotype in the United States for most of the past century—despite anecdotal and research evidence that a significant proportion of elders are able to function physically and mentally at the level of those in midlife. Moreover, there appear to be things each of us can do to raise the probability of maximizing the quality of our later years.

This myth is dangerous on two counts. First, it is the basis of age-based discrimination because the skills of all older people are presumed to decline at the same rate. These mandatory retirement laws have been overturned, but much informal age discrimination remains. Second, it is the basis for self-inflicted ageism. In this case, the older individual is both the victim and the perpetrator. After a particular birthday, there is sometimes a tendency to blame an embarrassing moment or a bad year at work on being "too old" rather than looking for other, more realistic reasons for the problems.

Studies of high-functioning older physicians found they were more often engaged in moderate exercise, read for fun as well as challenge, had more frequent contact with the younger generations, and felt joy or confidence in some portion of their lives. Other suggestions for aging optimally involve avoiding self-inflicted ageism. Louise's case illustrated how to overcome self-inflicted ageism by seeing the problem as within her control, seeing that improvement was possible, and deciding that she could take concrete steps to turn things around. In addition, it is useful to practice ways for controlling anxiety, a growing problem for older individuals. Both problem-focused responses (confronting a stressful situation directly) and emotion-focused responses (talking to friends, medications, relaxation techniques, suppression) are useful. Finally, selection, optimization, and compensation are qualities that many optimal agers share. Selection involves narrowing the range of activities in which we engage; optimization entails maximizing our performance by practice and scheduling what we select; and compensation consists of doing everything we can to bolster our capacities.

3

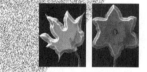

MYTH THREE:
AN UNSOUND BODY
EQUALS AN UNSOUND MIND

$\mathbf{O}$f all the accumulated lore about aging, the statement that struck me instantly as the most believable was "An unsound body equals an unsound mind." What could be more obvious? The mind is part of the body. It stands to reason that people with thick medical charts may have a weakened intellect. Besides, every student in psychology and medicine is taught from the beginning about how certain diseases and injuries impair mental operations. Every day our clinical work confronts us with patients whose physical problems result in greatly diminished intelligence, giving validation to the idea that an unsound body can result in an unsound mind. An excellent book on neuropsychological evaluation devotes a chapter to all the physical conditions that compromise intelligence. The list is long: head injuries, strokes, infections, tumors of the brain, toxic exposure, drug and alcohol abuse, and nutritional deficiency. Physicians, psychologists, or other practitioners constantly see patients devastated by these physical conditions. In my own clinical training and practice, I don't recall ever hearing my supervisors or senior colleagues saying in public that the correlation between mind and body vigor may diminish in an older nonpatient population.

This belief is especially worrisome for those of us getting along in years. From our family and friends, we have first-hand knowledge of the deterioration in health that accompanies growing older—Grandmother is diagnosed with diabetes, one uncle has a brain tumor, another a heart attack, and a cousin is diagnosed with epilepsy. At 60 something, we are not in very good shape either—a former smoker, we still drink more than one glass of wine a day, have had surgery for cancer, and are taking medications for high blood pressure, glaucoma, and vertigo. With this list of medical problems and daily medications, we begin to wonder whether our mind isn't weakening at the same rate as our body.

THE REALITY

The truth is that we should not automatically assume that physical deterioration inevitably leads to mental decline. We can have a great deal wrong with us physically and remain intellectually competent. Moreover, we should not be shocked to discover that community-dwelling seniors functioning normally will report a history detailing a number of problems that we know are often associated with diminished mental faculties— learning disabilities, smoking, depression, neurological problems—and still be keen. I don't have trouble understanding how psychologists and physicians come to believe in the "unsound body equals unsound mind" theory. But we should not generalize from a clinical population seeking professional help to seniors who are not patients. Among a large proportion of com-

munity-dwelling older people, physical state is not highly correlated to mental ability.

The evidence calling into question the "unsound body equals
unsound mind" thesis came from our own studies and from
research at the Mayo Clinic. The logic of the "unsound body
equals unsound mind" theory had seemed so obvious that
before our study no one had tested this idea with a normal community-dwelling elderly population. In the summer of 1988, we
created a medical questionnaire that was given to each of our
participants on the same day they took MicroCog, our mental
ability test. This comprehensive form queried the individuals
about a history of twenty different medical events—head
trauma, heart condition, cancer, thyroid deficiency, high blood
pressure, epilepsy, diabetes, Parkinson's disease, and other neurological illnesses known to be associated with cognitive
deficits. In addition, we inquired about a history of other physical problems that could compromise thinking—learning or
attentional problems in school, alcohol or drug abuse, smoking,
cataracts, and toxic exposure. Then, we obtained a detailed list
of medications the participants were taking as well as their history of hospitalizations. Finally, because health includes mental
health, we asked the subjects whether they had been depressed.
We left nothing out.

The first group we looked at were fifty retired Harvard faculty and staff living independently in the Boston area. Expecting
to find that the professors in the worst health would obtain the
lowest scores, we were surprised to discover that little correlation existed between their medical history and how well they
scored on our test. One professor in his ninth decade whose
medical record included a stroke, hypertension, diabetes, and
cancer obtained one of the highest scores. A 77-year-old who
arrived in a wheelchair told me with an ironic smile that he was
able to answer "Yes" to all but two items on the medical questionnaire. His score was in the top 20 percent of these scholars.
At the other end of the spectrum were two apparently robust
men who reported almost no physical problems. The scores of
both were so low that they suggested the presence of
Alzheimer's disease.

I vividly recall looking at the high test scores obtained by men and women with serious medical problems and thinking, "Is it really true that an unsound body equals an unsound mind?" But because we were working hard on the development of our test and preparing to give it to over a thousand physicians and several hundred others, this question was pushed out of my mind. Two years later, we again looked at the relationship between the reported health of the older physicians and their scores on cognitive testing. We found confirmation for what we had discovered earlier—there is only a tiny connection between physical and mental vigor. This time we knew we were on to something. We presented these findings at the annual meeting of the American Association for the Advancement of Science in the winter of 1991.

To our surprise, many in the audience reacted to our findings with disbelief. One eminent scientist must have found our data so dissonant that he couldn't even hear what we said. After my paper, he stood up and said, "I'm glad you verified my belief that as long as I stay physically fit, I'll keep mentally sharp!" Several commented that our research must have been flawed in some way because "everyone knows" that any number of physical problems are associated with compromised intelligence. Several mumbled about "other studies" that were said to contradict our findings.

A later review in the *Journal of the American Medical Association* labeled as "surprising" our published findings that health status in our subjects was only slightly related to cognitive functions. Another said this was a "troublesome conclusion." It continued: "Readers are advised to exercise interpretive caution . . . in accepting these conclusions." No evidence was cited to rebut our findings.

What was the finding about the mind-body relationship that caused such a negative reaction? It was the finding that the mental ability scores of most of the physicians who responded positively to each of the medical questions differed little from those of the healthiest participants. The major point of our results was that, with a few very important exceptions, mental ability was not much influenced by medical history—at least in this population of volunteers. For example, physicians who reported preexisting conditions (such as learning or attentional disabilities) that we had believed might lower intelligence scores were no different from all other physicians. Ditto for those with a history of strokes and neurological problems (excluding Parkinson's' disease), and for those with treated hypertension and diabetes. Neither did reported exposure to toxic chemicals, smoking, and alcohol and drug abuse result in lower cognitive test scores.

Most of the physicians had been in the hospital at one point or another in their lives, and nearly half were presently taking medication. Overall, no relationship was apparent between being in the hospital or taking medication and mental acuity. "But," you might wonder, "how about hospitalization for conditions that might affect our thinking, such as a brain tumor? Or, how about medications such as tranquilizers?" To answer this question, a senior psychiatric colleague identified those subjects with hospitalizations and/or medications that he thought might have the potential to disrupt intellectual functioning. Ten physicians who were hospitalized or were taking medications for motor problems, such as myasthenia gravis, had a substantially lower performance on the mental test—perhaps because of the necessity of operating a computer keyboard. No other relationships were found.

One medical condition was moderately correlated with lower intelligence scores—a history of heart problems. Our medical questionnaire did not inquire further into the nature of the cardiac difficulties. In retrospect, it would have been helpful to know whether their symptoms were sufficiently severe to require heart surgery. Testing at Long Island Jewish-Hillside Hospital of patients awaiting coronary bypass or valvular replacement surgery has found lower than average attention, organizational skills, and reasoning. Unfortunately, surgery did not seem to improve the mental functions in many patients.

This time when we uncovered the low correlation between the body and the mind, we looked for other investigations that had found similar results but had used techniques and volunteers different from ours. Then, we could be more certain that our reservations about the "unsound body equals unsound mind" theory were valid. We found a similar study at the Mayo

Clinic, a medical center located about ninety miles south of Minneapolis, MN. It is famous worldwide as the place to go for sophisticated medical treatment. In addition, it provides primary medical care for a large population in the Upper Midwest. With access to the medical records of a large number of individuals using the Mayo Clinic, researchers there recruited over 500 volunteers to participate in a study comparing health to scores on intelligence tests. The volunteers spanned the ages 56 to 97, averaging just over 72. Individuals were included if they were living independently in the community and were considered to be cognitively normal by their primary care physicians.

A unique aspect of this study was that the medical information on each volunteer was provided by his or her Mayo Clinic personal physician and was up to date. That is, the health status of the volunteers did not depend on a self-report as it did in our study. Although there is no reason to suspect that the physicians in our study were not completely open in completing their medical history, the results would be more convincing had we had access to their medical records.

The Mayo research team looked at three measures of health for each volunteer: the number of diagnoses assigned, the number of physical systems involved, and the number of medicines prescribed. The participants were divided into three groups: The top third were called the "best," the middle third were labeled "common," and the bottom third were called the "worst." Then the relationship between these measures of health and scores on IQ tests were compared.

The story told by their analyses is that they, like us, were able to discover only a small relationship between objectively measured health and intelligence. Take, for example, how the number of medical diagnoses corresponded to IQ scores. Those with the best health had two or fewer diagnoses and obtained an average Full Scale IQ of 107; those in the worst health scored 105, a negligible difference. The Verbal IQ was exactly the same (105) for both groups—those in the best and the worst health. The Performance IQs were 109 for the Mayo volunteers with zero to two diagnoses and 105 for those with four or more. Although statistically significant, this difference is very small. When the IQ scores of those with the smallest and largest number of physical systems compromised by illness were compared, no differences at all were discovered.

Finally, the Mayo Clinic researchers looked at the question of whether the number of medications taken were associated with lower IQ. Those taking the most medications (four to seven) obtained a Full Scale IQ of 106, precisely the same as those in the best group, who filled no more than one or two prescriptions regularly. Again, the Verbal and Performance IQs of both the "best" and the "worst" subjects were not different.

Of course, we need to be careful about assuming that the physicians in our study or the Mayo Clinic subjects are just like everyone else. It could be that those physicians who volunteered to be tested were an unusually superior group of individuals who were not representative of all the physicians in Florida, where we did most of the testing, and that those people in the Upper Midwest who participated in the research at the Mayo Clinic were not the same as their neighbors who preferred to stay at home. Perhaps the nonvolunteers might have been sicker and would have scored lower on the tests. We don't know whether this is true or not. What we do know is that research reported by others in Berkeley, CA, and Atlanta, GA, support our findings and those at the Mayo Clinic—an unsound body does not inevitably lead to an unsound mind.

"Surely you are not saying that being physically unfit is the way to be mentally sharp at 70 or 80 or 90," a student listening to a lecture on this topic inquired. No, that is not the take-home message from studies finding a low correlation between health and intelligence in elders. The bottom line from all these findings is that the "unsound body equals unsound mind" equation is a half-truth. We can have a great deal wrong with us—as measured by medical events or hospitalizations or the number of diagnoses or the number of medications we take—and remain mentally vigorous. Our physical whole is greater than the sum of its parts. That having been said, it is also true that there are physical functions that we must take particular care to maintain if we aspire to continued mental vigor.

As I write these words, my mind drifts to Dr. Hale, an 84-year-old medical researcher who has continued his unusually productive career well beyond the retirement time of most of his contemporaries. He performed heart surgery into his 60s and less complex procedures until he was 75. Still carrying on research and teaching medical students in Boston, Dr. Hale was working on procedures to reduce the complications following valvular replacement when I met him. Hearing of our research on cognitive aging, he called to ask me if he could be tested. His motivation, as it turned out, stemmed from a recent encounter with one of his medical school classmates. His colleague said somewhat nastily, "Are you still working? With all you've got wrong with you physically, there is no way you can still be sharp enough to do research." So the physician came in to see whether his mind was in fact following the same decline curve as his body. His scores on our aptitude test put him in the top 10 percent of physicians 50 years of age. Dr. Hale thought he should have done better. Most interesting was his medical history. He reported having glaucoma, ringing in the ears, a hip replacement, prostate cancer, and diabetes. The last time I saw him, he had just coauthored a revision of his 2,200-page textbook on cardiac surgery. When I asked about his future plans, Dr. Hale replied that he was planning to attend the quincentenary celebration of the Royal College of Surgeons in Edinburgh, Scotland, in 2005. "After that," he said, "I'm flexible."

▓ Maintaining a Sound Mind

How can we maintain a sound mind in a body that may become increasingly unsound with every passing year? One answer is to focus our attention on those aspects of our health that are known to influence our mental powers and over which we have the most control. If the bad news about getting older is that our bodies usually wage a losing battle against the effects of aging, surely the good news is that those physical systems that most influence cognitive vigor are those over which we have the most control. There are some lessons for all of us in the life of Dr. Hale. For instance, he did not have two physical problems we know are especially hard on mental skills—he avoided cardiac problems and kept his blood pressure within normal limits. And he took several preventative measures every week to preserve that keen edge on his mental powers—he maintained a moderate exercise schedule and kept his blood sugar up. His lifestyle represents a good model for all of us.

Avoid Heart Problems

Dr. Hale had no heart problems. Recall that earlier in this chapter the point was made that those physicians in our study with heart problems had lower scores on the aptitude tests. These findings would not surprise investigators in the Pacific Northwest and at Duke University in North Carolina. These researchers have followed thousands of older normal women and men living independently in their communities. As part of their research, the health of the subjects was monitored and IQ tests given. Both sets of investigations found that volunteers with cardiovascular disease (CVD) had lower mental ability scores. CVD embraces a large number of conditions including atherosclerosis (for example, blockage of blood vessels leading to the heart), congestive heart failure, and cerebrovascular disease (for example, narrowing or weakening of blood vessels leading to transient ischemic attacks and cerebral embolisms or hemorrhages). In Seattle, the researchers were interested in finding out what the future impact of CVD today might be on mental ability later. They divided their participants into two groups: those with significant CVD and those without CVD. Both groups were given an aptitude test at the beginning of the study when they were about 56 and then seven years later. When the Seattle men and women were tested again at about age 63, those with CVD had substantially lower scores on overall intelligence than those with no heart disease. Among the Duke volunteers, those with severe heart problems had a greater decline in intelligence than those without CVD. The conclusion—heart disease is strongly associated with lower mental aptitude.

In the last decade, the number of reports appearing about the beneficial effects of exercise programs for older individuals has jumped dramatically. A decade ago, it was rare to read of training programs for seniors. Today, articles in papers and books on exercising elders spill out from all over the world. Research carried out in universities and medical centers across the United States point emphatically to the conclusion that women and men in their seventh and eighth decades of life and beyond can dramatically improve their cardiovascular fitness by adhering to a regular workout program. In fact, in 1989, a medical task force article said that an appropriate exercise program can improve the cardiovascular fitness of a 70-year-old woman or man to the level of a sedentary 30-year-old. A Philadelphia researcher followed 184 previously sedentary individuals 60 to 86 who completed a four-month exercise program. Two years later, only 2.5 percent of those had new-onset CVD. A matched nonexercise control group had a 13 percent occurrence of new heart problems.

Keep Your Blood Pressure Normal

Dr. Hale had normal blood pressure. This seems obvious, doesn't it? What could be less debatable than the recommendation that high blood pressure levels are bad for brain cells. Keeping our blood pressure normal gives our cerebrum the nourishment it needs, whereas hypertension stresses the vessels of the brain.

But, believe it or not, there have been investigations that have reported findings that contradict this common sense. For example, scientists conducting the Seattle Longitudinal Study found that a mildly hypertensive group did not show a decline in most mental skills from 56 to 63. These results were supported on the East Coast a decade later. Nearly 2,000 participants in the Framingham Study have been followed every two years since 1950. They had their blood pressure taken and were given a battery of mental ability tests later on. The news from this study was the same as that from Seattle. No relationship was found between blood pressure at the time of testing and IQ scores.

These findings remind me of the last time I saw my mother-in-law. She was 76 at the time and had battled hypertension all of her life. The dinner conversation that night turned to how IQ tests were constructed. I posed several sample questions, such as general information ("Where is Zimbabwe?" or, "Who wrote Hamlet?"), reasoning ("How are a mosquito and a flower the same?"), and vocabulary ("What does *infrangible* mean?") Our teenage children were amazed to find that their elderly grandmother answered the questions as quickly and accurately as they did. She died the following fall of a massive stroke, doubtless due to the hypertension that had weakened her blood vessels.

Her mental keenness at the end was always a wonder to me, because it seemed that her high blood pressure should have had a greater impact on her mind. But as I thought about it, the answer became obvious. She had been on hypertensive medication for decades. Although her blood pressure was still elevated, it may well have been that the medication she was on helped to control her hypertension enough so that she could remain mentally keen to the end. And doubtless this is why those with high blood pressure in the Seattle and Boston areas were able to retain high-level cognition—their hypertension was treated.

What happens to intelligence when chronic high blood pressure is not treated? The answer comes again from other studies of the Framingham volunteers. Researchers looked at the records of women and men who were given physical examinations biannually from 1956 to 1964. During that time, few individuals in the United States were being treated for high blood pressure. When they compared the blood pressure readings in these early years with mental tests given in 1976 and 1978, those with untreated hypertension scored lower on cognitive tests than those with normal blood pressure. More specifically, increased diastolic blood pressure (that is, the low reading, the pressure when the arteries are at rest) seemed to have particularly negative consequences for intelligence. Every 10-mmHg increase in diastolic blood pressure decreased scores on the cognitive test battery about 2.5 percent. Not a large amount, you might think. But it is more than the average normal decline in overall intelligence from one year to the next at age 70.

Studies elsewhere confirm the findings that elevated diastolic blood pressure is moderately correlated with lower mental aptitudes. Two recent reports also show that the intellectual consequences of high blood pressure are far more serious for younger hypertensives than those beyond midlife. Hypertensives under 40 had far lower scores on cognitive tests of attention, memory, mental flexibility, and reasoning than age-matched normals. The differences on the same measures did not differentiate among older subjects with high and normal blood pressure. The reasons for these differences in the younger groups may be because those with normal blood pressure in their 30s are likely to be functioning at their peak. Thus if the mental acuity of the young hypertensives were compromised just a little bit, it would show up as statistically significant. By contrast, the older group would have started to decline a bit cognitively so that the 45+ hypertensives could score less well on these ability tests and still be in the range of those with normal blood pressure.

The moral of this story for those who wish to remain mentally keen is that hypertension should concern everyone, but most especially young adults.

Exercise Benefits the Mind, Too

One way of avoiding cardiac problems is by exercise. It also improves cognitive functions. Dr. Hale walked 2.5 miles back and forth to work each day. He still loved to hike in the White Mountains of New Hampshire. "Why should I take up jogging just to live a little longer?" a 40-year-old chubby cousin once remarked. "Somewhere I read that if I burned 2,000 calories a week in exercise, I would live 2.15 years longer. By my calculation, that means if I start right now I will be spending all of that extra 25 months on a stairmaster to nowhere." That amusing comment misses the point. The value of exercise is not just to add years to our life expectancy, it is to add years of *high-quality* life expectancy, mentally as well as physically.

"Where's the evidence for this?" my young cousin queries. The evidence accumulating from all quadrants of the country confirms that exercise increases blood flow to the brain. Increased cerebral blood flow in turn results in a quicker, sharper mind. At the Baylor College of Medicine in Houston, physicians

studied the effect of activity on cerebral blood flow. They measured the cerebral blood flow of women and men just prior to
the normal retirement age and then followed these volunteers
for the next four years. They divided the participants into three
groups: working, retired and physically active, and retired and
sedentary. The last two groups were classified on the basis of
how much they exercised. At age 64, there was no difference in
cerebral blood flow in the three groups. Two years later, cerebral
blood flow in the working and retired-active groups was no different from the baseline measurement, whereas flow in the
retired-sedentary subjects had declined. Four years after the
beginning of the study, the gap had widened even further. The
cerebral blood flow scores of the retired and inactive individuals
were far lower than those of the two other groups. Even more
interesting were the results of cognitive tests. The working and
retired-active volunteers scored much higher on cognitive tests
than the sedentary retirees did.

"Just how active do we have to be to get that blood moving
through the brain fast enough to stay sharp?" you ask. One
opinion comes from research on over 1,000 volunteers, 70 to 79,
from around Boston, MA, New Haven, CT, and Durham, NC.
This study concluded that for physical activity to have a beneficial effect on intelligence, it has to be relatively strenuous—as in
working out vigorously about three times a week.

Psychologists in Salt Lake City, UT, might disagree. The
Utah researchers took a group of older adults and divided them
into groups who would receive four months of either moderate
aerobic or anaerobic training. Then they compared their results
with a sedentary group. All were given mental tests before and
after the training. The regimen for the aerobic group consisted
of a moderately stressful workout that varied from fast walking
to light jogging and occurred three times a week. The anaerobic
volunteers did stretching and moderate weight training. At the
end of four months, the two exercise groups scored much
higher on the cognitive test battery than they had in the beginning. There was no difference on the same tests for the sedentary volunteers. The abilities on which the subjects who exercised scored higher spanned a wide range of aptitudes: faster

reaction time, better attention, speedier reading, and greater intellectual flexibility.

So, the jury is still out on how much exercise is necessary to maintain higher levels of intellectual functioning as we age. My guess is that it has to do with how physically fit we are to begin with; those of us in the best shape will need more strenuous exercise to benefit, whereas those who are less fit will require only moderate exercise to make the same gains. The bottom line is that exercise that will help us maintain our mental capacities in the years ahead, whether we are 35 or 75, needs to be regular and at least moderately taxing.

Men Need to Exercise More

When I think of an older couch potato, I always visualize a male. There he is, sitting in the Barcalounger, surfing through the channels, snacking on high-calorie junk food. This man needs cardiovascular fitness training. But how about his spouse? Some interesting male-female differences emerged in several of the fitness reports. It turns out that, if you take a group of older women and men who rate themselves as "sedentary" and give them a regular workout program, there is quite a difference in how much each sex improves. One study found that fitness training raised the vital capacity of the average 65-year-old man almost 80 percent. The typical woman gained 60 percent, a significant gain, but substantially less than that for men in the same program.

"Why might that be?" I asked a couple in their early 70s in our neighborhood. "It's probably because men have more athletic ability," smiled the man. "Not at all," snapped his wife. "While I say that I am relatively sedentary at 73 compared to when I was at 50, I am still far more active than my husband." She went on to describe running up and down three flights of stairs during the day while doing laundry, cleaning, and cooking. Although her husband takes care of some of the yardwork and putters around his workshop, he clearly makes fewer demands on his cardiovascular system than she does. Because the average older woman is likely to be at a higher level of cardiac fitness to begin with than men of the same age, her gains following an exercise regimen are likely to be smaller than his. What this means is that it is important for older men to engage in cardiovascular training if they want to retain their physical and mental vigor.

Keep Your Blood Sugar Up

Dr. Hale took time out in the afternoon for a cup of tea with sugar in it and a cookie. If we are planning to continue to work at an intellectually challenging job in our later years, we need to keep our body fueled. It is no secret that our memory and other mental skills decline with age. One reason is that intellectual functioning is influenced by the amount of glucose (sugar) in our bloodstream. As we grow older, maintaining optimal levels of glucose in the blood is correlated with better cognition. Because many older people eat irregularly and erratically, their mental skills suffer.

The evidence for this recommendation comes from the work done by psychologists at the University of Virginia. These investigators wondered whether normal senior adults would exhibit better memory following the intake of glucose. To answer this question, they gave volunteers who had fasted the night before a beverage containing either glucose or saccharin. Then the individuals took memory tests. The next day they repeated the process but switched drinks. Those participants who had had glucose the day before received saccharin drinks; those who had had saccharin were given glucose. Then they repeated the testing. Memory test scores of each volunteer on sugar and on saccharin were compared, and the results showed that both short- and long-term verbal memory were better on glucose. For instance, the volunteers who had ingested sugar recalled 38 percent more words right after hearing them than when they had drunk saccharine. Long-term memory also increased. On glucose, they could remember more elements of the five-minute audiotaped story a half an hour after hearing it.

These two skills, short- and long-term verbal memory, usually decline dramatically with age. Glucose intake benefits older people in precisely those intellectual domains that are adversely affected by age. The moral is don't starve yourself during the day as you get older. Don't go to work without something in your stomach. Find time to eat a bagel or an apple. Have a cup of tea with sugar late in the afternoon. It will lower your stress level as well as help you keep a sounder mind.

RECAPPING

The "unsound body equals unsound mind" myth is hazardous to optimal aging because it presumes that our minds will follow the same inevitable age-related decline as our bodies. Believing this myth could result in the idea that we are as powerless to retain our mental skills as we have been in keeping 20/20 eyesight, so we may as well give in gracefully to our waning intellectual powers, scale back our expectations for ourselves, cut back at work, and begin to look for a nice retirement community. The truth coming from investigations of the mind-body relationship is that we can remain mentally vigorous despite serious physical wear and tear.

But to raise the probability of our optimal cognitive aging, we must avoid two physical problems we know are related to mental decline: cardiovascular disease and untreated high blood pressure. Exercise—regular and moderate—either reduces the probability of developing these physical problems or lessens their impact. Exercise programs benefit older men more than women because, as a group, females are generally more active than males. Medication to reduce high blood pressure helps us retain our intellectual acuity. And if we plan to remain mentally sharp in the afternoon, we must keep our blood sugar up.

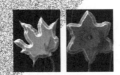

MYTH FOUR:
MEMORY IS THE FIRST THING TO GO

4

"**W**hat *is* his name?" I agonized as I was about to introduce my brother-in-law of 30 years to my next door neighbor, whom we had met while out walking the dog. "When my sister hears this, she will kill me!" I thought as my mind spun its wheels, gaining no traction in the frantic search for his name. Then I heard myself saying, "Helen, I'd like you to meet . . . umm . . . my beloved brother-in-law . . . uh . . . Helen, meet . . . umm . . . well, it's . . . uh . . . well, they say memory is the first thing to go!" Later Bob and I laughed about my failing powers of recall and traded Alzheimer's jokes. That was last month. Last Friday, I forgot we were invited to a Halloween party on Saturday (I had even bought a smashing Dracula outfit at the five and dime) and was reminded of this by my wife when I asked her if she'd like to rent a video to watch that night. Then this morning I could not, for the life of me, remember what you call that thing that you turn eggs over with.

These recent personal experiences seem to be ample evidence that memory—most especially memory for names, events, and things—is certainly adversely affected by getting older. The increasing popularity of jokes about failing memory bears witness to this assumption. In fact, a number of physicians and social scientists have said that we can experience a mild decline in memory in later adulthood in the absence of other cognitive losses. Physicians working with the elderly have labeled these memory problems as "benign senescent forgetfulness." As in the illustration above, it is characterized by intermittent inability to recall familiar names, events, or words. Someone with this condition is usually aware of the trouble and later will be able to bring back this momentarily forgotten material. The condition may gradually worsen with age, and while troublesome and occasionally embarrassing, it does not usually lead to more serious conditions such as Alzheimer's disease.

Another term for this forgetfulness is Age-Associated Memory Impairment (AAMI). To qualify for AAMI, you have to be over 50 with normal intelligence, and have difficulty remembering names of individuals whom you have recently met, misplace objects, and block on telephone numbers or zip codes. These memory problems have to be severe enough to place you in the bottom 15 percent of normal adults on tests of memory. A requirement of both AAMI and benign senescent forgetfulness is that the problems with recall have to come on gradually and not be associated with medical problems such as a stroke or head injury that could account for the difficulties remembering.

A problem with these characterizations of cognitive aging is that they both limit their attention to a specific type of memory loss—blockages in remembering names, events, and things. Although you might think that recall of words and numbers is the primary component of memory, in fact, the process we call memory comprises many different subsystems. There are, for instance, spatial recall and working memory, which we will meet shortly. The real danger in the myth that memory is the first thing to go is that the myth both oversimplifies the concept of memory and obscures the more dramatic decline of other aptitudes while memory is slowly gliding downhill.

⚡ THE REALITY

The idea that memory for names, events, and things is the first thing to go is not so much a myth as a half-truth. This type of memory does weaken with advancing years. But other abilities drop off more precipitously—spatial and reasoning skills, processing speed, working memory, and the ability to do two things at once. If these losses are not recognized and not compensated for, they can have far more serious consequences than the failure to recall someone's name or phone number.

Our aging study produced evidence that memory for names and numbers is not the first ability to decline. We measured the abilities of over 1,000 physicians ages 25 to 92 and nearly 600 normals in the development of MicroCog so that we could see for ourselves when aptitudes first nosed down. We calculated the average scores by age decade (for example, 45 to 54, 55 to 64) for verbal memory (short- and long-term) of story content. We did the same computations with other aptitudes such as recall of number strings forward and backward, spatial ability (remembering the placement of three to five squares lighted for one second on a three by three grid), reasoning (analogies), simple arithmetic, and attention (deciding whether two names shown side by side were spelled the same way).

Then we charted the relative decline in test scores for each ability from the youngest to the oldest group. Not surprisingly, most, but not all, of the aptitude scores were lower with each advancing decade. Because of the belief that memory would be the first ability to fall off, we thought the decline in long-term story recall would be the most noticeable. Instead, we discovered the sharpest decline occurred in spatial relations. The 50-year-old physicians scored 20 percent lower than the 30-year-old physicians. From 50 to 70, the physicians lost another

27 percent of their spatial aptitude. In second place in rate of decline was not verbal memory but reasoning, as measured by the ability to pick which of three choices best completed an analogy.

Was this a quirk specific to the physicians in our sample, we wondered? We would have had more confidence in the thought that memory was not the first ability to deteriorate with age if findings similar to those that occurred with the physicians happened with different subjects. So we looked at the aptitude scores of 581 normals and found precisely the same result. Again, spatial abilities exhibited the earliest and steepest age-associated decline, followed by reasoning. Trailing well behind in third place for both groups was verbal memory. Among the physicians, memory for story content diminished only 6 percent from 30 to 50, and 9 percent from 50 to 70.

When we came up with findings in our research that ran counter to popular opinion, we looked for evidence collected by other researchers who had used other tests with different subjects. We uncovered support for our findings in the work of Timothy Salthouse. He and his colleagues at Georgia Tech searched the literature for reports of age-associated trends in spatial ability, reasoning, and verbal memory. These trends were measured in many different ways, including the types of tests we had employed. When Salthouse drew charts showing the rate of decline in spatial ability, reasoning, and memory from 35 to 75, the results looked very much like our findings. The downward trend in verbal memory was not as rapid as the decline in other abilities, especially spatial relations and reasoning.

Salthouse and other scientists have asserted that other cognitive abilities—processing speed, working memory, and dual-task attention—are more vulnerable to the aging process than memory is. All these functions have been demonstrated to diminish rapidly with age. Take processing speed. Unlike simple reaction time (for example, push this button when that light goes on), processing speed is the rate at which we complete a task involving complicated thinking. Tests of processing speed include learning a symbol-digit code and applying this knowledge under timed conditions, or judging whether two complex figures shown side by side are the same or different. In real life, processing speed might be measured by determining how long it takes us to balance a checking account without a calculator, proofread a letter, or decide the next move in a chess game.

Working memory refers to the ability to store important information while simultaneously working on a related task. Scientists might assess working memory by asking a volunteer to recall a list of five words after first putting them in alphabetical order, or repeat a series of digits in the reverse sequence of presentation. A description more familiar to the computer-literate reader is random access memory, or RAM. For me, an analogy for working memory is my desktop. At the top left are pages of this chapter already written; at the top right are other completed chapters; in the bottom right corner are a stack of rough notes containing the ideas of this chapter arranged more or less in order; and at the bottom left of my desk are piled references I intend to include. In front of me is a yellow pad to write on. As these words are being written, my attention is constantly sweeping the desktop, moving back and forth between the ideas I am presently putting on paper, glancing at my notes to help me decide where I want to take this thought, paging through the references for specific information supporting the text, and looking at the other chapters to be sure what I am writing is consistent with what has already been written. To accomplish complicated tasks, we likewise have to access various stacks of information in our working memory.

Dual-task attention, as you might imagine, is the ability to do two things at one time—the intellectual equivalent of simultaneously rubbing your tummy and patting your head. Researchers studying this ability to carry out two activities simultaneously might have volunteers push a key with their left hand whenever the letter X appears on a computer screen while adding three two-digit numbers heard through earphones and entering the sum on the numeric keypad with their right hand. In real life, dual-task activities might include talking on the telephone to a friend while writing a grocery list, or driving down California Highway 5 ("the Five") while studying the map to determine where to turn off to get to the San Diego Zoo.

⬛ REMAINING AS MENTALLY SHARP AS POSSIBLE WHILE GROWING OLDER

All of these abilities ordinarily trend downward with advancing years. We forget where we left our car in the parking lot: it takes us longer to solve complicated problems; our "desktop" of working memory shrinks from three by six to two by four; and when we do two things at one time, we are in danger of doing both badly. "So, why do I need to know the details of how my mind is going to fall apart?" the 40-year-old wonders. Having the knowledge of what skills are likely to decline first enables us to anticipate these potential weaknesses and plan what we might do to minimize the negative effects of these changes. If we know what some of our weaknesses may be as we advance in years, we can compensate for them so that we can maximize our mental acuity. Here are four suggestions for coping with the most predictable soft spots in our intellectual functioning as we mature: anticipate and rehearse solutions to spatial problems; set aside plenty of time for complicated tasks; augment working memory; and avoid doing two things at once.

Anticipate and Rehearse
Solutions to Spatial Tasks

Not only do I know from our research that spatial capacities are adversely affected by age, but informal observation also confirms this effect. My "laboratory" is the local supermarket parking lot. The management at this new supermarket insists that the employees wheel your groceries to your car. As we walked out the exit, I had a moment of panic: "Where is my car?" Then the memory surfaced—two rows to the left, halfway back on the right. Because I was working on this book at the time and have a theory that remembering where you parked your car is hard for many adults, I asked the high school student pushing my shopping cart, "Anyone ever have trouble finding their car?" "Every day," she smiled. "Yesterday I followed a woman up and down six lines of cars before she located her minivan." Now I always ask that question of the person wheeling our groceries. And the answer is always the same: Lots of people have lots of difficulties finding their cars. But it is a bigger problem for older people. Recently I asked another adolescent about people who had trouble remembering where they had left their vehicles. After thinking about it for a moment, he said, "I think women may have a little more trouble."

In fact, females as a group have predictably more difficulty with certain types of spatial tasks. They are called spatial rotation tasks. Suppose you are facing north; you turn 90 degrees to your left and then another 90 degrees left; then 90 degrees to your right; and finally 90 degrees to your left. What direction would you be facing? (The answer is south.) Some researchers believe that males have evolved special skills in spatial abilities. This aptitude is associated with being a skilled hunter. Our early ancestors had to accurately visualize the trajectory and velocity of the spear he was throwing, as well as the track and speed of the running woolly mammoth, so that they would intersect at a given point. Otherwise, no dinner tonight back at the cave.

Today's men have far fewer challenges that require the application of spatial abilities. An ordinary task at which males of my acquaintance excel is packing the car trunk for a long trip. Men seem to be able to stuff more into the trunk than women can. This may be because they can mentally rotate this bag and that box, or a bag of toys, so that the space is filled completely. Males have been known to get more things in a dishwasher for the same reason.

It is reasonable to imagine that you and I will need to start finding ways to cope with the inevitable weakening of this skill from midlife onward. Here are some things we can do to compensate for diminishing spatial abilities. Take particular care in parking lots to remember where you left your car. In large multilevel parking lots, don't assume that three days from now you will remember where you hurriedly parked your station wagon. Write it down: fourth level, K-13. In shopping malls, always exit by the same door you entered. Plus, before entering the mall, walk to the door and imagine you have completed your shopping and are going to your car. Where is it? Ah, there it is, three rows to the right, about halfway back on the left, near the second lamp post.

Practice navigation. In particular, read and understand the route you plan to take before leaving on a trip to visit a friend in the southern part of the state. Avoid trying to read a map upside down at sixty miles an hour on a crowded two-lane highway. Take advantage of automobile clubs, which will send you maps with the precise route highlighted to your destination. Or use the Internet. Several services like MapQuest provide maps showing how to reach where it is you want to go from where you are. Or, if you prefer the written word, another service will print the exact instructions for how to get from here to there (TripQuest). I have tried both and they work well.

Beware of being rushed. Rushing triggers anxiety, which disrupts navigation. Just how badly this can affect getting from here to there was brought painfully to my attention two years ago. I was asked to speak to that year's Harvard fortieth reunion class about cognitive aging. The reunion was being held in Newport, RI, the weekend after graduation. I had been to Newport several times—the most recent visit had been about five years earlier—so I had the idea that I knew where Newport was. When the day came for the talk, I was a little nervous and spent some extra time reviewing the lecture and adding some new material before starting the trip to Newport. Believing I knew how to get there, I didn't refresh my memory by glancing at the map in my glove compartment. An hour later, to my horror, I found myself in Providence, RI. *Then* I looked at the map and discovered that I had taken the wrong highway and was forty miles south of my destination.

When the lecture began a half-hour late, the Harvard Class of '54 was relaxed and forgiving. They were especially amused by the slide showing that spatial abilities are the first casualty of the aging process.

Set Aside Plenty of Time
for Complicated Tasks

We know that we think more slowly as we grow older. But the effect is far greater with more complicated problems. Age differences in processing speed apply far more to the most difficult tasks and far less to the simpler ones. For example, Georgia Tech researchers found that older and younger people differed very little on simple ("Shoe is to foot as hat is to ____?") and medium-hard ("9 is to 3 as 25 is to ____?") analogy questions, even though the time pressure was substantial—ninety seconds to complete eighteen questions. However, the accuracy scores of 65-year-old subjects fell off relative to those of the younger test-takers on the hardest of the analogies (for example, "Fission is to fusion as splitting is to ____?").

The moral here is that at 60 and beyond we have a greater need than the 35-year-old in the next cubicle to anticipate the complexity of problems that we may deal with in the coming week. Therefore, we need to use our experience to sort the tasks into piles of easy, medium, and hard. We can expect to handle all of the easy, and most of the medium challenges, at about our usual pace. But when we face the week's most complicated problems, we should allocate far more time to reason our way to a solution. So we plan to use our lunch hour to try to entice a reluctant, frightened first grade boy to read; we come in early and stay late to design a new ad campaign for a sneaker company whose sales are plummeting; we spend much of our weekend reviewing our medical literature because we wonder whether a 30-year-old who is tired all the time has Gulf War Syndrome; or we stay up much of the night reading the Web pages of a potential new client company we are pitching the day after tomorrow.

Prepare especially thoroughly for those infrequent occasions when you have to think fast about unfamiliar intricate matters and make a decision. For instance, it is time for me to get a new car. When I trade in my old Volvo for a new one, should I buy or lease? About half my friends are leasing cars, and the rest buy. Before I talk to a 40-year-old sales representative, I had better recognize that my machine speed is going to be substantially slower than the salesperson's. Also, he or she is going to be able to tap-dance through the thicket of financial complexities, making a convincing argument for me to buy or lease so quickly that I will not be able to follow. So how do I prepare for this ordeal? Well, I talk to my friends who have both leased and bought, noting their reasons for their choices. My accountant's opinion is sought. Although he seems to be able to argue both sides with equal logic, I discover he paid cash for his Cherokee. Then I spend a weekend afternoon at the library, paging through automotive magazines where there is an astonishing amount of information. I take notes.

Next Tuesday I will be ready to negotiate. Even though that 40-year-old's processing speed is a lot quicker than mine, and he has negotiated more deals in a week than I have in my life-time, I can keep up with the rapid pace of the discussion because the terms are familiar. And I have an idea of the argu-ments for both sides. This preparation puts me in the best posi-tion to get a fair deal on a new car.

Remember that being slower doesn't mean that we can't do complex problems. It merely means it takes us a little longer. A few heartbeats more for understanding a complicated problem, a couple of hours or so for the most complex challenges. If we respect these realities, we can handle whatever comes our way.

Augment Working Memory

There you are at 62, comfortably working as a claims adjuster in a large insurance company. You have been there fifteen years and hope to continue working. Then on Monday morning comes the announcement that all claims adjusters now have to be licensed in your state. This requires passing a multiple choice examination. Classes start Wednesday and the exam is a week from Friday. If you don't pass the exam with a score of 70 per-cent or higher, the company will have to let you go.

Your heart rate jumps alarmingly. Perspiration washes down your sides. You are sure you have no chance to pass this exami-nation. It has been almost forty years since you dropped out of school, and you have not tackled anything more challenging than the morning scrabble game in your newspaper. There is another matter—the other claims adjusters are between 25 and 45, and all are college graduates. Then this afternoon they hand out the textbook they'll be using for the course. It's 386 pages of microprint covering all the types of property and casualty insur-ance there are—dwelling insurance, homeowner insurance, auto insurance, business and professional liability insurance, boiler insurance. You are convinced you will never be able to memorize 10 percent of all the material, let alone 70 percent.

What advice do we have for you?

Being anxious disrupts our attention. Because we cannot focus, we have trouble remembering. The first piece of advice then is to control your nerves. About 25 percent of high school and college students fail exams because of test-taking nervousness. The negative effects of anxiety in test-taking performance are excessive worry and emotional upset. The worrying is usually about feeling inadequate, failing the test, embarrassing ourselves relative to others, and losing our job. The emotional upset expresses itself in physical responses to stress—nausea, diarrhea, sweating, and increased heart rate. These unpleasant stress-related symptoms are sometimes so distracting that they cause someone to be unable to focus on the exam itself. We also know that anxiety levels rise with age.

Remember that the mind that makes us nervous is also the same mind that can soothe us. In Chapter 2, we learned that people calm themselves down by using problem-focused and emotion-focused coping techniques. Examples of the latter methods are regular moderate exercise, which not only reduces anxiety but also improves mood and sharpens memory and other cognitive abilities. Meditation, relaxation tapes, Yoga, and Qi Gong also wind down an overactive nervous system. So does prayer.

The second recommendation is to work hard. This is the best problem-focused coping technique. Most people fail exams because they don't put in enough time. Pay attention in your classes. Review the day's material in the evening over a beer or a cup of green tea. The next morning, look at the lesson for that day with your decaf. Take plenty of practice tests. Especially useful are old exams. Isolate your weak spots. Too, recognize that your working memory will need boosting. Make notes of material you need to remember. Looking at the list of terms to be recalled while saying them out loud enhances your memory.

Third, work with others. In small groups, go over the material you need to learn. Don't be afraid to admit that you are clueless about the intricacies of marine insurance. Someone in your group will understand the difference between barraty and the Inchmaree clause and will be able to explain it to you. Go over multiple choice questions together. Then discuss why choice "d" was the correct answer when you thought for sure it was "b."

Finally, if you are still having trouble, get professional help. Hire a tutor. You would be surprised what two hours a week of one-on-one tutoring can do for your ability to retain information you need to recall on next Friday's exam. Three out of four highly anxious individuals with a history of failing tests were successful after a brief period of applying these problem-focused and emotion-focused anxiety management strategies.

These tactics to improve working memory work just as well with other types of challenges—a staff assistant needs to learn how to use Windows 2000; a stockbroker is trying to figure out how the new variable annuity works; or an airplane captain is asked to upgrade to the new Boeing 777. The older person's working memory can be augmented by anxiety management, working hard, being a member of a study group, and obtaining professional assistance.

Avoid Doing Two Things at a Time

Zipping past you on the interstate this morning are cars driven by the boomers, the dinks, and the generation Xers conversing on their cellular phones, accessing their voice mail, returning yesterday's phone calls, making appointments, doing deals. Two miles later, you sit in a traffic jam for fifteen minutes. In the surrounding cars, you catch glimpses of your younger fellow commuters sitting in their virtual offices while you sit irritably listening to the news. Over there is a woman talking on her mobile phone; on the right is a man reaching down to peck something into his laptop; behind you, you swear the driver is pulling a fax out of his glove compartment. You have the distinct sense that these young tigers are already half an hour ahead of you before your workday has even started.

Maybe it is time you modernized, used your time more efficiently. At 63, you believe it might give you a little edge. It might. But it also might result in your driving your car into a tree. Not much edge there. This is because our capacity for dual-task attention falls off sharply with age. It is hard to imagine a better test of dual-task attention than having to navigate a car down a highway filled with other vehicles while at the same time punching in a number on your cellular phone.

In fact, even younger people have trouble with this type of dual-task attention. A 1996 study reported that there has been a significant increase in accidents associated with using a mobile phone while driving. The article calculated that using a cellular phone increased the probability of an accident nearly sixfold—the same proportional increased risk associated with driving drunk.

Respect the fact that your capacity to do two things at once drops off dramatically after age 55. If you can, once you become eligible for membership in AARP, resist talking on the phone or dictating or both while driving. If you must use electronics when you drive, be aware you are putting yourself at risk. Drive more slowly and carefully even when you are on a familiar road. Use these devices when the traffic is light or when you are stopped. It is hard to react swiftly to emergencies in the middle of an intense conversation with someone.

On the job, try to focus on only one task at a time. Well established is the fact that oldsters have little tolerance for being interrupted when they are concentrating on finishing a task, whether at home or on the job. If you are a staff assistant, train your boss not to interrupt you to send a fax while you are word-processing a complicated document. If you are an executive, don't respond to your e-mail while making a phone call. You wind up either making errors in your correspondence or not paying attention to the person on the other end of the line. Or both. You can get just as much done by taking things one item at a time. And the quality of your work will be far higher.

◼ RECAPPING

The myth that memory for names, events, and things is the first faculty to go is a half-truth, obscuring the complexity of memory, which consists of many components. This piece of folk wisdom is potentially dangerous because it may cause us to disregard the potential problems created by the decline in those other abilities that fall off more sharply than verbal memory. The facts are that spatial ability and reasoning, how fast we can solve complicated problems, working memory, and dual-task attention all decline with age well ahead of memory for names, numbers, and words.

Suggestions for remaining as sharp as possible in our later years include anticipating and rehearsing solutions to spatial tasks. This tactic includes taking special care to remember where we parked our vehicle, practicing well ahead when driving somewhere unfamiliar, and trying to avoid being rushed. Also, prepare thoroughly and set aside plenty of time for complicated tasks. Working memory can be augmented through anxiety management, putting in more effort than usual, working with others, and, if necessary, obtaining professional assistance. In the last quarter of life, avoid doing two things at once as much as possible, especially when driving. These strategies will help us older workers stay abreast of our younger colleagues.

MYTH FIVE:
USE IT OR LOSE IT

Perhaps the single cherished and most passionately held myth about cognitive aging is that using it prevents losing it. That is, if we continue to exercise our mental muscles, we'll retain our intellectual skills while those who do not use it will find themselves losing ground cognitively with the passing years. Support for this idea is widespread and dates back at least a half-century. When we were completing our study of 1,002 physicians, we sent them a questionnaire asking whether they thought the use-it-or-lose-it theory applied to cognitive aging. Ninety-three percent said that they believed it was true. The rationale is straightforward and plausible: If we apply our mental ability to solve challenges on a regular basis as we grow older, these faculties will be preserved until very late in life.

Take, for instance, Keith Sward, a California psychologist, who examined the use-it-or-lose-it question more than fifty years ago. He gave aptitude tests to older and younger professors at two West Coast universities. The older professors were eminent scientists and were still working. Because they had remained active in their fields, Sward thought that this would be a good way to see whether their continuing use of their mental abilities prevented decline. They were matched with younger up-and-coming instructors in the same fields—English, math, science. Eight different mental tests were given to both groups, including arithmetic, analogies, code learning, and word knowledge.

When he looked at the results, the news was not good for the use-it-or-lose-it theory: 95 percent of the younger faculty had higher total scores than the older ones did. In other words, only about one senior professor in twenty did as well on the overall test as their average junior colleague. Despite the obvious superiority of the younger faculty members over the active older professors on these tests—results that should have given him a pause about continuing to embrace the use-it-or-lose-it theory, listen to the conclusions Sward reached: "the older man may be rusty, but only in a set of specific habits in performances which he has neither the occasion nor the desire to preserve in active use." In other words, even if a decline in particular aptitudes occurs, it can be attributed to lack of practice, just as our typing speed drops when we have been away from the keyboard for several months. Thus the so-called decline in mental ability test scores found in older adults is caused by lack of recent experience in the type of activities that make up IQ tests—putting blocks together to make a design, solving math problems in your head.

Since then, nearly everyone who has looked carefully at groups of older and younger individuals in the same occupation who were still working has come up with the same findings. Older and younger teachers and truck drivers, nuns and executives, pilots, architects, and nurses, it doesn't matter what the vocation, the results were still the same. Younger people outscored their older colleagues. But this idea is hard to sell, even when the evidence is right in front of your nose.

"Older people do different things than younger ones in the same field," the true believer of the use-it-or-lose-it theory might point out. "So you really can't say that the older professors are using the same skills as the junior faculty." For instance, they may be more likely to work as administrators. By contrast, the younger ones may be doing more actual teaching, which requires more reading and faster processing of new information. It is therefore possible to argue that all this research is flawed because older and younger people aren't involved in the same activities.

Suppose we were to see how older and younger people do on activities that both carry out on a regular basis. According to the use-it-or-lose-it logic, if we test older and younger adults on familiar tasks, ones older individuals have done for years, the differences would be minimal. That is just what two occupational therapists in Colorado did. They gave twenty younger (age 28) and twenty older (age 71) women familiar household chores to carry out. They were asked to choose two jobs from a list that included cooking eggs, making toast and coffee, preparing a fruit or tossed salad, making a sandwich, repotting a houseplant, vacuuming the living room, or changing the sheets on the bed. The researchers videotaped the subjects doing these familiar activities and rated them on how efficiently each task was carried out. The investigators discovered that the older women were much less effective at performing these familiar household chores than the younger women were. For these older women, years of experience using it did not prevent losing it.

Despite 50+ years of research showing the decline of cognitive skills with age, an eminent gerontologist wrote recently that the "observed decline in many community-dwelling older people is likely to be a function of disuse and is often reversible." Dozens of other quotations could be cited, each one arguing that continuing to exercise our mental powers will enable us to maintain them. This is an all too common illustration of what happens when theory and hard facts collide. We throw out the evidence in order to keep the theory intact.

These days, and in the decades ahead, the use-it-or-lose-it theory can become a particularly dangerous myth, for two reasons: First, this myth brings with it both a false optimism and, perhaps, a dangerous cynicism to those of us who are getting older. "All I have to do to stay up with the young hotshots is to keep on keeping on," we may say to ourselves. But then the evidence becomes clear to anyone paying serious attention: that most of us will not be as mentally sharp at 70 or 80 as we were at 30 or 40. The danger is that we will give up, believing that nothing can help. Because using it has not kept us from losing it, we might as well pack it in. Like the baseball hall-of-famer, Willie Mays, who couldn't hit the fastball after 35 and was forced out of the game, we may assume our life as a competent human being is pretty much over when we witness ourselves a few heartbeats slower and more uncertain than when we were in midlife.

The second reason the use-it-or-lose-it myth is dangerous is because it seems to assume that older individuals won't require particular types of environmental support or instruction to help them remain mentally vigorous at work. The logic of the use-it-or-lose-it theory argues that older workers can stay sharp by continuing to do whatever their job has required. Because employees will be needed beyond the time of normal retirement and certain skills decline with age, organizations must confront the reality that frequent retraining will be necessary. Programs designed especially to upgrade the skills of seniors who may be a little slower and more anxious than their junior coworkers, should pay dividends in the form of greater enthusiasm and competence among older employees.

The Reality

In the past decade, our own research with physicians and other volunteers has shown that mental abilities decline with age. We tested the use-it-or-lose-it theory by comparing older physicians who continued to work with those who had retired. Would those physicians who still practiced have higher scores than those who were no longer working? We divided the subjects into five-year age groups from 60 onward and compared their mental test scores. We discovered no differences in the working and retired physicians from 60 to 69. After 70, the working physicians had slightly higher total aptitude scores. One explanation for the stronger showing on the mental tests among the working physicians is that they continued to exercise their mental abilities. But other explanations come to mind. Perhaps the physicians who retired did so because they were aware of a diminished capacity relative to what they believed was needed to continue in competent medical practice. Most older physicians we tested were more sensitive to their mental state than most nonphysicians. Probably most of those who continued to work had reached the conclusion that they were still mentally sharp enough to do their job capably.

It has been shown that physicians who retire remain just as mentally active as when they were working full time. The beneficial effects of an active retirement was shown by a Texas study of men and women. The question examined in this investigation was whether the amount of physical and social activity that retirees engaged in was correlated with greater blood flow to the brain and higher mental test scores. To carry out this experiment, they divided a panel of 64-year-old volunteers into three groups: (1) those who planned to continue to work; (2) those planning to retire and remain physically and socially active; (3) those planning to retire to a relatively sedentary lifestyle.

At 64, there was no difference in cerebral perfusion, that is, blood flow to the brain. Two years later, they measured the cerebral perfusion of the three groups. The retired sedentary men and women were 6 percent lower than those who continued to work or were retired and active. Four years later, the difference was nearly 9 percent. This decline in blood flow to the brain was mirrored in cognitive test scores, which showed that the retired sedentary individuals scored 10 percent lower than the other two groups.

Let's assume for the moment that the physicians over 70 benefitted mentally from continuing to use their skills. As a result, a typical physician of, let's say, 75 scored higher on our ability test relative to others in his age group who had retired, were sedentary, and were not using their mental skills regularly. But how do the working 75-year-olds compare with younger physicians? This is *the* essential part of the use-it-or-lose-it theory: Does continuing to exercise our mental aptitudes on the job reduce the rate at which they decline? The results were once more disappointing for the use-it-or-lose-it proponents. In every case after 65, groups of working physicians scored lower than a typical physician five years younger, including younger physicians who had retired. In other words, a 75-year-old physician continuing to practice may outscore other 75-year-old physicians, but his intellectual skills are still significantly lower than 70-year-old physicians, retired or working.

So it seems that, if there is any truth in the use-it-or-lose-it theory, it is this: Using it may help us retain our mental skills relative to our age group in the young-old years, but the inevitable decline relative to those ten or twenty years younger continues. This conclusion reminds me of the story of two middle-aged men hiking in the Maine woods. As they turned the corner on a remote portion of the Appalachian Trail, they came upon a large menacing black bear, who immediately charged at them. One of the hikers took off his boots, reached into his knapsack, and began to put on a pair of running shoes. "Why are you doing that?" said the other. "Don't you know that the black bear is one of the fastest animals there is for a short distance? You'll never be able to outrun him." "No," said the other hiker, double-knotting his Nike's, "but I'll be able to outrun you!" In some ways, I suppose this is the essential truth of the use-it-or-lose-it theory. Using it may help us outstrip those in our age group, but the inevitable decline continues relative to those in their prime.

AGING OPTIMALLY WHILE USING IT AND STILL LOSING IT

Recognizing the use-it-or-lose-it theory as a myth enables us to take constructive actions to compensate for some of our waning mental powers. Plenty of other evidence exists that most of us will be able to continue to perform effectively on the job, at home, or elsewhere into the eighth and possibly the ninth decades of our lives. But we need to face the reality of diminishing intellectual powers, just as we've confronted arthritic joints and dimming eyesight. If we recognize that there is a strong probability that we will have difficulty remembering where we left our purse and car keys or the names of the new people we meet, or that we will learn how to operate a new software program more slowly, we can take specific steps to remedy the situation. These steps include valuing experience, working smarter, being ready to educate your organization as to your training needs, mobilizing environmental support, remaining committed, and avoiding self-inflicted ageism.

Value Experience

When we face a new challenge at 60 or 70 or 80, experience matters. Sometimes we've lived through the same problem before and know the likely answer: We know that broken hearts heal; that low interest rates are associated with bull markets; that saying "no" is harder than just saying "yes" when someone asks us to volunteer our time for a difficult task. Or we know what the process is to find the answer: We know that expert help is useful in making out our income tax; that when we are feeling stressed out and short-tempered, talking to a good friend can help us sort things out and feel better. Experience, too, teaches us something about the rhythm of things, allowing us to predict what comes next. We know that people at work react negatively to changes at first, need time to process them, but then eventually come around. When a loved one has hurt us, we know forgiveness benefits us more than holding a grudge, but it will take time. We also know something about the pattern of our own reactions to a crisis situation, knowledge that can be very helpful.

Here is a personal note about the value of experience. At age 60, I decided that I needed to take a course in intermediate statistics at Harvard. At the time, I thought it was important to bring myself more up to date on the advances in research design and statistical methods of analyzing data that had occurred in the nearly four decades since I last took courses in this subject. Fearing that I would not stick it out when the going got rough, I signed up to take the course for credit—and for a grade.

I entered the class with an optimistic attitude because I had been "using it" over my career. At the first meeting, I began to worry. In a class of twenty-nine, there was no one even half my age unless you counted Dan, a 31-year-old MD/Ph.D. candidate, and Xiaoli, a visiting professor of statistics from the University of Beijing. The average age was quite low—the two freshmen in the class looked about 14.

After the second meeting, I knew I was in big trouble. Lots of changes had occurred in the field since my graduate student days. Furthermore, the professor presented ideas at what seemed to me warp speed. My younger classmates had no trouble absorbing information at this pace. When he asked the class a question that I could answer, my reaction was about three heartbeats slower than anyone else's. On those rare occasions when I did manage to blurt out an answer before anyone else, my response was incorrect more times than I care to remember. It was so bad that the one time I happened to answer a question correctly, before anyone else, the class gave me a spontaneous ovation, much like people clapping for the distance runner who gamely finishes dead last. At the first midterm, I was tied with two others for the lowest grade in the class. Bob, the professor, and a friend, asked me gently if I would rather take the class as an auditor, the way many faculty do. I shook my head doggedly, knowing that if I didn't have a grade to work for, I would eventually drop it and not learn what I very much needed to know. I mumbled something about not worrying about me and "running my own race." I didn't care what grade I got. Which was a lie. I lusted for an A.

At some point, my experience came into play. This experience had nothing to do with how much I knew about the field of psychology or statistics. The experience had to do with having had to learn difficult things before. I knew what I had to do. For example, I knew the value of hard work. To this day, I hate to admit how much time I spent doing problem sets or studying for exams—perhaps two or three times more than the other class members. My experience also had taught me the value of expert assistance. I hired a young tutor, Mark, who worked with me regularly and patiently, giving me lots of practice and reassurance. Moreover, I knew from my own teaching that the largest share of the course content was compressed into the first half of the semester. If I could just survive until Halloween, I would be okay.

Knowing how I typically reacted to this kind of stress was a comfort when the going got rough. I was aware that situations like this always made me anxious and that this nervousness caused me to have trouble focusing. Therefore it was hard to take in new ideas. I knew these feelings would eventually subside; after I became less anxious, my learning curve would rise. Over the years I have discovered that my mind absorbs the written word better than the spoken word, especially when complicated, unfamiliar concepts are involved. As a result, I forced myself to do all the required reading in advance, so that the lecture material would be more familiar. My classroom notes filled two large spiral binders. Sometimes I even brought a recorder to the lectures.

As a result of my self-knowledge, based on years of living with me, I passed the course—in that half of the class that makes the top half possible, but with an honors grade. Without experience, I would not have survived. Today, much of what I learned has been put into use in my research on aging.

Work Smarter

For most of us in the fourth quarter of our lives, an undeniable fact is that certain mental skills are degraded by the aging process. Even if our job has not changed much and we have been doing it well for decades, most of us will be a little slower to discover the answer to complex problems; we will have difficulties doing two things at one time; and we may be sharper in the morning than in the afternoon. Because many of us are part of an aging workforce, we need to be able to work smarter to compensate for these declines. Here are several "work smarter" tips.

First, do only one thing at a time. Older workers have trouble carrying out multiple tasks simultaneously. As we learned in Chapter 4, dual-task attention—the capacity to attend to and carry out two or more jobs simultaneously—trends downhill with age. Because our bosses are not mind readers, they may not be aware that this executive or that executive secretary, who could juggle several major projects at a time at 45, can't at 65. We need to let those we work with know that we're more effective when we can complete one project before beginning another. The total number of large projects we can accomplish will not be much less than when we were at our best; it's just that we do better when we can cope with them in sequence and not all at once.

Seniors don't perform as capably when schedules or priorities suddenly change. A veteran salesman planning to call on accounts in Atlanta on Tuesday, Chattanooga on Wednesday, and Nashville on Thursday, doesn't respond well to the request from his boss to work in a breakfast meeting in Birmingham sometime during the trip. New items suddenly added to the "Do Now!" list should be discussed as far in advance as possible so that they can be programmed into the schedule.

Second, pay attention to your diurnal cycle and use this knowledge. The diurnal cycle is our biological twenty-four-hour clock. During different portions of the day, we normally work, relax, and sleep. There are periods during the cycle when we are considerably sharper, more mentally acute, than others. Older women and men are, on the whole, livelier in the morning than later in the day. Psychologists at Duke University gave younger (18 to 22) and older (66 to 78) volunteers a "Morning-Eveningness" questionnaire. It contained questions asking when they felt best and when they were most alert. Age dictated their preferences: 96 percent of the older women and men said they were at their most alert during the morning. This tendency among the older volunteers was even more striking because they were all retired and able to set their own schedules. Among the younger volunteers, a mere 12 percent said they were AM people. This finding is not a surprise for those of us in our 60s and beyond who remember working late into the night in our 30s but now tackle our most challenging work in the early morning.

The Duke research showed that older and younger adults perform at about the same level in the morning on a test of memory. In the afternoon, however, recall by the 20-year-olds greatly improved, whereas the memories of those in their 60s and 70s dropped off. Older workers, then, who work closely with younger people are well advised to schedule meetings in the morning when they are not at a cognitive disadvantage. This also means that those of us who are older should take on our most challenging projects as early as possible in the day, leaving midafternoon and beyond for less taxing activities. The salesman on the road should make his toughest calls in the morning and save the later afternoon for visiting pleasant, established clients who are happy to see him.

Third, work through others. The most productive senior executives, professionals, and scientists are those who in midlife learned to extend their own productivity by enlisting others to share the load. Those whose productivity pivots too much on their own efforts have far more difficulty keeping up in the seventh and eighth decades of their lives.

My mother was neither an executive nor a professional. She worked as a bookkeeper in a bowling alley until she was 75. She also commanded the nursery, coordinated the bowling leagues, and ruled over the office staff and maintenance men. "What was her secret?" people asked. How could she keep all those balls in the air at once? Delegation was the answer. In her 40s, she learned that she could be more effective if she let others take over as much responsibility as they could handle. Even though these people may not have run the nursery, supervised the maintenance crew, or handled the accounts payable as well as she did, this tactic allowed her to do what she did best, which was handling the corporate checkbook. This model worked for her through the eighth decade of her life.

Mobilize Environmental Support

Long before we are eligible for membership in AARP, most of us need various types of assistance to function productively. Eyeglasses and hearing aids for weakened senses, medication and orthopedic support for bad backs, creaky joints, and falling arches help all of us cope in midlife.

Look for ways to boost declining cognitive functions. Because spatial memory is an early casualty of the aging process, begin to develop ways of remembering where you parked your car. Recognize that this is an age-related weakness like poor eyesight, and compensate. Seek electronic assistance. The ritual of remembering where you left your car can be accomplished easily by using small battery-operated recording devices that fit in a shirt pocket or a small purse. They have a tiny microchip into which we can dictate, "My car is parked in H-1, third level" or "Remember to pick up the laundry this afternoon" or "Call Aunt Rose on Thursday to wish her a happy birthday." Just under half of my aging friends admit to carrying around these small memory aids.

I am less technologically sophisticated. Suction-cupped to the inside of my car's windshield is a small notepad where I scribble notes to myself.

Sometimes we find ourselves in situations where it might not be seemly to whip out our electronic memory-minder or notepad—say, at a barbecue in our new neighbor's backyard. In attendance are a dozen of their friends, whom we don't know but are about to meet. At 60+, we know we don't remember names as quickly and easily as we did 30 years before. How are we possibly going to recall their names? If we decide we're going to try (and we don't always have to try; it's amazing how long one can converse with people without using their names), we need a strategy. The strategy should involve a system that we have already practiced and found to work. The one I use is the so-called method of loci. This technique involves associating each person's name with something we are familiar with. I use the rooms of my house. I am ready when I am introduced to Jack and Jill, Hansel and Gretel, Harold and Maude, Bonnie and Clyde, Thelma and Louise, and John and Marsha. In my mind, Jack is placed in the basement and Jill in the family room, Hansel in the kitchen and Gretel in the dining room, Harold in the living room and Maude in the downstairs bathroom, Bonnie in the foyer and Clyde on the stairs, Thelma in the study and Louise in the upstairs bathroom, John in the blue bedroom and Marcia in the guest bedroom. You might choose to connect names to familiar landmarks or subway stops.

This system works for me because I have practiced it in advance. Numerous other memory support systems work just as well. Ways of remembering people's names are regularly advertised on infomercials and in the newspapers. Bookstores have sections devoted to the topic. The key is to practice whatever system you decide to use before you meet those twelve strangers in your neighbor's backyard.

Rely on technology when you have to analyze a pile of material. Facing the fact that, as we age, you and I will not be able to keep as many items in working memory as we once were able to allows us to experiment with relying on technology for a larger "virtual" memory. With this technology, we no longer need to store vast amounts of data in our heads. For instance, as part of my annual physical, my blood and urine are analyzed by the laboratory. My physician then receives a report telling how I did on the four dozen or so indicators of my health. He doesn't have to remember what the normal ranges are for white and red blood cell counts, or for serum albumin and the other chemistries, because the normal ranges are indicated on the printout from the lab. He only has to think about what these numerical patterns indicate about my health.

Extensive and easily accessible databases exist on just about every topic imaginable. I subscribe to many fewer professional journals than I did a decade ago because I can access them, as well as hundreds of others, from the libraries around the world, through my computer. If I need to know something about a particular subject—say, how older people can improve their memories—I can gather in one afternoon all the information available on that topic from the last two dozen years. Last spring, we started a project on cognitive training for the elderly. We reviewed the published literature to bring ourselves up to date on what some of the best and newest techniques were for cognitive training. We then e-mailed several people who were doing this work to see whether they were using any new ideas that had not yet been published. We heard back from Martha in St. Louis, Paul in Germany, and John on the West Coast, all of whom shared with us some of their most recent ideas.

You don't have to have a university office to do this. Many public libraries have similar capacities. Internet and e-mail bring other technological advantages to the older worker looking to maintain an edge over the competition. A 68-year-old salesman consults his corporate clients' Web pages on the Internet before making his calls. This tactic provides him with up-to-the-minute information on each of his customers. When he later visits his clients, they are appropriately dazzled by how much he knows about them. As long as we are willing to muster environmental support, older individuals can continue to function effectively at home and in the workplace.

Be Ready to Educate Your Organization About Your Training Needs

In an ideal world, organizations would be aware of the needs for regular training and upgrading for all its employees. This is even more important today as the growth of technology influences the way things are done. Plus, larger numbers of healthier, energetic, older people will want to stay on the job in the years ahead—an entitlement of most, if they so choose. Because there will be substantially fewer workers in the generation behind them, baby boomers will be needed to fill positions in the workforce. So there will be a growing need to upgrade the knowledge and skills of gray-haired employees. Right now, the professions have led the way. Airline pilots are recertified every six months. To retain my license as a psychologist, I must attend three days of continuing education each year. Most other professions—physicians, teachers, accountants, social workers—have similar requirements. Top-level managers stay current by frequent exposure to workshops and conferences.

The people I worry about most are the middle-level executives and the staff assistants who make up the engine that drives most organizations, large and small. It is up to them to implement and execute the new ideas and systems that keep the organizations current and competitive. I worry about whether their bosses have thought enough about the training needed to help them master a whole new series of procedures at 55, 65, or 75: the librarian who left the Dewey decimal system behind to learn the Library of Congress alphanumeric classification four years ago and has just been told that a new computer-based expert system for cataloging books will be installed shortly after the first of the year; the staff assistant in a physician's office who has to negotiate the labyrinth of managed care and this month's new sheaf of forms; the traveling salesman who used to return at the end of the week, orders in hand, but now is required to submit them daily by laptop—a new practice designed to enable him to stay on the road longer and be more productive. These workers and others like them will need, not only our very best training programs in the years ahead, but also our support and encouragement.

Support and encouragement are as important for older workers as the actual technical training itself, because oldsters are likely to be a little more anxious about mastering new technology and procedures than the youngsters are. Consider an example that has struck fear into me and several of my senior colleagues who teach in Harvard's Extension Program. I am now being "strongly encouraged" to create Web pages for my classes. We can load in the syllabus, slides, old exams, CD-ROM material, and required articles and whatever else makes up the content of our classes. My guess is that next year the choice will not be optional because many other institutions now require a Web page for each class a faculty member teaches. Even though I have been working with a computer for the past three years and have taken many courses, I still feel slightly apprehensive because I don't honestly know what a Web page is.

I am a little nervous, but a number of my nonscientific colleagues are terrified. "I'll never learn it," lamented a 60-year-old. "I still can't work my VCR." Another, in his early 50s, whined, "There is no way I can do a Web page. I've never worked a computer in my life and have no plans to start." When I recently shared these anxieties with my son-in-law, George, who is a teacher, his response was, "What are they worried about? Any of my seventh graders can make a Web page in an afternoon." Well, what George says may be true for 12-year-olds, but those of us in our late prime have not, like them, been brought up with computers. And, thank you, we have been successfully teaching a particular way for decades.

In part, of course, these reactions by senior faculty are a rationalization because we are wary of the new technology, which seems to change every year. Furthermore, we recognize that we are not as quick to learn as we once were. Many of us older workers will react negatively when told we must learn new ways of doing things. Most will be a little on the anxious side and more than a few may seem a trifle negative at first. This doesn't mean we can't learn it or won't; we can and will master whatever needs to be understood to carry on our work confidently.

Executives in educational institutions, government agencies, and private-sector companies are not mind readers. Moreover, they recognize that their performance depends on the effectiveness of workers who are growing older. Therefore, we need to be able to tell them when we need more training, a slower pace, or a different approach. This feedback has helped in organizations where there is a channel available for employees to "manage upward." Such communication provides a forum for the brass to hear the gripes, whines, complaints, and legitimate concerns of those of us who want to make the new ideas work. Sometimes the managers will respond positively to these concerns by making the necessary adjustments. Just as often, the bosses can't or won't do anything about it, but the workers still feel better and are more effective, knowing they have been heard.

Organizations who want to continue to get the best out of their employees need to recognize that seniors will need more reassurance than do younger workers that the company wants them to learn new technology and procedures, that the pace will be adjusted so that everyone can keep up, that individual tutoring is available, and that mistakes are to be expected for a period while the new system is being implemented.

Remain Committed

In the years just before Ted retired, his attitude changed dramatically. Instead of being involved in his work, he became increasingly disengaged; instead of being full of energy, he was dispirited; instead of being enthusiastic, he seemed uncaring; and instead of being pleasant and cooperative, he was increasingly disgruntled and disagreeable. This behavior was in sharp contrast to the way Ted had been in the previous quarter-century. Until his early 60s, he had contributed energy and ideas to our organization, had built an empire, and had been a prime mover in two creations that won national acclaim. Now Ted seemed negative about everything, lacked energy, and filled the air with remarks like, "The best years of this place are behind it." "There are too many changes, most of them for the worse." "It's a good time to be getting out." It wasn't long before we all thought that his retirement was a good idea.

Why such a change in attitude in such a short time? What had happened? Eight months after he retired, I asked Ted about this while having dinner at his house. At that time, he was enthusiastically developing a consulting practice and, with the help of his son-in-law, building a small cabin on a lake in New Hampshire. He couldn't wait to show me the plans and tell me about this new laser-aimed power saw that he had just learned to use. Sometime that evening, I asked Ted if he had been taking those new supplements that I had seen advertised. Was that where this new enthusiasm and energy was coming from?

Ted and I talked late into the evening about those last years of our work together. He explained that he had become increasingly aware of the short time he had left with the organization. He admitted feeling a sense of loss and resentment. "How could I participate in the development of a new program when I knew I was not going to be there to see it get off the ground?" he said. "Why should I plant an acorn if I'll never see the oak tree?" The only way he could continue to function was by pulling away, investing less in our work. And his anger, that things weren't the way they used to be, helped him break the bond of caring he had about the organization and his friends in it. The loss of his work and friends didn't hurt as much that way.

If there is a moral in Ted's story, it is this: If we're going to continue to work, we need to remain committed. This means continuing to participate and to think about new projects, even though we may not be there to see them mature. It means attending meetings and paying attention even if we've heard it all before—*especially* if we've heard it all before. Younger generations nearly always think that they were the first to come up with a new idea. The fact that we may have tried the same idea earlier—and gained hard-won experience about what happens when you try to implement this particular vision—can be useful to our younger colleagues. If we're going to be a player, then we must play, let our enthusiasm show, and remain involved and committed.

Watch Out for Self-Inflicted Ageism

Even though we're doing our best to stay sharp, we will notice a decline in our mental powers. Like our physical abilities, our mental capabilities will be less at 65 or 75 than they were at 40. How we react to this inevitable weakening makes a huge difference in the quality of the last third of our lives.

Major hazards are resentment of this natural decline and punishment of ourselves. Internalized anger can result in an inaccurate assessment of our abilities. Just because we are not the same as we were in our prime does not mean we are ready for the nursing home. We may see ourselves as less capable than we really are. We then live down to these expectations. Vivid in memory is the 62-year-old professor, part of our research study, who complained, "Until a few years ago, I could read the *New York Sunday Times* from cover to cover and remember everything that was in it. Now, I can't remember *anything*." As a result of this selfappraisal, he had given up teaching a course for which he was justly famous and was thinking about retiring the next year.

Believing that this was an overreaction to the normal aging process and knowing that our test data on him found that he was still functioning quite well, I took time to discuss his reasoning with him. As we talked, his logic became apparent: He had always been at the very top of whatever class he had belonged to, from preschool through a Ph.D. His academic career was packed with accomplishments—writing influential books, chairing a department, acting as a government consultant, and on and on. But as he got older, he noticed that he was beginning to lose these remarkable skills. Reading the *New York Sunday Times* and being able to recall its contents was the way he gauged his mental powers. When he found his memory was declining, he was devastated. "I always thought I could bank on my memory," he said, "but now that it's going, I guess it's time to pack it in. I can't stand embarrassing myself." Behind this conclusion was the belief that, with his diminishing skills, he couldn't do his work the same way or at the same high level as in the past. No other alternatives existed for him.

P.S. The story has a happy ending. After we talked—only twice—the professor heard himself saying that he was slipping irretrievably because he couldn't remember everything in a Sunday paper. On further reflection, he thought that perhaps that didn't mean that he'd lost everything, and he might have overreacted by thinking he was over the hill. When I mentioned that some professionals in my field call this "catastrophic thinking," jumping to the conclusion that all is lost on the basis of a single setback, he smiled and said that he didn't agree. "It was more like self-loathing," he countered, "I hated myself for getting old, which made me unable to do the things I've always done so well. Then I realized something: I was both the victim and the perpetrator [of ageism]." Once he recognized this pattern, the professor forgave himself for getting older and losing some of his powers. Then he could value his remaining, still powerful mental skills. "I am still good enough to do what I want to do," he said. "And I haven't lost any of the knowledge I have learned from experience; experience is a knowledge that is unique to me. That makes me valuable." Last summer I ran into him in Harvard Square. Now 72, he had given up his department chairmanship two years earlier and declined a major consulting job with the government. When I asked him how he was, he said with a wry smile, "I guess I've lost a little bit more, but I still like what I do. The best part is, I don't hate myself for being older now."

This professor's experience contains lessons for us all about how to avoid self-inflicted ageism. First, accepting any decline is difficult for most of us, not just those with photographic memories. Second, we may react with mixed emotions—frustration, despair, anger—which may lead to catastrophic thinking such as, "I can't do anything anymore." Third, talking to loved ones, colleagues, older relatives, or even experts can be helpful in judging whether our reactions are consistent with reality. Fourth, an objective reappraisal of just how serious the decline is, and whether our initial response was appropriate or should be tempered, can lead to realistic strategies to cope with these changes. Finally, instead of feeling resentful and bitter about those things that we can no longer do as well as we once did, we can identify those mental activities that are still available to us and will continue to give us a sense of confidence and enjoyment.

◾ RECAPPING

The use-it-or-lose-it myth implies that our mental powers will remain strong until very late in life if we continue to exercise them. Even with fifty years of evidence dispelling this myth, it remains alive and well. The truth is that age-related declines in cognitive abilities occur naturally whether we use our abilities or not. It may be that exercising our intelligence routinely at 70 or 80 will enable us to outperform our age-mates who do not, but we are unlikely to score as well on mental tests as colleagues a decade or two younger. As it applies to mental powers, the use-it-or-lose-it belief is dangerous for two reasons. First, it may create an initial false optimism that all we have to do is "keep on keeping on" and our intellectual aptitudes will be maintained. When this turns out not to be the case, we may conclude that we can do nothing to help ourselves as our abilities inevitably decline with age. Second, this myth is hazardous for organizations because it may block the recognition that their older employees will require not only regular retraining but also a slightly different approach and a slower pace.

Considerable evidence exists that we can take steps to retain a high level of functioning as we grow older. These steps include valuing experience—having seen a problem before and knowing the answer, knowing the process to find the right answer, being able to predict what comes next, and understanding our reactions to stress; working smarter—doing one thing at a time, respecting our diurnal cycle, and working through others; mobilizing environmental support—using electronic assistance, learning methods for augmenting working memory, and accessing databases; being ready to educate our organization about our training needs; remaining committed late in our careers; and avoiding being both the victim and the perpetrator of ageism.

6

MYTH SIX:
OLD DOGS CAN'T
LEARN NEW TRICKS

Not long ago, the BBC aired a program about aging in the workplace. A survey by the Institute for Employment Consultants in the United Kingdom showed that three-quarters of the companies wanted to fill openings with people under the age of 35. A manager of a computer company said that their company "needs to have lively minds who are aggressive, robust, and hardy." He was looking for someone no older than 33.

Stereotypes about older workers abounded in their broadcast: set in their ways, unmotivated, lacking flexibility, no taste for hard work or overtime, unwilling or unable because of waning intellect to keep up with the pace of technology and change. Someone too old to cut the mustard could be astonishingly youthful. At 37, with fifteen years of secretarial experience, a candidate was told by a recruiter that most of the clients were looking for secretaries in their early 20s "because young people are more flexible." After age 50, jobs were just about impossible to find. A company manager looking for salespeople said he didn't feel that anyone over 40 could do the job of driving 50,000 miles a year because they "might become lonely on the road" and be unable to sell. Asked how old he was, he whispered in an embarrassed tone that he was 51! But he was sure that he had the mental and physical powers of someone twenty years younger. He didn't apply this same logic to people he was looking to hire.

In England, they do not yet have laws forbidding mandatory retirement or protecting older workers from age discrimination in the workplace. Therefore, the comments made by employers and employment agencies were not softened by the need to make statements that are politically correct by US standards. Whereas it is now manifestly illegal, the same age discrimination exists in the United States—although it is less overt. After listening to the BBC broadcast, I talked with a senior vice-president of a Wall Street firm. In his organization, it is common for partners to retire at about 50. "There's very little gray hair in our organization," this executive said. "We have taken the best out of them by the time they reach a half-century." When I inquired why older people couldn't do the job, he responded in phrases reminiscent of the English executive, "They just don't seem to have the stamina of the 30-year-old or, maybe that fire in their belly has died out." At the end of the interview, I asked the executive how old he was. "Sixty next November," he snapped irritably, and stood up to end the conversation.

Age discrimination is not limited to Wall Street. *USA Today* recently featured stories of men and women in the advertising industry being fired because they were "too old." An avid skier, racquetball player, and recent father, one ad man was let go because, at 53, he was thought to be excessively elderly for the job. Prime-of-life women in the advertising world feel especially targeted: Among top female executives, age bias was cited as a major career concern for women over 40. Advertising agencies defend their decisions because they are trying to sell younger adults their products and believe that only younger executives can create campaigns that will appeal to the 25 to 44 crowd. A 50-year-old jingle writer was terminated with these words from his 30-something boss: "How can you write rock and roll at your age?"

These examples indicate the extent of the myth that beyond a certain age it is impossible for someone to work at the level necessary to carry out a particular job. So powerful is the strength of this misapprehension that even those older workers who are living proof that old dogs can indeed learn new tricks continue to embrace the myth.

Even those in their prime who work relentlessly to keep pace with their younger colleagues have a hard time. Take Chris Toal, 54, the topic of a feature article in the *Wall Street Journal* in the spring of 1997. To remain employed over the past fifteen years, Chris has reinvented himself again and again. Once a production manager, he learned marketing and then purchasing. Following two layoffs, Chris mastered finance, sales, and most recently, customer service.

A generation ago, most managers at 50 had job security. Functioning as the organization's institutional memory and as mentors to younger workers, they had paid their dues and could settle comfortably into their jobs in their final decade. Now the hierarchy is turned upside down. Chris's bosses are in their early 40s; the younger folks don't approach him as a mentor because they are more secure than he is. Instead, they mock his coat and tie and come to work in green khakis and work shirts; they kid him about his modest computer skills and the fact that he can be found on the stairmaster in the gym before work most mornings.

Twice a month, Chris meets with a men's group, all 50+, who discuss how their working lives are changing and what they can do to cope. When the eyes turned to him, Chris said, "Things are not what any of us anticipated—we believed that with natural talent, hard work, and good moral values there would be a sense of job stability. There is no security and no stability." Asked what the future holds, Chris replied, "No clue. I feel like

I've peaked in my career, but I don't think I've peaked as a human being." One thing he is sure about: He will be back on the stairmaster tomorrow at 6:45 AM.

☀ THE REALITY

In no case could the executives and recruiters who were unwilling to hire or retain older people point to any evidence showing that the older workers could not carry out their jobs as effectively as younger employees, or benefit as much from training to upgrade their skills. These comments were based entirely on what many of us, including individuals who themselves are older and still functioning competently, believe to be true. What does the evidence actually have to say?

The scientific evidence contradicting the myth that you can't teach old dogs new tricks begins in the laboratory of Marian Diamond, a professor of anatomy at the University of California at Berkeley. Over the past thirty years, she and her colleagues have demonstrated the effects of environmental changes on brain function. Early in her career, she became fascinated by the discovery that "maze bright and maze dumb" laboratory animals could be reared from the same litter. Some animals learned quickly how to find their way through mazes and solve problems, whereas some littermates were far slower. Excited by these discoveries, she began to wonder whether the structure of the brain could be altered by external experience. She was among the very first to discover that laboratory animals who were raised in an enriched environment developed a thicker frontal cortex—the thinking part of the brain—than did those living in normal cages. Enriched environments, in this case, were those filled with things that laboratory animals found interesting—exercise wheels, tunnels, and toys.

Diamond and her coworkers varied the age at which the animals were placed in enriched environments. They discovered that both young and middle-aged lab rats raised in enriched cages had a thicker frontal cortex than did littermates placed in unstimulating cages. Then Diamond wondered whether the brains of older lab animals would exhibit the same changes after being exposed to an enriched environment. She put the animals in stimulating cages when they were 766 days old—a rat age equivalent to a human age of 65. She then compared differences in the thickness of several parts of the brains between these animals and animals not given enrichment. She discovered that the thickness of two sections of the cortex in the animals from the enriched cages were between 4 and 10 percent thicker than those of rats who spent their days in more boring environments. The increased thickness came, not from an increase in the number of brain cells, but from an increase in the number of connections (called dendrite branching) produced by the existing nerve cells in response to outside stimulation. The nerve cells themselves also became larger.

What happened to those rats whose fate it was to live out their days in impoverished surroundings? Their brain cells actually decreased in size. Paradoxically, the body weight (as opposed to brain weight) of the animals in unstimulating cages increased 7 percent over that of the littermates reared in settings with a variety of things to do. Is it possible that the waistlines of the couch potatoes among us are expanding while their brain cells are shrinking? Diamond's conclusions lead in that direction. Older brains can continue to develop when stimulated by new activities. But, more important, the brain cell losses among those rats in unstimulating environments was far greater than the gains made in the brains of rats in the enriched environments.

In other words, we might not be able to improve our minds a great deal by engaging in diverse activities, but we can be reasonably certain that maintaining an unstimulating lifestyle will result in declining brain functions.

The argument that engaging in novel activities stimulates brain growth would be more compelling if similar evidence could be collected in humans. Obviously, we cannot manipulate the environments of human beings and then examine the thickness of their cortexes after they die. But it is possible to correlate the degree to which older people are engaged in stimulating activities with the size of brain cells after they die. A research team at UCLA looked at the brains of twenty adults at autopsy. Then they correlated the size of the nerve cells in the brain's cortex with the activities reported by these individuals prior to death. The UCLA team found the cortexes of those older people who were more mentally and socially active to be thicker than the cortexes of those who were not. Among those who were active was a 79-year-old woman who was physically infirm but kept up with politics. Another was said to be exceptionally active socially; she was taking college courses for self-improvement at the time of her death. Even more striking were the brains of those who were sedentary and lethargic, and had few interests. Like the animals in Diamond's laboratory, their brain cells were smaller.

Looking at these scientific results, the skeptic might say, "What's the big deal? Sure they were able to show that rats that played with toys had slightly thicker brain parts than animals who didn't, but the differences are really tiny—3 percent here, 5 percent there, 10 percent in another place. These small differences don't add up to much." Whenever I hear a comment like this, it reminds me of something William James said a century ago. A philosopher and a doctor, he spent much of his career thinking about what made people happy and life fulfilling. A critic once said to James that it seemed to him that most people were pretty much the same. James responded, "There is very little difference between one man and another; but what little difference there is, *is very important.*" Ah, these "little differences": A baseball pitcher with a 92-mph fastball strikes out major league sluggers; but at 85 mph, he's back in the minors. A 5 percent majority is a landslide majority in a presidential election. These "little differences" can make all the difference in the quality of our lives.

OLD DOGS CAN LEARN NEW TRICKS

In Chapter 5, I made the point that age-related decline occurs in the normal course of our lives. "Using it" does not completely prevent cognitive as well as physical losses. In Chapters 4 and 5, I discussed ways to compensate for this decline. This section will add to the list of activities that can enrich our minds while shallowing the downward glide in our cognitive skills.

Seek New Learning Experiences

Apply the lessons from the laboratory to your everyday life by seeking new learning experiences. The results can be dramatic. Here is an example. Several years ago at a holiday gathering hosted by new friends on the west coast of Florida, I was introduced to two older women who were standing in a corner by themselves. Both had spent their careers teaching at a large Florida university and were a year away from retirement. Dressed identically in shades of gray, shod in ground grippers, and wearing little jewelry or makeup, they stood apart from other female (and male) guests who were dressed to kill. Because we were from New England and used to interesting minds cloaked in unassuming garb, I was prepared to find that appearances were deceiving. This turned out to be a faulty assumption. The two women expressed no enthusiasm for anything—their work, what was happening in the world, the state university system, or their city. They seemed uncomfortable and made me edgy. Conversation was impossible and, to my shame, I fled at the earliest opportunity. On the way home, talking to my wife, I referred to these women as "the Professors Boring."

Two years later, we were invited to that very same holiday event. After a short time, I noticed several people engaged in a lively conversation and wandered over. In the center of an animated rapid-fire discussion on topics leaping from Italian art to Greek culture to the political climate of Russia were two vivacious, articulate, and, to me, attractive, older women. Afterward, I recounted to my wife how interesting the conversation with them was. It might be enjoyable to see more of them, but their names escaped me. Did she know who they were? "They are the same women we met here two years ago," she smiled. "You referred to them as the Professors Boring."

What could have happened in the intervening twenty-four months to cause such a change in these two women? Two days later, I asked them. I learned that they had retired the year after we first met. In the following twelve months, they pursued their lifelong dream of studying Italian art, enrolling in a series of Elderhostel programs consisting of one- to four-week courses of study of art and history in Italy. They lived for a time in a small hill town on Lake Como, absorbing their surroundings. Then the two women decided to follow the same pattern in Greece. Right after the New Year, they were off for another course, this time in St. Petersburg, because they had decided they should study Russia. The "Professors Boring" fulfilled a long-held dream by studying the Italian (and Greek and Russian) culture and art. These programs raised their spirits and opened their minds, making them seem much more vivacious and interesting than they had been two years before. I also believe they would have scored far higher on a test of cognitive functioning after their studies abroad.

The Elderhostel program is worldwide, offering opportunities for study at nearly 2,000 colleges and schools. It offers short courses on just about any subject imaginable. And you don't have to have a doctorate to attend. If you can sign your name on a check, you are admitted. The programs are relatively inexpensive. Room and board in a college dormitory and classes usually cost less than five hundred dollars. And, unlike high school, there are no grades and you don't get detention for cutting class and going to the beach.

The positive effect of the Elderhostel programs on the two retired professors was possible because they possessed the desire and the adventuresome spirit to seek out new stimulating activities. They needed these qualities because neither had ever been to Italy before and both had only a rudimentary knowledge of Italian prior to their travels. Spending time in foreign countries taking courses in unfamiliar settings, some with only limited amenities in an environment where little English is heard day to day, was not without its hazards and frustrations. But they successfully coped with these difficulties and returned enriched and invigorated, setting themselves on the path to years of optimal aging.

Challenge Yourself

Like the Professors Boring, many high-functioning older people share a willingness to challenge themselves to learn or experience something intellectually or physically new. Often this challenge involves doing something unfamiliar, for which you have no demonstrated competence. You may be a little apprehensive about the ability to pull off the new undertaking. Take my friend Fran, who had played the piano in midlife. In her more recent pursuit of music, she learned to play the viola da gamba (an ancestor of the cello). She found that she not only enjoyed it but had a musical talent she had never fully developed. After five years of lessons, Fran was invited to play with three other women who were capable amateur musicians. Though uncertain about her ability to play at their level, she joined and fit in perfectly. She still does, at 82. Their string quartet, specializing in early chamber music, now performs regularly in churches and at community functions in the Boston area.

Then there is the feminist author Betty Friedan. A city dweller all her life, she decided, as she neared her sixtieth birthday, that she would take an Outward Bound program. In an amusing chapter journalizing her experience, Friedan begins by summing up her doctor's response when she asked him to fill out a four-page medical form. "Betty, are you out of your mind?" Although she was terrified of heights and had never spent a single night of her life separated from indoor plumbing, she decided to do it. She attended a ten-day program with a group of other 55+ Outward Bounders. They were Jerry (56), who ran a midwestern computer business; Earl (72), a retired insurance broker; Bob (60), who had recently sold his Madison Avenue advertising agency; Cece (64), also from New York City; Ruth, a teacher and mother; and Letha, a widowed social worker. They chose to participate in the Outward Bound program because all, in their own way, wanted to go beyond the boundaries of their present lives, challenging themselves with new adventures and risks, allowing their spirits to grow.

Friedan describes her growing feelings of competence as she backpacked through the North Carolina mountains, slept outside in clean cool air, paddled a rubber raft through the rapids on the Chattooga River, dug a hole for a toilet, climbed up a difficult mountain, rappelled down a dangerous cliff, and spent twenty-four hours alone in the midst of a crashing thunderstorm. After successfully completing the trip, Friedan described how impressed the young Outward Bound instructors were with her group of 55+-year-olds. They had imagined the oldsters would not have the stamina required to trek long distances, possess the strength to paddle through treacherous white water, and develop the skill needed to negotiate shear rock faces. In fact, Friedan reports that her group came through in good health, renewed in body, uplifted in spirit, and possessed of a firmer sense of their essential selves.

As a feminist, Friedan could not resist male-female comparisons. She noted that this was the first Outward Bound group where women and men were represented in equal numbers. Programs for younger generations attract many more men than women. She speculated that females may become more adventuresome with age: "Are women more likely to risk or relish new ways to test themselves than men?" she wondered. "Could that be one reason why women live longer?" She goes on to speculate that older males may be more reluctant to take on the challenges of the Outward Bound experience because of the fear of being shown up by the 25-year-olds. "Maybe this just applies to those who have the money to go on one of these elite programs," you might say. It turns out that others looking at the lives of older women and men from blue-collar backgrounds uncovered similar patterns. More females than males felt they needed greater novelty and challenges and excitement in their lives. Most, however, perhaps because they found few opportunities to engage in an Outward Bound program or similar activities to gratify these needs, did very little about it. The jury is still out on these questions. What does seem to be true, however, is that the diverse and stimulating experiences of Friedan's wilderness adventure enriched the spirits of both the men and the women.

Other challenges don't require hiking boots and a tent. Although possessing neither background nor talent, I've always been drawn to ballet and small modern dance groups; I especially love Merce Cunningham, Twyla Tharp, Alvin Ailey, and José Limon. During the intermission of a delightful Mark Morris production at Jacob's Pillow in Becket, MA, I wandered through the gift shop while reflecting on the intricate, graceful, athletic moves of the young dancers. Suddenly, a picture among the posters of dancers stunned me. It was a photo of Liz Lerman and several other dancers in a pose in which they were all looking right, each with the toes of the right foot touching the inside of the left knee, dancing the "Four Swans" from *Swan Lake*. What took my breath away was the realization that two of the dancers were in their 80s. Accompanying the poster was Lerman's book, *Teaching Dance to Senior Adults*. The pages of her book were filled with pictures of elders who had accepted the challenge of training to do ballet moves that I could not imagine executing myself.

Not all challenges need to be physical. After remarriage to a younger woman who believed that household activities should be divided evenly, including meal preparation, a 75-year-old friend of mine who had never boiled water in his life took up cooking. His first two courses in the adult education center were just right for him: "Boiling Water I" and "Boiling Water II" they were called. Soon he progressed to simple dishes and then more elaborate ones. A year ago, he prepared a good soup-to-salad five-course meal for us. This year he proudly announced that he had mastered mincemeat pie and jambalaya. We are invited for dinner next weekend. I wonder what jambalaya is.

Engage the New Technology

Almost ten years ago, I led a team of experts given the task of devising a test that would accurately distinguish between those older individuals whose minds were aging normally and those who were beginning to exhibit signs of mild Alzheimer's disease. This project is described in the Introduction. The team decided that MicroCog, the test's name, should be administered by personal computer (PC). Over the seven years that I worked on this project, I had a secret—a morbid dread of computers. A frequent nightmare was that I would find myself in a situation where my inability to carry out the simplest operations on a computer not only would be humiliating but also would under-mine the project in some important way. Fortunately, I finished the project without having either my ignorance or my anxiety revealed.

Learning how to work a PC was a good idea, I kept telling myself, but I was always "too busy" to learn. The truth was that I honestly didn't think that I had it in me to learn how to operate one. The thought of trying to master the imagined complexities of the computer evoked painful memories of my struggles with geometry. If I couldn't handle simple math as a teenager, how could I do it at 60-some? Besides, all the computer jocks I knew were about 17 and had IQs of 200.

Then a neighbor of mine told me that her 3-year-old grand-daughter could work the family PC even though she could not read. That did it. If a 3-year-old could learn to work a computer, I certainly could. So, that fall I signed up for a four-hour course introducing personal computers. The textbook was appropriately called *The Personal Computer for Dummies.* Although full of well-deserved doubt about my capacity to learn how to manage the little beast, and worried about being taught by someone who was younger than my own children, I found, after a short course of hands-on training, that I could actually make the PC do what I wanted most of the time. The effort required to master the elementary operations of a computer was much easier for me than overcoming the doubt as to whether it was possible to learn. Since then, I have taken three more courses. I can actually do my own word processing—at the two-fingered speed of fifteen words per minute—and make most of my own charts for slides and overheads. I even have my own e-mail address. Now an advanced beginner, I can be heard speaking with casual familiarity of "files," "bauds," and "megs of RAM," not to mention A and C drives, Web pages, and MUDS. No one from 5 to 55 is impressed, but I command the respect of the post-60 crowd.

As it turns out, my experience was not unique. A Penn State professor decided to see whether older adults could learn a specific computer skill, in this case, the Lotus 1-2-3 spreadsheet program. This research was motivated particularly by the recognition that today's workers will more and more often find it necessary to access the "information superhighway," using micro-computer skills. Present predictions are that the average worker will have to upgrade his or her skills eight to ten times in a career. But older workers must overcome the current negative stereotypes about being unable or unwilling to try to master new skills. In this research, none of the subjects (whose average age was 67) had previous computer experience. At the time, Lotus 1-2-3 was a popular and widely sold spreadsheet. The participants were taught how to construct an electronic monthly bookkeeping ledger and a checking account statement. Then they were tested on how accurately they formatted the information and used the spreadsheet formulas to calculate profits and losses, and balance the checkbook. After just three hours of instruction, one of which involved learning how to work a personal computer, the individuals completed over half the operations successfully.

Anyone who has tried to learn Lotus 1-2-3 in three hours will be impressed with these results. And I'll bet the volunteers for this project had some of the same fears in the beginning as I did. The biggest problem in learning how to work a PC is getting past the fear: fear of being overwhelmed with too much to learn; fear of not being able to learn as fast as the others; fear of being taught by teenage geniuses with no idea what it's like to be old and slow; and maybe even a fear of being seen by the other "students" as being too old to learn. Maybe it is because we are so scared in the beginning, and so doubtful of our own capabilities, that acquiring any new knowledge or mastering any new techniques is so exciting. It seemed to me that I could feel the dendrites starting to send out their little branches while I was learning how to work a PC. I don't know if my brain cells were actually growing, but I felt a lot smarter after learning something new.

Improve Declining Skills Through Training

We can't remember a friend's name, or find our way back to our car in the supermarket parking lot, or recall our own zip code. At 45, we don't worry about these lapses; at 55, we are briefly concerned and joke about having "early Alzheimer's"; at 65, it's not a joke anymore, and we worry that we may in fact be losing it.

Memory training has been a popular topic for several years. Infomercials regularly show the wonders in recall that can be achieved by this videotape or that audiocassette series. The self-help section of a bookstore I browsed last fall featured a shelf bulging with "improve your memory" books. All promised a "cure for absentmindedness," "total recall of names, numbers, faces, and places," and "the rapid mastery of assignments." None that I skimmed through targeted older people as those who would benefit especially from their techniques. That's a pity. They are missing a big market. Growing numbers of elders are worried about their memories; they are able to benefit from training; and most have the money to buy the books.

If the bad news is that many of our abilities have declined noticeably by age 60, surely the good news is that there are many available aids that have been scientifically demonstrated to reverse the downward trend. Yes, not only can the loss of memory be stopped as well as the decline of other functions such as reasoning and spatial ability, but some programs restore these abilities to the level of a decade or two younger. More important, it seems that those particular cognitive functions that are most likely to decline with age are those that can be improved.

Here's just a small example of the proven approaches that improve the mental agility of older people. Want to improve your memory? My research assistant, Norman, and I have found seventy-two studies that have been written since 1990 and report the positive benefits of mnemonic instruction (that's memory training). Nine out of ten studies found that the program participants reported improved memory, whereas volunteers who did not receive instruction exhibited little or no change. More than a dozen different approaches were used.

One of the most common techniques of improving memory is the so-called method of loci. As noted in Chapter 5, this is the one I use. The central element in this method is to acquire a mental map of fixed locations and then link each of the words or other things to be recalled from one of the locations. For instance, suppose I wanted to remember ten items to be picked up at the supermarket but didn't want to write them down. The items are celery and onions, bagels and cream cheese, orange juice and coffee, soup and pasta sauce, and notepads and rug cleaner. To go about memorizing this list using the method of loci, I try to associate the celery with the basement, onions with the kitchen, bagels with the living room, cream cheese with the dining room, orange juice with the family room, coffee with the stairs, soup with the bathroom, pasta sauce with the north bedroom, notepads with the east bedroom, and rug cleaner with the west bedroom. Other strategies work just as well. You can cluster words to be memorized in categories to cue recall. For instance, vegetables (celery and onions); things to drink (orange juice and coffee); cans (soup and pasta sauce); natural pairs (bagels and cream cheese); and other (notepads and rug cleaner). These examples are only two of many approaches that have been demonstrated to improve memory.

Can we be helped if we have already noticeably started to "lose it"? The short answer from the laboratory is "definitely yes." Sherry Willis and K. Warner Schaie, two of the world's most eminent gerontologists, tested volunteers from the Seattle Longitudinal Study at intervals from 1970 to 1984. In 1984, they selected subjects whose past scores had remained stable during this period and volunteers whose test performances had declined to about half of what they had been fourteen years earlier. At the time, the subjects ranged in age from 64 to 95, with an average age of 73. Both groups were given five hours of individual training. As we might expect, the stable group improved about 20 percent. But what was most interesting was that those whose cognitive scores had declined previously by about 50 percent improved to the level of their performance fourteen years earlier.

"Could it all be a placebo effect?" I thought to myself as I looked at these reports of elders' mental skills improving with training. "Maybe if you just pay some attention to older people, their test scores will jump up." But then, as I paged through these studies, I was intrigued to find that only those mental skills selected for training improved. Those *not* targeted for tutorial work remained the same as when the instruction began. Thus if the goal of the program was to improve the ability to remember a list of words, the subjects didn't exhibit stronger calculation skills at the end of training.

Suppose that, instead of receiving tutoring, we decided to buy a self-help book and try to improve on our own. Will that work? Paul Baltes at the Max Planck Institute in Berlin answered the question this way: He gathered a group of volunteers, ages 63 to 90. Half were given five tutoring sessions. The other half were given ten minutes of introduction and booklets on memory training to read on their own. These self-help volunteers spent the same amount of time working independently as those receiving the training. The self-help group posted scores as high as those in the training groups on tests of spatial skills and reasoning. Their gains were maintained six months later.

If we use improved test scores as a criterion, all abilities can be improved with training, including those aptitudes that are most vulnerable to the aging process—spatial ability, reasoning, and verbal memory. So far, the evidence that cognitive training improves mental abilities is limited to laboratory settings. The effects of the training has not been tested in real life. We do not know for certain that a man who has just completed a course on memory improvement will be better able to recall a list of errands he has to run tomorrow morning or that a woman will be able to more easily find her car in a large mall when she has finished her shopping. A small group of us in Cambridge have just begun a study of how much cognitive improvement through training extends beyond improved test scores to the real world and is maintained over time.

Indirect Approaches Work, Too

Suppose we really would like to improve our memory but don't feel like going through a memory training program, or are unable to locate one nearby, and those "how to" books for memory enhancement seem too complicated. What can we do then? Sometimes, just testing ourselves over and over helps. I have a vivid picture of a physician in Orlando, now in his 80s, who swears that he stays mentally sharp by taking the Law School Aptitude Test (LSAT) every year. He couldn't have known that studies of older volunteers in Europe and the United States have verified his hunch. In Berlin, volunteers improved on tests measuring memory and spatial abilities just by taking the tests several times. At Scripps University in California, psychologists found that those subjects who took tests a month apart did just as well on measures of reaction time, vocabulary, and spatial relations as those given training.

Other indirect approaches also worked well. It's known that tutoring programs that include relaxation components result in cognitive gains. Because anxiety impedes our capacity to focus, anything that lowers anxiety improves mental function. But what happens if we just use relaxation or meditation by themselves? A study demonstrating the powers of these techniques was carried out by psychologists at Harvard University and Maharishi International University. They looked at a group of 80-year-olds to see how they would perform on three ability tests after being taught transcendental meditation and relaxation. The results were remarkable. Those receiving transcendental meditation improved in memory, word fluency (name as many words as possible beginning with the letter *s* in one minute), and reasoning. No improvement occurred among individuals receiving no treatment. Of additional interest was the follow-up three years later. All of those receiving transcendental meditation were still alive, despite an overall survival rate for this age group of 63 percent.

Then there is exercise. We already know that aerobic conditioning has a positive effect in lowering anxiety, raising mood, and enhancing self-concept. Did you know that aerobic training also improves cognitive functions? In Salt Lake City, relatively sedentary individuals 55 to 75 were recruited to participate in a light exercise program. This exercise consisted mostly of fast walking and occasional slow jogging for three one-hour sessions weekly over a four-month period. Like the other research, the participants were given a battery of aptitude tests before and after the exercise program. Those receiving aerobic training improved in reaction time, reasoning, and attention. Volunteers who did not exercise failed to improve in any of these measures. Our own investigations of older physicians confirmed the benefit of moderate exercise. Those who reported that they walked regularly had higher overall scores on our cognitive test.

Before we take out a life membership in a nearby gym, we should remind ourselves that not all studies correlating physical and intellectual vigor have come up with the same positive findings, and nothing lasts forever. For instance, scientists in the Midwest have failed to find a consistent connection between aerobic fitness and scores on their cognitive tests. In Alabama, volunteers who had benefitted from cognitive training three years earlier showed a normal decline. However, their memory test scores three years later were still considerably higher than those who did not participate in the exercise. At present, the weight of scientific findings is on the side of the argument that moderate exercise positively influences our mental operations. Regular moderate exercise has about the same impact on the quality of our lives as stopping smoking. That's enough evidence to suggest that a morning walk or an evening stroll, or maybe a trial membership in a health club, might not be such a bad idea.

How Long Can We Keep Improving?

We know for certain that up through the mid-70s people can achieve remarkable gains in the quality of their thinking with very little instruction or through indirect activities such as meditation or exercise. But, a nagging question remains: How long can old dogs keep learning new tricks? The answer: Quite a bit longer than we might have imagined. Evidence comes from three different countries. One piece of evidence comes from the Seattle Longitudinal Study: 67- and 81-year-olds were given five hours of training in spatial and reasoning skills. All had been tested fourteen years earlier, and their scores had declined on mental tests during this period. Not surprisingly, those who were 67 raised their scores to the same level they had achieved in their 50s. Those who were 81 were able to improve, too. Their test performance after training was at the same level they had achieved when they were 67. A Swedish report found identical results with memory training: 80-year-old Swedes improved their memory by the same amount as those in their early 70s.

The third piece of evidence comes from psychologists at the Max Planck Institute in Berlin. They recruited a group of older (65 to 83) well-educated subjects to see whether they could improve their memory. Their task was to remember a list of thirty nouns (car, flower, desk, airplane, and so on). When the words were presented at a speed of about one word every two seconds, most people of any age recall only about five words from this list. Then they were taught the method of loci memory strategy, which involved associating each word with a Berlin landmark. They were given an opportunity to practice this technique until they had reached their peak and could improve no further. This training took about twenty sessions. At their peak, the average older person was able to recall about fourteen of the thirty words. In other words, the older adults improved their memory 180 percent.

As with physical fitness and improved cognition, not all efforts to raise the level of intellectual functioning of older adults have been successful. And the improvement of the oldest-old is modest relative to the remarkable gains in cognitive function that training brings to those in midlife, or even to the young-olds. Finally, we don't know how much these improved test scores apply to real life. Current evidence indicates that the mind continues, amid the inevitable losses accompanying the normal aging process, to retain a potential for growth for those who wish to age optimally.

No magic birthday exists after which we can no longer improve our intellectual skills. Given reasonable health and freedom from Alzheimer's disease or other forms of cognitive impairment, chances are we can boost our memory, if we choose to do so, until late into the final chapter. And many avenues can lead to cognitive enhancement: training sessions, self-study, relaxation, meditation, and exercise. There is something for everyone. To be able to improve memory for names and faces, to be able to refresh our reasoning or spatial skills at 70 or 80 or 90, can matter a great deal to elders who value staying as sharp as possible for as long as possible. Even if the improvements are relatively small, these "little differences" in the quality of our thinking make an enormous difference in our sense of being competent human beings.

RECAPPING

The myth that after a particular age you and I are too old to handle our job, to upgrade our skills, or to grow by meeting new challenges is alive and well in many sectors of the United States and the rest of the world. This patently false belief results in competent older workers being laid off or having their responsibilities reduced. It also can occasion feelings that beyond a certain age we are "too old" to develop new competencies, extend the horizons of our experience and refresh declining skills. Actions that can help us continue to grow include seeking diverse experiences and challenges: whitewater rafting; learning to speak Chinese; engaging the new technologies (especially the personal computer); and enhancing declining cognitive skills through short training programs; using relaxation, meditation, and exercise. These approaches can benefit mental skills until very late in life.

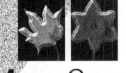

MYTH SEVEN:
OLD PEOPLE ARE
ISOLATED AND LONELY

Becoming socially isolated and lonely as we grow older is a common negative belief about aging. The reason is straightforward and compelling. Moving into our later years entails losing people close to us. These loved ones give our lives definition and pleasure. Because these losses occur in the context of growing physical problems that make it harder to get around, it is not hard to imagine elders feeling marginalized, ignored, and lonesome.

The probability of losing a spouse or life partner grows dramatically in the years after 55. The death of a loved one, someone with whom we have shared most of our life, tops the list of stressful events people must endure. All of us have seen first hand what one of our grandparents or parents has gone through when his or her spouse dies: grief, disarray, the inability to find pleasure in things that used to be enjoyed with a spouse.

If that loss isn't bad enough, widows and widowers find the distance opening between themselves and friends who are in couples. Widowers report that couples they have known for decades seem uncomfortable with them as single men. "They don't seem to be relaxed with just me," a widower sighed. "They keep trying to fix me up." Widows have an even harder time. Two women told me almost identical stories about their sudden isolation from old friends following the death of their husbands. "Married couples, who were old friends of ours, just stopped calling me," one 67-year-old woman said. "I guess the wives didn't want competition from a single woman." The other widow, who experienced a sudden evaporation of her coupled friends, had a slightly different and more self-deprecating take on the problem. "I just don't think I am as interesting alone as when John and I were together. The two of us made a good combination. We were always interesting and fun. By myself, I am not as good."

Even without the loss of a spouse, advancing age opens gaps in the ranks of close friends. Long-term friends can be as dear to us as husbands or wives and nearly as irreplaceable. They were our first, best friends, part of a select inner circle who shared our most intimate thoughts and feelings. Together we learned how to swim, put on makeup, buy our first bra or jock strap; we helped one another struggle with parents, school, and romance. Maybe we went to camp or college together. With them, we shared the sunset and the sunrise, the view from Mr. Katahdin, a canoe trip through the white water of the Au Sable, or the pleasure of sitting in silence fishing for perch off a pier in Lake Michigan. They were with us in our early adult years and as we started our careers; and they were part of our wedding. They rejoiced with us at the birth of our children and shared our tears at the death of our parents. There, by our side, they helped us endure a divorce, a layoff, a serious illness or self-inflicted injuries. Sharing these memories with old friends enables us to revisit our childhood, youth, and midlife, reliving our excitement and wonder, lusts and loves, aspirations and realities, and the laughing, particularly the laughing, laughing until our bellies ached, at stories worn to a fine gloss by re-telling, but just as funny to us now as forty or sixty years ago. When old friends depart our company, part of our memory of ourselves, and enjoyment of our lives, goes with them.

These age-associated losses—marital and personal—would be close to unbearable for women and men in their prime. It stands to reason that it would be worse for an elder already struggling with the illnesses of old age, declining eyesight, diminished hearing, arthritic joints, insomnia, and those other limitations that late life brings. Unable to physically move about like they used to, and with many fewer old friends, what could be more reasonable than to believe that old people are isolated and lonely?

▓ THE REALITY

There is no denying that the loss of a spouse or a life-long friend can be a devastating event. But this myth is especially danger-ous because it leads to the conclusions that we can do nothing to avoid the depopulation of our world of loved ones and that only loneliness lies ahead. To predict that isolation and loneli-ness are inevitable outcomes of these serious losses is to ignore what happens in the everyday lives of most elders. In fact, most people cope with the loss of loved ones and resume a normal, if altered, lifestyle within two years.

Social activities change in ways we might anticipate: Closer relationships with family members and former friends develop in the first year after conjugal loss. The connections may be fewer but stronger. As we might expect, there is much indi-vidual variation in relationships, depending on the quality of the contacts prior to the loss. Some who are suddenly alone rapidly knit themselves into their family networks. For others, for whom family relationships have been less intimate, contacts with kin decrease while associations with close friends grow.

And, some, who have been caring for invalided partners, report greatly increased social relationships because of more free time and energy.

Substantial gender differences are apparent after the loss of a loved one. Older males are seven times more likely to remarry than females are. Whether fewer females remarry because fewer age-appropriate men are available or because females are more capable of living by themselves than males are is difficult to determine. But we do know that remarriage is about the only place older men hold an edge. The loss of a spouse causes a greater shrinkage of the social contacts of men than of women. And widowers have a much greater risk of illness and death than widows do.

Until the middle of the eighth decade, little difference exists in the actual number of people in the lives of most women and men. When we ask younger and older adults of both sexes to name their close friends and relatives, we find that the average number of close associations is about ten at all checkpoints from 30 to 75. Dramatic differences exist among the post-65 group in the size of their social networks, just as the variability in their cognitive and physical vigor increases with age. Some choose to retain fewer intimates rather than repopulating their cadre of friends with persons whom they can never be as close to. Seniors who continue to work or have more financial resources say they have more friends than do retirees or those with less money.

In the 70s, the circle of people we can count on shrinks. Old friends die, become disabled, or move away. Not surprisingly, contacts with relatives take on greater importance. Only one in ten older Americans has not personally seen a family member in the past thirty days. Half have been in the company of a relative yesterday or today. These connections are informal (calling or dropping in for a chat), ceremonial (birthdays and holidays), or assisting (helping and being helped).

Being alone and being lonely are not synonymous with being older. Unquestionably, elders spend more time by themselves than younger adults do. People over 65 are alone about half of their waking hours, whereas those who are not yet 65 spend about 30 percent of their time alone. Lots of seniors, however, enjoy their privacy. This is especially true when it's a voluntary choice, and when they have the security of knowing that they are loved and wanted. Being alone only turns to loneliness when we feel this condition is imposed upon us. Approximately 12 percent of senior citizens say they are alone more than they desire. For many, however, these feelings of isolation have not suddenly come upon them in their later years. Because of problems in their environment or in their psychological responses to stress, many felt isolated and lonely as young and midlife adults.

When I think about these research findings, I think of my mother. When she became a single parent and a working mother simultaneously in midlife, most of her large group of friends melted away. Mother repopulated her social network this way: Her inner circle consisted of the three women she played bridge with once a month for the next twenty-five years and her two younger sisters, who moved in with us. The middle circle contained the extended matrilineal family—great aunts, numerous cousins, and nieces. Although ours was the smallest house, it was at our home that the family gathered to share major holidays and ceremonial occasions. The outer rings comprised friends at work and at church. These relationships sustained her until the day she moved into a retirement home when she was almost 80.

In the retirement home in this medium-sized midwestern town, she rediscovered old female friends from her youth, Betty and Elaine. She added two more, Gladys and Elsie. She also maintained an active correspondence with her grandchildren. Finally, she found a cause, the plight of the Native Americans. "I always thought the Indians got a raw deal," she once told me. But I had no idea until after she died how deeply involved she was with their programs. She regularly donated a portion of her small discretionary income to the Native American Prep School in New Mexico and became a pen pal to one of the teenagers there.

As she grew older, mother liked her solitude. And so did most of the women in the retirement home. One of the features she liked most about living there was that she could close her door. She put it this way: "All of the women on the corridor have a rule: If the door is open, we don't mind visitors; if it's closed, we want privacy. Most of us on the corridor like to be able to close our apartment doors. We never could when we were wives and mothers."

In short then, serious investigators have refuted the theory that advancing age is synonymous with increasing loneliness. Most elders, at least those living in the community, do not feel isolated from friends and family. Contact with kin, especially adult children, is frequent. Those who feel lonely in the last quarter are often those who felt isolated earlier in their adult life.

■ OPTIMAL SOCIAL AGING IN THE FACE OF PREDICTABLE LOSSES

What can we do to cope with the predictable losses of loved ones that go hand and hand with growing older? Fortunately, a lot of potentially useful information is available. The advice falls into these categories: Begin early to reweave social networks. Seek virtual friendships. Choose quality over quantity. Recognize that men and women may have different social needs. Avoid learned dependency.

Begin Early to Reweave Social Networks

Friends don't just melt away suddenly when we retire or when our spouse dies. For most of us, the decimation of our group of friends begins when we leave home or graduate from college in our 20s; we move from Atlanta to Seattle and then from Seattle to Denver in our 30s; our friends get promoted or fired, separated, divorced, remarried, or otherwise leave town in our 40s. Once we reach our 50s and 60s, more people drop out of our lives; older friends move to Myrtle Beach or downsize to a condo in the city. At work, we find ourselves to be the oldest person in the room more often than we care to think about. That in itself is not so bad, but increasingly we find ourselves not knowing most of the new people who are two or three decades younger. Furthermore, they may be strikingly different from the cadre of individuals with whom we entered the organization. The new arrivals are far more diverse than the cohort of people from similar backgrounds with whom we joined the workforce. They are often females of color, and the mother tongue of some is not English.

I am speaking for my generation of white men, of course. When I began working at Harvard in the early 1960s, my contemporaries were all white males. Gradually we have entered the twentieth century, and now the genders are equally divided and we have a rainbow of racial and ethnic backgrounds. My colleagues from backgrounds different from mine seem to have much less trouble relating to the new arrivals in our department; maybe it's because they are closer in age, or perhaps they share common experiences unfamiliar to my generation.

The growing social vacuum may not hit us full force until our children leave home. Up to that point, our lives are filled with their activities and friends as well as the parents of their friends. This social swirl slows dramatically when we pack our last child off to college or move a daughter into an apartment in Chicago. People stop dropping by, no messages blink for us on the answering machine when we arrive home at night; and we ask ourselves, "Where *is* everyone?"

If we wait until this time to begin trying to fill the rapidly expanding social void, we have our work cut out for us. So start early. In your 40s, begin replenishing your pool of friends as old friends depart. At home, reach out. Seek out and talk to your new neighbors or the new people who have joined your church or temple. Find a new regular racquetball partner when someone you played with regularly blows out her knee or is promoted to the home office in Cincinnati. Fill in those foursomes of golf or bridge when someone departs, ideally with younger people. Introduce yourself to those young people at work, especially those whose life experiences may be different from your own. They have probably heard about you, and may even want to get to know you. Besides, they may be looking for a mentor. Remember when you were their age, standing in the corner of the room, feeling overwhelmed and scared? Did you ever wish one of the seniors would take the slightest interest in you?

Recognize that younger coworkers will be as edgy as you were when you make a welcoming gesture. They may not have had that much experience with oldsters being nice to them. So your first efforts are likely to be greeted with surprise and an awkward unresponsiveness. Take your time getting to know them. You will probably find that they are at least as interesting as you were when you were just starting out.

This is hard work. And you have to be creative. Tom, a contemporary of mine and a busy dentist, has been teaching Sunday school for a decade. Last year over a glass of iced tea following a morning workout, he said, "It keeps me connected. In fact, I stay connected to two generations—the kids and their parents." I am less creative, but I try. Every fall a half-dozen trainees join us for the year. Always I volunteer to teach a seminar for them in an effort to create bonds between us. I don't bat 100 percent, but over five years I have made two or three new friends among these trainees, a small yield but one that makes up for other losses. New neighbors have been in the house next door for four months and I have yet to introduce myself with anything other than a wave, but I'm working at it. I did invite their two sons, Eli (11) and Josh (8), over to shoot baskets in my driveway, which is more level than theirs. They were there when I came in the driveway tonight. Maybe this will result in an introduction to their parents.

Limited as my efforts have been, I can see positive results. Our Christmas card list continues to fill with the names of former students and younger colleagues, the young adult children of our friends, and the friends of our children. One of them, John, now 37 with a family of his own, calls me most years on my birthday. The gaps in family networks created by the departure of parents, aunts and uncles, and favorite cousins fill with nieces and nephews and grandchildren. Especially grandchildren. They hold a special place in my inner circle of intimates.

▓ SEEK VIRTUAL FRIENDS

Most older people don't mind having more time to themselves. But about one older person in eight says he or she has too much time on his or her hands. The majority of these few are 75+ and physically frail. So, there we sit, at 75 or 85 or 95, old and creaky, living alone, not able to get out much anymore, most of our old friends gone, and the new younger ones too busy to pay much attention to us, one child on one coast and a second living in New Guinea. We are not one of those "successful" oldsters with the mind and body of a 50-year-old; we're closer to 100 than 60 and feel every minute of it. Sure we enjoy our privacy, but enough is enough. How can we "reweave" social networks?

The solution? Make virtual friends on the Internet. The Internet is a worldwide network of computers that allows their users to share information. Computers used to be merely tools, little more than high-speed adding machines or word processors. In her second horizon-expanding book on the effect of computers on our lives, MIT professor Sherry Turkle details the effects of the Internet. She talks of the computer having the potential to open doors to an array of social contacts unimaginable a decade ago. For those needing contact with other human beings, there are e-mail, chat groups, and forums as well as games to play with participants from around the globe.

For a frail elderly person, especially someone living in a nasty climate or in isolated circumstances, the Internet is a godsend, because it enables these people to remain mentally active. We can shop, pay bills, reposition investments, and make reservations to visit our grandchildren with a few keystrokes. In some cases, we can even keyboard in questions about worrisome drug interactions or physical problems to a medical on-line service.

Electronic mail (e-mail) connects us to a whole world of real and virtual friends. One man who just learned how to work a computer e-mailed his grandson, who was away at college. Immediately came back the reply: "Hi, Grandpa. Glad you were on-line! Could you send me $20? I am a little short. Love, Nick."

Computers are not inexpensive, but the prices are coming down every month. Today a perfectly adequate machine can be had for under a thousand dollars. Used ones are cheaper. Less expensive yet are the computers available through senior centers and organized by SeniorNet. Now just over ten years old, SeniorNet is a booming on-line service tailored to the needs and interests of older people around the world. Founder Mary

Furlong started SeniorNet in San Francisco senior centers, church basements, and schools in 1986. Her goal was to teach older people to use computers and to communicate with one another. Her first class had twenty-two students in it. But, with the backing of powerhouses such as Microsoft and several foundations, there are currently eighty-three centers visited by over 20,000 members each year. They are taught by older volunteers, some of them retired computer industry executives. In 1996, about 30 percent of people age 55+ owned computers, up from 21 percent the previous year. Seniors with computers are logged on about twelve hours a week, more time than either high school or college students spend at similar activities. Using the SeniorNet is not expensive, costing about $25 for an annual membership.

When we can't get out physically, we can bring new virtual friends to us on-line via SeniorNet. They can be people who share particular interests such as Amish culture or the North African campaign in World War II. Jim, living in a nursing home in Eau Claire, WI, says that his view into the cyberspace window is much larger than the view from the single window in his room. On his computer screen, he can "smell the savory aroma of a Holly Springs, TX, barbecue, tremble as a New Zealand earthquake shakes me . . . and chuckle at the wit of an Oregon sage."

As you might guess, romance sometimes flourishes when virtual friends become real-life companions. Following the death of her husband four years earlier, Marge heard about Senior-Net. As she met more and more people on-line, she told her daughter, "This is what I want to do, meet people I wouldn't otherwise meet and not be alone anymore." Then Marge met Dick on-line in October. They discovered they lived near each other. The chemistry must have been transmitted electronically because they agreed to meet at a SeniorNet get-together in the fall. The following January they were married.

One of the best advantages of contacting people via the computer is that we can communicate when we are at our best. So often as we grow older, we just aren't in the mood to see others when they want to call or stop by. Then when we feel motivated to have company, there is no one around. With the Internet, we can send our message to people on our own schedule and they can respond on theirs.

Choose Quality over Quantity

In the old-old years, the number of people we can count on to be there for us emotionally and physically shrinks. But as we mature, a few close friends are more beneficial than a large number of acquaintances. This statement seems so obvious that it needs no elaboration. But there are two good reasons we are selecting quality over quantity in our friends.

The first reason we should pick our friends for quality is because our tolerance for people who bring up negative emotions in us, no matter how interesting or amusing these individuals may be, decreases dramatically with age. Advancing age brings with it a growing intolerance for women and men who disturb the emotional status quo.

Stanford psychologists had a theory that older individuals grow to be more selective in their social contacts because they are disinclined to choose to be with individuals who stimulate high levels of emotion. So these scientists thought that when women and men were near the end of their lives they would choose to spend this time with familiar friends and family members who don't ruffle their emotions. They called a large number of people from 11 to 92 and asked them to imagine that they had thirty minutes free. This free time could be spent in one of three ways: with an old friend or family member, with a recent acquaintance with whom they had much in common, or with the author of a book they had recently read. The younger group selected each of the choices with about the same frequency. The older volunteers preferred familiar intimates. What confirmed the idea that the sense of having little time left causes people to choose older, rather than new or unfamiliar individuals, was when the younger volunteers were queried: "How would you spend thirty minutes if you knew you were going to move across the country in a few weeks?" This time the younger people reacted just as the older participants had: They preferred to be with their closest friends and family. They just didn't have time to waste with people who upset them.

The Stanford investigators theorized that the choice of who to spend time with is more a function of how much time we believe we have to live rather than our chronological age. To test this theory, they asked gay young men in the San Francisco area the same questions. One-third of these men tested negative for HIV; one-third tested positive for HIV but had no symptoms of AIDS; the remaining one-third were HIV positive and were experiencing AIDS symptoms. Those who tested negative for HIV made choices of social partners similar to the choices of other young adults. In contrast, the young men with AIDS overwhelmingly picked familiar friends and relatives to share their remaining time with.

A second reason that we can get along with fewer contacts is that in older age we prefer to spend time with those we have helped in the past. Because many of us do not particularly enjoy asking for the assistance of others, and elders are no exception to this rule, we are often more comfortable soliciting the care of those in our social network whom we have helped in the past. This is known as the "bank account" model of social relationships. Thus, a frail 85-year-old, living in an assisted-living facility, who has nursed her children through their growing-up years and has comforted them during crises in their lives, knows she has made "deposits" in an emotional bank account. Therefore, she is entitled to ask for their help when she needs some things at the drugstore, has to be taken to the doctor, or would like her winter clothes moved down into storage and the summer ones brought up.

Having positive contacts with a few close friends and relatives benefits our health too. Psychologists at Rutgers compared how often elderly volunteers were ill in the past month with gastrointestinal problems, upper respiratory infections, and other ailments. They also recorded the number of people these elders knew well. The investigators discovered that how many friends they had was *not* correlated with the health of these oldsters. What mattered most was the quality of these relationships. Those who were the most satisfied with their relationships were the healthiest. Specifically, these healthier elders said that they had family and friends who did things for them. No surprises here. But many also reported that their friends were available for them to confide in or just to relax with.

If the quality versus quantity recommendation has a moral, it's that we need to begin early in developing multilevel relationships with people who will later be important to us. "Be nice to your children: They will pick your nursing home," read a bumper sticker I saw recently. In fact, with life expectancy increasing, our progeny may well spend more time taking care of us than we have spent raising them. This will be especially true for those people having children in their late 30s and 40s. We also need to work hard to maintain contact with old friends. Never again will there be friends quite like these. Avoid relying on one-dimensional friendships that evaporate when you retire, can't bowl anymore, or move out of the neighborhood. While still in your prime, be sure to make some emotional "deposits" with others in need. And continue as long as it gives you pleasure. Studies of mature adults find that those who go out of their way to give to others are healthier and better adjusted, and report being less lonely than others who do not.

Women and Men May Have Different Social Needs

About five years ago, I became aware of the correlation between the size of social networks and illness or death: The larger our social networks are (the more relatives and friends we can count on), the less likely we are to fall ill or to die. For instance, the relative risk of catching a cold for those exposed to a virus is four times greater among those with one or two friends than among those with a social network of six or more. Six months after a heart attack, socially isolated people die twice as often as those with two or more sources of social support. These findings remain constant whether the subjects were rich or poor, black or white, rural or urban, living in this country or abroad. These associations held up when controlled for age, previous health, and how much the subjects smoked and drank.

What caught my eye when I looked at the lines charting the relationship between the size of social networks and morbidity/mortality statistics were the male-female differences. How many people you were close to meant less to females than to males. Women on the whole needed fewer people in their lives than males to live just as healthfully. For example, men with few friends died at a rate of 164 percent greater than those with the most intimates. But, for women, the ratio was significantly lower. There was only about a 37 percent difference in mortality between females with the fewest and most friends.

The following week, I presented these findings to my class on aging, highlighting the male-female differences. The men looked perplexed; the women nodded understandingly. "I have fewer friends, but I have far better and closer friends than my husband," said one gray-haired lady. She went on to say of her spouse, "His friends are all 'one thing' friends: He has friends at work, he has friends he plays cards with, but not both." A 40-year-old woman in computer sales chimed in, "My boyfriend doesn't have anyone I would call a friend. He also always has to *do* something with them—fish, play racquetball, drink. I almost never 'do' anything with my friends except invite them over for a cup of coffee and unload." Then she smiled and went on, "I don't think my boyfriend could ever call on one of his buddies and say, 'Hi, Ralph. Why don't you stop over for a cup of tea this afternoon.'" Another woman recalled that she once asked her high school boyfriend—a macho, smart, future neurologist— what he and his best friend talked about. "Oh, cars, stereo systems, the Green Bay Packers." he replied. She asked if they ever talked about their plans, hopes, or things they worried about (the boyfriend's father was dying of cancer). He responded in total shock, "No! That's what *girls* are for!"

The comments of the class anticipated what I discovered in the research of others on male-female differences in friendships. The reason that women can get along with fewer close relationships than males is because they have more rigorous standards for what constitutes a friend. Far more often, their friendships are multidimensional, that is, a wide range of experiences and feelings are shared.

In essence, then, we should be aware that, for both genders, having more friends is better for our health than being socially isolated. Women, especially older women, may be able to get along just as well with smaller social networks than males because their friendships are more likely to be multidimensional.

Avoid Learned Dependency

Two decades ago, a pair of young Yale graduate students, now among today's most prominent psychologists, wondered whether giving institutionalized elderly people a tiny amount of control over something in their lives would have a positive influence on their personalities. What they did was to give a houseplant to each elderly resident in a nursing home in Connecticut. Half of the residents were told that the plants would be cared for by the nursing staff. The other half were told that they were responsible for the care of the plant. They were to decide when to water the plant and how much sun it should have. Also they were encouraged to make decisions for themselves: choosing when and where to receive visitors and on what day they would see a movie. At the beginning of the study, the two groups were similar in physical and mental vigor.

Three weeks later, there was no difference in the health of the plants. But there was a lot of difference in the psychological adjustment of those residents who were put in charge of caring for the plants and who were encouraged to take more control of their own lives. Prior to being given the plants, both groups filled out questionnaires inquiring about how much they participated in activities at the nursing homes and how happy they felt. After three weeks, a similar questionnaire was passed out. The group given more responsibility rated themselves as more alert, active, and vigorous than they were before the study, an observation confirmed by the nursing staff. Eighteen months later, their health had improved, whereas the physical state of the others not encouraged to take control of their lives had declined.

What's the take-home message for those of us elders who may not be in a nursing home? The message is that feeling in control of some portion of our experience is good for our physical and mental health. The amount of governance we have over the events in our lives changes dramatically during our life span. We grow from being largely helpless as infants and children to taking greater charge of what we eat, how we dress, who our friends are, and what goals we set for ourselves during the adolescent years. In young adulthood, we have a greater degree of choice as we select what we plan to work at, who we want to share our lives with, where we will live, and how we will fill our discretionary time. The amount of control we have in our day-to-day existence noses down slightly in the prime of life with the inevitable demands of career and family, but we still feel in charge of most of what happens to us.

Then in our 50s we start the process of relinquishing the management of many parts of our life. Our children leave our sphere of influence. By now we've peaked at work and we can see the spotlight moving away, illuminating others. Our bodies betray us; joints deteriorate so that a slight limp supplants our once springy step. After 60, osteoporosis shortens us a quarter of an inch a year. We don't need a crystal ball to see that old age (that's ten years beyond however old we are now) will bring with it decreasing power to govern our existence.

How do we continue to have as much control in our lives as possible as we mature from the young-old to the old-old stages of life? Two general principles to keep in mind can help us keep a workable balance of independence and dependence on others: (1) selection, optimization, and compensation; (2) and avoiding learned dependency.

We first met the concept of selection, optimization, and compensation in Chapter 2, using the examples of Arthur Rubenstein and Colonel Jarvis. Recall that the three steps in the process allow us to bend to the inevitable toll that aging takes while still being able to control large parts of our life. For instance, at work we choose to continue those activities that we are best at or find most gratifying, letting go of those that are less central. At 68, a college dean resigns her academic post so that she can focus her energies on teaching. In the next building on campus, a librarian one year her senior, having cut back to 60 percent time, has a passionate interest in accessing computerized databases for faculty researchers. He works at keeping current, optimizing his skills. Just back from a workshop in Ann Arbor, he is planning to attend a weekend seminar at UNC in October. Both are hard of hearing. They compensate for this loss in two ways: both use hearing aids but find conversation by phone taxing. So they encourage e-mail.

Selection, optimization, and compensation works well for people in their young-old years. Because of technical, economic, and educational advantages, the overall quality of life for the 60- to 75-year-olds is far better today than at any point in the past. But as we head into the last season of life, health deteriorates, so the need for the assistance of others grows. The proportion of 72-year-olds needing some help with the basic activities of daily living (shopping, errands, cooking) is about one in ten. That percentage doubles every five years thereafter; so at 77, it is about 20 percent, and at 85, close to one person in two requires some form of assistance.

Although they live longer than men, women are at considerably greater risk for functional impairments related to old age. Elders in Berlin from 70 to 103 were rated on about two dozen measures of how well they functioned, from good to poor. The investigators were not surprised to find that twice as many 70-year-olds were rated as having a "good" level of functioning as 80-year-olds, and octogenarians were five times more likely to be at the highest level of functioning than the 90-year-olds. A finding that raised my eyebrows was that the risk for older females of becoming disabled was about twice that of males. So, while women live longer than men, the quality of their later lives has a higher probability of being undesirable. It is possible that today's cohorts of women entering the post-menopausal years will be able to retain much higher levels of activity and self-care than their mothers and grandmothers because of better nutrition, improved fitness, and hormone replacement therapies. But this remains to be demonstrated in the old-old years.

Because many of us who will live "to a ripe old age" may need the help of others to live our lives as fully as possible, we need to continually balance and rebalance those parts of our lives we manage ourselves, and those parts we allow others to handle. Only by allowing ourselves to be dependent can we continue to live with maximal autonomy. A widow living alone in an apartment without a car can maintain her independent status by allowing the senior center van to transport her to the mall for shopping and her son-in-law to put on the storm windows in the fall. A few years later, she accepts a wheelchair at the airport so that she can fly to see her grandchildren. Later, the same woman, now frail and elderly, moves into an assisted-living facility. Although she regrets losing the independence of her apartment, she recognizes that she needs considerable assistance to care for herself. Because this support is now being provided by others, she is able to see her several children and grandchildren when she is at her best. They seem happy to see her, and she them. And she feels good about not being a burden to anyone.

The second way to help us maintain a workable balance of independence and dependence is to avoid learned dependency. In our last years, we need to be wary of giving up governance of segments of our lives because of premature loss of control that is reinforced by others. This undesirable outcome occurs because those caring for us may encourage us to be increasingly dependent on them to carry out activities of daily living that we might still be able to manage for ourselves. Some caregivers have a tendency to ignore, if not outright discourage, independent self-management and to positively reward dependent actions. The resulting behavior is called learned dependency.

A classic study of learned dependency discovered that nursing home staff regularly encouraged elderly residents to be dependent upon them for dressing, eating, and maintaining personal hygiene. In some ways, this is not so surprising, because the staff want to do things as easily and quickly as possible. It is easier for an attendant to put the sweater on an 85-year-old man who has trouble doing it quickly or to feed an elderly woman rather than wait for her to do it on her own.

When the elderly were living, *not* in a nursing home, but on their own, and the caregivers were family, not the nursing staff, exactly the same pattern occurred. Family members did things for their elderly relatives rather than encouraging them to be as independent as possible. By the same token, they ignored the efforts of older individuals to do things on their own. The daughter would say, "Here, Mom, let me help you button that shift," rather than waiting and perhaps encouraging her to do it herself. A son insists on mowing the lawn of his 80-year-old father's small house rather than allowing the older man to do it himself slowly, but capably. "Next you will be cutting my meatloaf for me," the older man sighs. The cost of the daughter's and son's efficiencies is a decrease in the self-sufficiency of their elder parents.

The trick for the loved ones of the elderly is to recognize that even the most enfeebled need some domains over which they have control. As much independence as possible needs to be encouraged while providing adequate care—maybe it is in dressing, eating, mowing the lawn, baiting the fishhook, or even taking care of a houseplant. Perhaps the sense of independence comes from having their opinions taken seriously: about the political situation in Israel, whether drugs should be legalized, what's wrong with HMO medicine or Medicare. Not having one's views ignored or trivialized because of age can do wonders for the mental vigor of elders.

And the trick for those of us getting on in years is to begin early getting comfortable with being a little more dependent on the younger generation. A few moments of dependence can yield far longer periods of higher quality independent actions. Begin early. When I think of this second principle, I picture my old friend, Rich, practicing his tennis game prior to a match with me and my skilled partner. With Rich is his son, Josh. We find that they have arrived a half-hour before us so that Rich can practice his game. Rich, now 60, with an arthritic elbow and a bad knee, is taking instruction from his 30-year-old son: "Keep the racquet in front of you in volleys, Dad. Punch those net shots, don't swing. Hit those returns right at their bodies." During the match, which we happened to be winning at the time, Josh took time out and whispered strategic hints to his father. Later they won the match in a sudden-death tie breaker when Rich volleyed my partner's forehand into my belly. Because of Rich's willingness to accept help from his son, he was able to continue to play the beloved game of tennis at a level he enjoyed.

Sitting on the porch overlooking the tennis courts on that warm Thursday afternoon, we reminisced about how much things have changed. I shared a vivid memory of sitting with Rich while the then 15-year-old Josh was playing in a New

England high school tournament. I remember Rich agonizing over his mistakes and yelling encouragement and advice. Josh smiled, "Yes, I remember that. I was a lot harder to teach than Dad is now." I have the feeling that the growing comfort with which Rich is now able to accept Josh's support bodes well for his being more gracious in the last season of his life when he will inevitably need far more help and support than playing winning tennis. This practice will give him a head start in learning to accept being dependent in some areas of life so that he can be as independent as possible in the rest.

RECAPPING

Being isolated and lonely as we grow older is a common belief about aging. This myth is especially dangerous because it leads to the assumption that nothing can be done to control the inevitable depopulation of our lives and the loneliness that results. In fact, most of those in the young-old age group name about the same number of relatives and friends that they named before, because networks of loved ones are rebuilt through the eight decades of life. Even those in the old-old years find that there is a difference between being alone and being lonely.

Coping with age-associated gaps that occur naturally in our circle of friends include practicing these strategies. Begin early reweaving of social networks, because close friends and relatives begin to depart from early adulthood onward. To overcome social isolation, seek virtual friends via the Internet and e-mail. Because we lose our taste for stimulating but aggravating people as we grow older, opt for quality more than quantity in friends. Women tend to have more multilevel friends, so they may be able to get along with fewer intimates than males. And, in the last season of life, maintain a workable balance of independence and dependence by selection, optimization, and compensation and by avoiding learned dependency.

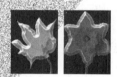

MYTH EIGHT:
OLD PEOPLE ARE DEPRESSED,
AND HAVE EVERY RIGHT TO BE

When the idea for this chapter first occurred to me, I honestly wondered what the scientific evidence would show. A formidable case can be made that old age brings with it serious losses. In the last chapter, we surveyed the shrinking social networks that occur as old friends and life partners leave us. Then there is the matter of retirement and declining health. Last week you and I were employed in a job that provided us with a role in society, a rewarding function to carry out, and a sense of being useful and competent. Plus, it provided a network of coworkers—some of whom we had cordial and friendly relationships with. This week we are retired, pensioned off, out of work. It's not hard to imagine that this change in roles causes us to feel devalued. And it is not difficult to visualize the sense of separation from friends and colleagues on the job. For a brief period, they seem happy to hear from us; but after a few weeks, they stop returning our phone calls. We no longer play a role in their lives.

Because each of these losses is known to be correlated with depression, who wouldn't predict that old age and depression go hand in hand? I was not surprised, then, to come upon the findings about depression from the Duke Longitudinal Study. In two different decades, their investigators queried North Carolina participants as to whether they experienced any of a dozen or so symptoms of depression. About one-third acknowledged the presence of insomnia, thoughts of death, feeling blue, or other signs of a mood disorder. More recently, the National Institutes of Health convened a Conference on Depression in Late Life. The conclusion of the conferees was that "because of the many physical illnesses and social and economic problems of the elderly, individual health care providers often conclude that depression is a normal consequence of these problems." This must be why older people, especially white men, have a higher risk for suicide. Just 13 percent of the population, those 65+, account for 19 percent of all suicides. How could anyone doubt that old people are often depressed and have every reason to be?

■ THE REALITY

The reality for the majority of older women and men departs considerably from these pessimistic conclusions, because the logic predicting that decimated social networks, unemployment, and the growing reality of illness and death lead to depression among elders in our society omits several critical truths. Few question that the death of a husband or wife will be among the most painful experiences that those of us who lose a life partner will have to bear. Health and emotional stability decline in many in the first year of bereavement. Illnesses increase and visits to the hospital rise. Depressive symptoms are visible in the first few months after a beloved's death. After six months, how-ever, the morbidity/mortality risk for widows and widowers returns to average: 90 to 95 percent of those who have lost a spouse recover their emotional balance within twelve to twenty-four months.

Similar findings apply to retirement. Nearly a half-century of studies of retirees came to the same conclusion: The over-whelming majority of men and women don't find that leaving their occupations has an adverse effect on their mental adjust-ment. Cornell scientists studied 2,007 men at age 64, when nearly all were employed, and then two years later when the majority had stopped working. They came from all the lower forty-eight states and held jobs at every level. The investigators discovered that seven out of ten retirees said that they were rel-atively satisfied with retirement. They didn't miss their jobs or the people there very much; and they also had no wish to return to full-time work.

Would those who continued their careers be less depressed and better adjusted than those who left the workforce? The short answer is "no." The Cornell Study compared the mental status of men who had retired with that of those who continued on the job. Among those still working, 77 percent said that they felt their life was useful and rarely felt depressed; 75 percent of the retirees answered the same way—no difference. Did those who were well adjusted prior to retirement experience a decline in their mental health when they quit working? Again the answer is in the negative. Among the men who said they were sound psychologically prior to retirement, 83 percent reported a good adjustment later when they were no longer employed. The proportion of well-adjusted men who continued their employ-ment was just about the same.

How about those who said they were poorly adjusted before retirement? Would they be worse off when they stopped going to work every day? Once more, the result showed that retirement was not a negative influence on emotional state. In fact, over half the men who said they were in a poor state of mind before retirement said they were well adjusted after leaving the work-force. A reason for their improved adjustment after retirement may have been that their work was toxic to their mental health. These same results have been reproduced many times in the intervening years.

Did prior attitudes about retirement influence how these men adjusted to life after 65? This time the answer is "yes." A higher proportion of the men who were happy in retirement were those who had thought positively about retirement while they were still working. By the same token, people who had negative attitudes toward retirement while employed tended to be dissatisfied with their lives when they were no longer working.

There are other good reasons to be depressed as we get older. Suppose we were to survey the mood of older people all over the country? Would we discover that depression is an inevitable consequence of growing older? Several thousand volunteers from 16 to over 65 were given a questionnaire inquiring about their mental health in the past six months. These volunteers were drawn from Baltimore, MD, St. Louis, MO, and New Haven, CT, as well as the area around Duke University in North Carolina. Analysis of the results found that fewer women and men 65+ reported symptoms of depression than those in the younger groups. That's just a superficial survey, doubters might say. If a thorough psychiatric evaluation were carried out, older people would show more depression. Again, comprehensive interviews using exacting diagnostic criteria for clinical depression found that those in the later years were less often seriously melancholic than midlife subjects.

This is not to say that no relationship exists between getting older and getting *periodically* depressed. Some of the things that can happen as we mature—physical disabilities and losing loved ones—have the potential to cause despair. But although most elders have periods of feeling blue, these feelings usually pass and they get on with their lives.

For example, more recent reports from the scientists studying a group of elders in the Duke Longitudinal Study have discovered a modest correlation between getting older and being depressed. What they also found was that other stresses were more strongly associated with being depressed than age. These factors can lead to depression at any age. They were, in order of magnitude, chronic physical disability, cognitive impairment (Alzheimer's disease), loss of social support, and poverty. Aging was less of a factor in becoming depressed than any of these.

"But how about those statistics telling us that old people kill themselves more often than younger adults?" you ask. Well, if we look carefully at the evidence, we see that not everyone over 65 is at the same risk for taking his or her life. For the young-olds, the suicide rate is no different from that of individuals 25 to 44. After 75, the risk of suicide grows, but it grows most dramatically among white males. Others, women and those of color, don't differ from those in younger census decades. Doubtless, many of those who do take their own lives suffer from some of the physical, financial, and social stresses mentioned earlier.

Suppose that, instead of asking people if they were depressed, we asked them, "Are you happy?" Would most older people respond with a negative and younger ones with a positive? The take-home message from every national survey in the second half of the twentieth century is that most people say they are very happy or pretty happy. The citizens of other affluent developed countries, notably Japan and France, answer in the same vein. Except the substantial number living in very poor countries, most of the world's inhabitants say their spirits are moderately good most of the time. Psychologists at the University of Illinois examined how different groups responded to the "Are you happy?" question. The subjects included college students, an elderly group, and disabled individuals. Generally those classified as "elderly" rated themselves above average on the measures of happiness about as often as other adults. More surprising were the happiness self-ratings of the disabled. Their scores exceeded the adult groups and were about in the same range as college students.

At any given point, most of us have excellent reasons to be unhappy with our lives, but these results indicate that the moods of most of us are not long depressed by these events. By far the greatest number of us are resilient, can recover from adversities, and regain a reasonably positive view of our life experience. It has been suggested that the reason people are happy is because they have satisfying close relationships, find their work absorbing, set goals for themselves in other parts of their lives, and work toward them. This logic explains why middle-aged people report being happy, but this thinking doesn't work at all when it comes to understanding the positive moods of the elderly and the disabled.

It turns out that heredity plays a role in our moods that is at least equal to environmental influences. Research using over 2,000 subjects from the Minnesota studies of twins found that over 80 percent of these individuals ranked themselves as very happy or pretty happy, just like other subjects worldwide. But then the Minnesota investigators looked at those identical twins separated at birth and raised apart to see how closely their happiness ratings corresponded at middle age. They found that 50 percent of what goes into the sense of positive well-being is hereditary and the other half is contributed by experience unique to the individual. Therefore, it seems that our nature has at least as strong a role as our nurture in determining our mood in midlife and beyond.

◼ KEEPING OUR SPIRITS UP WHILE GROWING OLDER

What can each of us do to keep our spirits up as we grow older? The lives of those who have been able to maintain a relatively positive mental attitude in the face of considerable stresses accompanying the aging process contain these lessons: Plan carefully and well ahead if you want to continue to work. Seize opportunities to play. Recognize that immunity to illness is influenced by stress and how we cope with it. Monitor depression and act if necessary. Conduct a life review.

Plan Carefully and Well Ahead If You Want to Continue to Work

Three out of four men and women in their 50s would like to stop working gradually, phasing down from full- to part-time employment rather than retiring all at once. Unfortunately, two out of three also said that they didn't think their present employers would allow an older worker to move to a less demanding job with less pay. For the most part, this is an accurate perception. Even though much has been written about the advantages of phased retirement, part-time work, contract work, and job redesigning to retain older workers, less than one organization in ten has implemented any of these innovative policies for retirement-age employees. It is not difficult to see the problem of part-time work from the organization's perspective. Finding ways to schedule and use a half-time firefighter, commercial airline pilot, or middle manager requires far more complex scheduling than employing full-time employees. As a result of not being able to wind down little by little, most employees plan to move from full-time jobs to full retirement when they reach retirement age.

About one person in six has an allergic reaction to retirement. For them, work is a vocation, a calling, not just a job. Without work, where is that sense of accomplishment going to come from, those good feelings that come from putting out a house fire, landing an airplane in bad weather, helping their small part of the organization run efficiently, relieving the suffering of a patient, or watching a light snap on in a student's eye. There is also the camaraderie. The kids are scattered to the corners of the Earth and there are no particularly close friends. All the people they enjoy are in the workplace. They want to stay on the job and will actively resist efforts to encourage them to stop working. If you think you might be a member of that fraction of the workforce, plan well ahead and plan carefully.

At least four options exist for those of us who need to continue working but on a reduced schedule: collaborating with our employer or constituents to design a mutually fulfilling part-time schedule, becoming a contract worker, starting our own new venture, or converting an avocation to a vocation. The first option—creating a part-time schedule—works well for physicians, accountants, dentists, lawyers, and others with technical skills in small independent practices. They can work fewer hours, taking more three-day weekends and adding a week or two to their vacations. A lawyer of my vintage says that he is no longer taking new clients. They go to his younger partners, and he handles only his pool of regulars. "The way I figure it, there will be a little less work each year," he says. "By the time I'm ready to hang it up, there won't be much business left, so it should just work out." Then he added, "And they don't mind if I return their phone calls or faxes from my corner office or the front deck of my condo in Jackson Hole."

Then there was John, an older physician in Ft. Lauderdale who volunteered to take MicroCog. He was 92 and still working. John told me that he liked his work and never considered retiring. When he reached 70, John developed a plan. He gave up his teaching at the University of Miami Medical School and reduced the number of weeks he worked from fifty to about forty. "When I am here, I work just as hard and just as long every day. But I don't work as many days." That gave him plenty of time to take up the piano, which he had given up fifty years earlier when he entered medical school. I asked him what type of medicine he practices, expecting to hear that he spent his day giving camp physicals and vetting applicants for life insurance. "General practice," he replied, "mostly with people my own age, give or take a decade or two. My patients are long past expecting medical miracles. What they like about me is that they know that I understand what getting old is all about."

You don't have to be a PhD or a computer jock to find part-time work after retirement. Mario, the uncle of one of my friends, had fewer than eight years of education but he was good with his hands. He worked as a silversmith in Rhode Island, making expensive silver-plated goblets and plates. When he retired, his coworkers gave him a set of tools and molds that he could use in his shop. For nineteen years, Mario created and sold pewter goblets and plates and other serving pieces that he crafted in his own basement on his own timetable.

Individuals in corporations have a harder time, because until recently, organizations have been eager to retire older, more expensive employees and replace them with less costly younger workers. But as the twenty-first century begins, and the pool of capable replacements dries up as a result of the baby bust generation that followed on the heels of the boomers, organizations will find it increasingly necessary to retain the talents of their young-old jobholders. Therefore, it is more likely that we will be able to negotiate a less demanding work schedule. And there are other options: Maybe we can share a job with a working mother, with a father from a dual-career household who doesn't want to work more than forty hours a week, or with someone else who needs to cut back from full time. But be sure to remember that it is far more difficult to schedule and manage two half-time employees than one full-time person.

Becoming a contract worker is a second option. Several of the physicians where I receive my health care have retired and then been hired back as "casual employees." That is, they are paid by the hour and are not on a salary. They live comfortably on that money and their retirement benefits. Millions of others in other occupations are doing this. Some are the computer design contract workers mentioned in Chapter 1 that my cousin hires. Others are academics. Upon reaching emeritus status, professors can sometimes keep their hand in by teaching one or two classes a year without the burden of committees and other responsibilities shouldered by the full-time faculty. Often they become members of what is known as the "freeway faculty." Nationwide, about 43 percent of those who listed their jobs as college teaching worked part-time, according to the US Bureau of Labor Statistics. Five years earlier, that figure was 28 percent. About half of all new faculty hired nationwide are part-timers.

For the employer, one of the great advantages of contract workers is that they are less expensive but provide needed expertise. The employers don't have to contribute to retirement plans, health and dental insurance, and other benefits. For the young worker, the lack of benefits presents a real problem. For older retired individuals who have put money into a retirement plan and also have Medicare, this situation is ideal. They have more control of their schedule, can take on one project at a time, and can set aside long moments for relaxation and hobbies.

The third option for those of us who need to work is starting our own business. Franchises attract many. On the same afternoon in a Southwest Florida town, I met two retired couples who had purchased franchises. One couple ran a mailing business and the other an upscale copy shop. Both pairs had devoted several years prior to their retirement investigating dozens of franchise opportunities. Although both couples complained about the long hours of work they put in after buying the businesses, they complained with a smile. As one of the women put it, "My husband and I would never have worked this hard for anybody else."

The cost of not planning ahead can be considerable. Consider Tom, a security guard at a condominium complex in Florida. About 66 when I first met him, he was bright, energetic, and interesting. One humid morning, I asked him what he had done prior to his present job. He replied, "I was a senior vice-president of the First National Bank in St. Louis." He thought he would enjoy having nothing to do after an exhausting forty years of seventy-hour weeks. He and his wife built their dream home and he took up golf, something that he'd never had time for as a bank executive. Eighteen months later, discovering that he hated golf, half mad with boredom and on the verge of splitting up with his wife, he took the first job he could find. "It gets me out of the house," Tom said, "and gives me some time to think about what I am going to do with myself." Then he added, "You know, I should have started this process ten years ago." Tom's story had a happy ending. By the following summer, he had teamed up with a retired Florida state trooper to set up sophisticated security systems in banks in Southwest Florida.

Then there is Gail, a clerk from whom I bought a pair of earrings for my wife. It was obvious Gail was just as underemployed as Tom. Because it was a slow day at the mall, we began talking about how she wound up selling jewelry. Gail's problems mirror those of a great many women of her generation who went back to work after raising children. At 25, she married, giving up her job to be a homemaker. After the last child left for college, Gail returned to school and obtained an MBA. She moved rapidly up the corporate ladder, becoming the CFO of a Fortune 500 company at 54. Just as she was reaching her peak, her husband, six years older, decided to leave the workforce after a long career and move to Florida. Gail reluctantly gave up her high-paying, prestigious position to maintain her marriage. Because no top executive positions existed where they live, she took a position in a jewelry store to have something to do. A year later, I stopped by the store and found that Gail had quit. "She wasn't a happy camper, that's for sure," said her boss. "I hear she's taking courses up at the University Extension in Ft. Meyers, something about being a Certified Financial Planner." A year later I saw an ad announcing that Gail was opening her own practice. Although both Tom and Gail landed on their feet, they had a tough time initially because they had not confronted how important it was for them to continue to work in a challenging position.

Often a preretirement hobby can be transformed into a vocation. A bank manager who loved sailing took early retirement so that he could buy a small ships' chandlery store in a small Maine coastal town. Alice, my mother's broker, was a retired second grade teacher. All her life, the stock market had interested her. At first, she invested imaginary money and calculated her winnings. Finding she did pretty well, Alice began to invest her own savings. The positive results continued. So, before retirement, Alice took courses to become licensed as a broker. Her investment advice carried my mother's small portfolio through the crash of 1987 with her assets intact.

My favorite early retirement story is about Mr. Goldman. I met him when he was 67 years old. The friend of the parents of a fellow graduate school classmate, Mr. Goldman ran a 300-acre farm just outside Bennington, VT. His farm had approximately eighty head of cattle in the flatland by the river, and beehives and maple syrup trees up the side of a mountain. When we drove up to meet him, Mr. Goldman was dressed in his farmer's garb—bib overalls, loose wool shirt, dung-speckled boots. He invited us into his comfortable farmhouse and showed us where the beer was. Forty-five minutes later, Mr. Goldman emerged in a sport coat, slacks, and button-down shirt and rep tie. When I commented that he looked like he had just stepped out of a Brooks Brothers showroom window, he smiled and said that he had to leave us to attend a cocktail party in Bennington. He would be back for dinner.

Over a simple dinner later in the evening, Mr. Goldman told us his story. He had been a highly paid, highly successful, and highly stressed Madison Avenue advertising executive. At 55, suffering from malignant hypertension, diabetes, and obesity, his physician despaired for his life and gave him three years to live. Divorced, with his children widely scattered, Mr. Goldman decided he would die doing something that he had always longed to do: live in Vermont and run a small farm. That was twelve years ago. Mr. Goldman looked in better health than any of us. Rarely have I met a happier older man.

In my experience, those who have landed on their feet after their first retirement are those who have planned well ahead, developed a scheme, tested the market, obtained the additional training they felt they would need, and then moved into the next phase of their work life relatively smoothly. And all the planning is worth it. Never have I met anyone of retirement age who wants to work, and is employed in an occupation suiting their skills and energies, who goes to the job reluctantly. Not one. Actually it is just the opposite. They brag a little to their fully retired friends that they can't play golf tomorrow because they've got some work that needs doing.

Seize Opportunities to Play

Not everyone misses their work, even those in impressive positions. Emerita Columbia professor Carolyn Heilbrun puts it succinctly: "I was shocked, almost from the moment I left Columbia, by how little I missed it." She goes on to describe a life of retirement impossible to imagine for a young mother in those years of being constantly needed at home and at work. Heilbrun sums up her feelings about entering this new phase of life in her seventh decade: "I discovered retirement to be a gift especially suited to my sixties, where I could relish its delicate flavor."

Engaging in playful activities can be a powerful antidepressant. Freed from many of the grinding responsibilities of work and family, the postretirement years provide the opportunity for us to live life more on our own terms than ever before. Instead of fitting ourselves to the demands of our occupations or our children, we can select from a range of recreational activities that correspond to our unique interests, talents, energies, and bank accounts. We can choose to learn to contradance, to tie flies, to operate a computer, or to speak Chinese. For the first time since youth we can wholeheartedly enjoy playing. As noted earlier, Mark Twain's Tom Sawyer identified an essential difference between work and play: Work is what we are obliged to do and play is what we are *not* obliged to do. Twain puts his finger on a significant feature of playing—the lack of obligation. Two other qualities distinguishing play are the freedom from the requirement for high-level achievement and malleability.

Playful activities don't demand our best, only our participation. The freedom from the need for high achievement can be invigorating. A woman who always wanted to sing but never had the time because of work and raising kids, now sings with the town amateur chorale group. She isn't very good, and neither are they, but they have a great time together. Some people just can't help taking everything they do to a high level of accomplishment, even playful ventures. My neighbor Jake is a biking enthusiast. Last week when I was out for a morning jog, Jake rode by. "Where are you headed," he inquired courteously. "A couple of miles around the neighborhood," I returned. "And how about you?" He smiled, "Orlando." Jake was headed to Orlando (that's Orlando, *Florida*) for the fifty-fifth anniversary of his graduating class from pilot training in World War II. Orlando is 1,600 miles south of our block. Jake figures he can bike it in forty days. "I can only bike about forty miles a day at my age," he said. Jake will be four score on his next birthday.

Just when you thought you had heard a story of an elder's accomplishment that is beyond anything else you could possibly imagine, you run into someone who has done something even more spectacular. On a late summer evening recently, I was invited to speak at a retirement community just west of Philadelphia. During the dinner before the talk, I recounted Jake's story. My hostess asked if I had heard about Julia, one of the residents. It seems that Julia decided to celebrate her eighty-second birthday by sailing a twenty-five-foot sloop from Nova Scotia to

Ireland. She did. Single-handedly. When I asked Julia later what the most difficult part of the journey was, she replied, "I forgot my passport, but they let me in anyway."

Playful enterprises are malleable. In contrast to the other provinces of our lives where we're locked in, we don't have to stick with the same old thing if a whim carries us in the other direction. In the thirty-five years I've known Charlie, he has worked for the same company and remained married to the same woman. Yet during this period, his avocational interests moved from photography to mountain climbing to golf to flying to sailing. His wife christened Charlie's boat "WHAT NEXT?" As Charlie's range of playing illustrates, many people thrive on new experiences. Regularly we read about some 78-year-old grandmother of nine who has taken up parachute jumping or skiing the double diamond trails. These people find a little terror exhilarating.

Many of us, however, whose work lives have been punctuated with enough thrills and terrors, don't want a lot of new sensations when we throttle back on a job. One octogenarian I know puts it this way, "You know, what I like most about retirement is that I can keep up with what's happening in the world almost every day. When I was working, it was rare for me to be able to do anything but skim *USA Today*, read the front page of *The Wall Street Journal*, and hear five minutes of news on the radio on the way to work. Yesterday, I read three newspapers. I plan to spend most of this afternoon watching C-Span. I love it!"

For those who have trouble getting around, the personal computer brings a galaxy of interesting playful opportunities. These come in the form of simple or complex games. PCs provide virtual thrilling experiences. Using an interactive CD-ROM, we can take a trip down the wild Colorado River. Clicking the mouse brings a map of the trip and vivid pictures of the river. It shows the flowers and animals on the shoreline, leaving out only the insects. Through the Internet, we can savor experiences and witty thoughts of others from around the world without leaving our chairs. And, if we are in the mood, we can enter people's fantasy worlds and see what they are all about. The PC is always there to play with us.

Recognize That Immunity to Illness Is Influenced by Stress and How We Cope With It

Among the strongest predictors of happiness in the last quarter of life is health. Numerous investigations of young-old and old-old volunteers from the Duke Longitudinal Study found that health, either self-rated or judged by physicians, was among the strongest correlates of life satisfaction, psychological well-being, and absence of depression.

Being sick is depressing. And illness is a more frequent companion as we age, because the immune system, our natural defense against disease, normally deteriorates with age. The job of the immune system is to detect, inactivate, and remove bacteria, viruses, tumors, and other foreign bodies from our body. The immune system also plays an important role in the repair of tissue following injury. It creates NK (for "natural killer"), T, and B cells, which all detect and destroy foreign substances. It also creates specific antibodies to combat diseases such as measles and chicken pox. Once someone has had these illnesses, the body's immune system develops antibodies that provide life-long resistance to them.

These are just the headlines. The immune system is exceedingly complex, consisting of scores of vital elements. While the scientific evidence points to an enormous amount of individual variation, the bottom line is that most of these functions decline with age. So most people will find themselves less able to escape illness as they grow older. The fall flu, the winter cold, and whatever viruses we contract from our grandchildren's last visit hang on and hang on, sapping our energies and lowering our spirits. In addition, bruises and cuts heal more slowly. The decline in NK cells means that the immune system is less able to destroy the tumor cells that lead to cancer.

The ability of the immune system to fight disease becomes increasingly variable among elders, just as the variability in cognitive function increased among the older physicians described in Chapter 2. Whereas a normal decline occurs in most, a large number of oldsters continue to have robust immune systems. Until recently, it has been assumed that the immune system functioned independently of psychological and social influences. Over the past ten years, however, evidence has accumulated that each of us has it within our power to enhance our resistance to disease, because the immune system is significantly influenced by our mental state—specifically, how much stress we confront in our lives, and how we deal with these unpleasant events.

The supporting evidence is of two kinds. First is the discovery that our mental state is highly correlated with our resistance to certain illnesses. For example, over 400 adult volunteers in Pittsburgh, PA, were given nose drops containing a common cold virus. Not surprisingly, a large number of the subjects developed a cold soon afterward. The Pittsburgh scientists also were interested in the extent to which the total amount of stress the individuals had to deal with in their lives, and how well they were coping with these unpleasant events, affected their vulnerability to colds. When the researchers divided the volunteers into high and low scorers on the stress scale, they found that those with more stress in their lives developed colds 50 percent more often than those whose stress scores were below average. An even more interesting finding was that those individuals who more often said that "the emotional demands in my life exceeded my capacity to cope" became infected with the viruses *twice* as often as those below average on this scale.

The second line of evidence indicating a connection between emotional and immune states consists of reports of psychosocial behaviors that strengthen immune system functions. For instance, we already know that regular, moderate exercise is associated with improved mood. It is also true that older adults who work out at least twice a week show higher levels of NK cell activity than those who do not.

Something else we can do to stimulate our immune system is to cope with stress effectively. How we respond to unpleasant events in our lives is as important to our health as how much stress we are under. Take, for example, the differences in survival rates among patients diagnosed with cancer at the John Wayne Clinic in Los Angeles. The ways they coped with this bad news were carefully analyzed, and the patients were followed for five years. The individuals who were still alive at the time of follow-up more often exhibited these characteristics: (1) higher levels of emotional distress at the time of diagnosis and early treatment; (2) the ability to express anger outwardly; (3) access to family, friends, and other resources; and (4) more efficient coping strategies. Among the patients I have known, those who survived cancer and other dreadful diseases were more often those who initially felt a psychic agony. They did not minimize the diagnosis. They cursed the fates and maybe the physicians who were trying to help them. They showed a fighting spirit, wanting to know why they were being given this treatment and not that one. They wanted to participate as fully as possible in their therapy. They were often seen as difficult patients. One physician described a feisty 78-year-old as "the patient from hell." But she was still alive five years later. Maybe this is scientific support for the adage that only the good die young.

At home, their loved ones noticed that they more often put themselves first, were less accommodating, and less agreeable. This behavior may come as a bit of a shock to the children and grandchildren of the woman with breast cancer who no longer suppresses her hostility, who is no longer compliant and appeasing, and who starts to think about satisfying herself before worrying about the needs of others.

There is no question that access to family and friends and other resources correlates with improved immune system operations. Remember that in Chapter 7 we looked at evidence showing that elders with more social ties had fewer colds than those with smaller networks. The more relationships we have with others, the healthier we are. And positive relationships with family and close friends is associated with longer rates of survival for cancer and HIV patients.

In Chapter 2, we went over two ways of coping with stress that enable us to reduce the amount of emotional pain we experience—namely, problem-focused coping and emotion-focused coping. The first involves taking direct action to reduce the stressor—for example, confronted a neighbor whose barking dog keeps us up at night. The second includes palliative actions that enable us to put unpleasant thoughts out of our mind. An illustration might be a man who has had a melanoma removed. This is the most lethal form of skin cancer. The surgeon's advice was, "If it recurs, don't buy any green bananas." After about six months of worrying about a metastasis, the man decided to get on with his life and to reduce the risk of recurrence by minimizing his exposure to the sun and using industrial strength skin block. Through these decisions and actions, he suppressed the day-to-day apprehension of a recurrence of the cancer, and his immune system was better for it.

This is not pseudoscience, not infomercial testimonials, not placebo effects, and not new-age healing. These positive influences on the immune system have been demonstrated in carefully designed investigations carried out in major hospital and university research centers by respected scientists looking for the truth. And the truth is that we can enhance our individual immune system functions by voluntary behaviors: getting exercise, exhibiting a fighting spirit, maintaining solid loving relationships, coping with stress effectively, and taking charge of as much our lives as possible.

Monitor Mood State and Act If Necessary

Dealing with bad news is a burden every aging individual carries. We confront separation from work, loss of loved ones, our own declining health, and a growing awareness that our personal story has only a few more pages in it. No wonder people old age is not for sissies.

As we cope with these challenges, most of us will have some bad days and some sleepless nights. But nearly all of us will recover within a reasonable period of time. In Chapter 7, we reviewed clinical studies showing that those who lost a life partner returned to normal functioning in a twelve- to twenty-four-month period. Among the older adults in the Duke Longitudinal Study who were confronting significant stresses of later adulthood, including a major medical problem in retirement, there was a lot of difference in how individuals reacted to these problems. But on the whole, the emotional balance of most of these women and men returned after several months.

What enabled these elders to cope with stress were resources and actions they had accumulated over a lifetime of facing difficult situations. These resources enabled elders to keep going in the face of serious losses that might have disabled midlife adults; they include freedom from physical disability, the size of social networks (we've heard this before), and higher intellectual ability. Investigations into the best ways to cope with depression have added other insights. For example, certain actions help: Talking to close friends about the pain we feel hurries its passage. Moderate physical exercise lifts spirits. Involving ourselves in activities that have given us pleasure in the past provides respite. And many find relief in prayer, the knowledge of being prayed for, and other spiritually stimulating activities.

Each of us has our own store of resources and a repertoire of antidepressive actions that are as unique as our own fingerprints. Some of us will withdraw from others, not wanting to talk about the distress we feel. The last thing we want to hear is, "How are you doing?" Others respond enthusiastically to this question, benefitting from talking by the hour to family, friends, and professionals. These persons are relieved because sharing their pain and tears is what they need most. Some widows and widowers suffer what is called "anhedonia" after a loss, the inability to enjoy activities that yesterday gave them pleasure. Others continue their avocational interests as though nothing had happened. Both groups explain their actions in the same way: "What do you expect me to do when I've just lost my spouse?"

Most of the time, our natural emotional resistance enables us to negotiate these moments so that our spirits and our amount of tension return to levels approximating normal within a year after the trauma. This is not to say that we don't have painful periods of feeling blue or sad years afterward. These melancholic moments can be triggered by a sight, a sound, a smell, or another funeral. I vividly recall standing beside the casket of my mother-in-law in a small midwestern town while people who had known her for decades passed by and paid their respects. An elderly gentleman started sobbing as he shook my hand. I mumbled something about how my mother-in-law would appreciate his expression of caring. As the tears streamed down his face, he replied, "No, that's not it. Seeing her reminded me of my own wife's funeral ten years ago." These periods are typically brief, a few hours to a few days, and they pass.

This feeling is unlike a clinical depression, which can extend over several months without relief.

How do we know whether we are coping competently or whether we need professional assistance? Again, huge individual variation exists. At the first sign of rough water, I might naturally turn to our family doctor, priest, minister, rabbi, or mental health counselor to help me with what I know will be troubled times. From experience, I know what they offer, whether it be a comforting ear or Prozac, or both. I also know they can help me monitor my mental state to be sure I'm not sliding over the edge.

You, on the other hand, may not be particularly interested in being helped by others. Toughing things out on your own is your style. You would rather endure the tears, fears, long nights, and loss of appetite, believing this is a natural process of working through the pain rather than seeking relief through counseling and medication. Intuitively, you understand that this temporary depressive reaction doesn't prefigure a clinical depression and are content to let it take its course.

The danger with the tough-it-out attitude is that we may tolerate depression too long, letting it absorb too much pleasure from our lives. In the year following a traumatic event, we need to monitor our mental state to see how we are adjusting. We need to enlist the help of others. If the consensus is that we are not ourselves and seem to be mired in a depressive mood, we should act—seek professional help. We shouldn't continue to think this is one more burden to endure because we are septua-, octo-, or nonagenarians. Suppose we were 40 and felt this bad. Would we obtain professional counseling for our moodiness? You bet we would.

Medication is often used to lift spirits. A new class of antidepressant "smart drugs" called SSRIs (for selective serotonin reuptake inhibitors—that's Zoloft, Prozac, and Paxil) are commonly prescribed. When they work, which is most of the time, the improvement in mood can be quite spectacular. Not all depressions, however, are biologically based. Low moods can also be raised by the traditional "talk" therapies and with the help of cognitive and behavioral therapy. Many people are astonished at how much better they feel after talking to a friend, a member of the clergy, or a counselor about their terrible loss and how they are going to put their lives back together.

Cognitive and behavior therapy aim at identifying and extinguishing thoughts and actions that sustain the depressive mood. A simplified example of thoughts nurturing the depressed state is the so-called A-B-C model of faulty thinking. A is the stress; B is how we believe it will affect our life; C is the resulting emotional behavior. Thus a woman's husband dies (A); she tells herself, "I can't live without him." (B); the depressed mood is maintained by the faulty belief that no happiness is possible without her husband (C). Cognitive therapy tries to help by gently pointing out that the widow has a life, quite a full life, without her husband—children, grandchildren, friends, a garden and a cat that she loves, and a part-time job she enjoys. Then there's the point that others have faced this horrible stress before and have gotten through it. New York psychologist Albert Ellis and Philadelphia psychiatrist Aaron Beck have spent most of the last three decades demonstrating the effectiveness of cognitive therapy with depression. It has been especially useful with mild to moderate depressions caused by acute stress.

Behavior therapy has yielded the same positive results for depression, especially among the elderly. These approaches, like cognitive therapy, effectively reduce negative thought patterns, but they use relaxation or controlling negative ideas with positive images. In addition, relatives and friends of the depressed elder may be recruited to reinforce positive statements and behavior by paying attention and ignoring negative attitudes.

Many mental health workers combine a number of these approaches in what is called multimodal or integrative, therapy. Thus, depressed widows and widowers may find themselves being listened to, given an SSRI, and provided with strategies for combating negative thoughts and behaviors.

Conduct a Life Review

A final strategy for lifting spirits, especially as the calendar is winding down our days on this planet, is to reflect backward, taking pleasure in appreciating the uniqueness of our own personal story. Photo albums help. Conducting a life review is a pleasure uniquely available to the omega generation (that's being among the oldest living members of one family). As we might guess, a life review entails looking back over the totality of our experience and then making an effort to understand what kind of life it has been for us. As elders, we are particularly well positioned to carry out our own personal life review. Almost all the chapters have been written. We are chronicling neither our adolescent turmoil nor our midlife crisis nor what it was like to lose a loved one, a job, or health. We're looking at nearly the whole picture from our beginning to the present.

A comfort that the last season of our life affords is time for reviewing what our experience on Earth has been like. And each of us has quite a story to tell. Oral histories are popular in some families. Among our children's most precious memories of their grandfather are the two nights around the fireplace during the Christmas holidays when he talked about his life. The story began with his growing up on a poor farm in Southwest Missouri. He recounted how he moved to Chicago and roared with the flappers in the speakeasies of the Roaring Twenties. He told about how he managed to stay employed during the depression when every third man was out of a job, about his alcoholism and about abandoning my mother and me, and about his recovery. This oral history, captured on two ninety-minute audiotapes, is a treasure we all love listening to again and again.

My father, 82 at the time, loved telling a story that revealed some flattering—and some not so flattering—qualities. What was noticeable in this most recent life review was how comfortable he was spinning the tale of his life in his ninth decade. I especially recall hearing much earlier accounts of some of the more difficult epochs of his personal saga, especially about his wilderness years separated from me. Then they had an edgy defensive quality to them, containing little of the humor and humility and enjoyment apparent in his last season.

But the life review is not for everyone. Some may not like its past orientation, preferring instead to think about the future. Others of us will dislike reliving miscalculations, failures to learn from experience, awful things we have done, good works we could have done but didn't, dreams nearly realized that slipped from our grasp. Sometimes, however, going over these events in the wisdom of our last years provides an opportunity to forgive ourselves for these wrong terms and missteps, letting ourselves also appreciate some of the things we did right. Perhaps, as a result, we find at last a greater inner peace.

Commenting on the personality changes accompanying the aging process, a friend of mine at Harvard remarked, "We become more like ourselves as we grow older." He was referring to particular character traits that evolve and are reinforced over time because they work, qualities like perfectionism, compassion and stubbornness. We can see these characteristics in the elders around us: the older friend with an increasing fascination for disasters who has been predicting monthly, with undiminished enthusiasm, stock market crashes as the bulls have surged upward; a grandmother who can't tolerate being interrupted by anyone when she's watching Jeopardy; a great uncle, a retired assembly-line worker, who becomes more British in manner and dress with every passing year; an elderly neighbor who has a growing soft spot in her heart for dogs and cats; and her spouse, who can't stand waiting in the supermarket line and consequently shops at the crack of dawn. These qualities often strengthen with age, while others melt away.

Studying this process from the vantage point of age-related neuronal loss in the brain, Northwestern medical school neurologist, M-Marsel Mesulam, has speculated that losing brain cells is not all bad. He wondered whether there is a fine tuning of the central nervous system that occurs because of neuronal attrition and results in an accentuation of certain qualities that "work" for us and become our most predictable traits as we age. He likens this subtractive process to chips that must fall from a slab of marble so that the underlying form may be revealed.

A life review entails looking at the "statue" of ourselves that has been revealed as the years fall away. Each of us will have a different approach. You may be comfortable scanning backward over your entire history: what kind of person you had hoped to be, and where your life journey has actually taken you; which youthful dreams were realized and which were not; those times when everything seemed to go according to plan and those long moments when absolutely nothing turned out as you expected; opportunities whose knock you heard and made the most of, and potential good fortune laid right in your lap that was ignored and lost forever; the hilltop experiences and the valleys of despair; and the people at particular stages of your life's journey who have made such a difference.

Others may have neither the taste nor the memory for compiling details of how their personal epic has been lived. Instead, their life review may consist of finding persistent patterns. For example, the themes around which my life has been organized over seven decades fall into the categories of enjoying competitive sports and the tendency to become bored with what I'm doing about every seven years or so and to seek new challenges. I have resigned myself to having a sense of humor that occasionally gets me into serious trouble and being taken advantage of by people who drive harder bargains than I care to. At 60+, I witness these patterns at an agreeable distance, which makes these moments in my life interesting and slightly amusing.

What happens if your life review brings out a sharp contrast between the sweet gifts of youth and the harder realities of old age? Take my neighbor, Caroline, as an example. When I first met her, she was in her mid-70s. One afternoon, Caroline was showing us pictures of herself as a young woman in World War II, in her nurse's uniform on a Pacific island. In the photo, the 20-year-old Caroline was stunningly attractive. I must have betrayed my shock at the difference between this beautiful young woman in the picture and the pleasant but no longer unusually attractive woman sitting beside me. "Quite a difference, wouldn't you say?" Caroline smiled. "I know what I look like now. But that's OK. I was beautiful then and that's still part of me." Then Caroline showed us photos of her mother when she was in her twenties. She could have been Caroline's twin sister. At the end of the evening, Caroline said, "You haven't met my daughter yet, she turns heads. But the beauty in the family is our granddaughter." That sense of beauty transcending years and being passed from generation to generation brings a comforting sense of identity. Other characteristics such as intelligence, energy, industriousness, loyalty, honesty, or a sense of humor, qualities that are uniquely us, run deeply in most families.

Sometimes you don't need a photo. Every time I look in the mirror to shave, I'm shocked by how much I'm beginning to look like my father: same hairline, crooked nose, brown eyes, receding chin, and left ear that protrudes asymmetrically. And my father was not a handsome man. But oddly, I'm comforted by this growing similarity because it reminds me of other qualities of my father—now gone for more than a decade—that I share. We both love the outdoors, like a drink, appreciate the outrageous, exhibit a wicked sense of humor, can sell others our ideas, and have a daredevil streak; and we remain closely connected to family. Several of these same traits are noticeable in my children and in my grandsons, although they have been improved by the addition of other gene pools.

In my case, and in Caroline's, we're comforted by knowing we are part of a generational process. We are part of the generations that preceded us and are connected to those that follow. We all have certain pronounced physical features, accumulated personal traits, particular habits, and specific vulnerabilities. For many, it's only later in life when we can look at these qualities in ourselves without blinking too much. And considerable comfort can come from the enterprise of a life review in older age. We can take pleasure enjoying the whole life we have lived rather than focusing merely on the last few ticks of the clock.

⬟ RECAPPING

The myth that aging inevitably leads to depression is inaccurate because most elderly women and men report positive moods. And all but a small proportion recover their emotional balance in a relatively short time following stressful events such as retirement, major illness, or the death of a life partner. This myth is especially insidious because it can lead to the thinking that our mental state is the result of the sum of only the negative events in our lives rather than the totality of our experiences.

In fact, many activities within our power help us maintain a
feeling of positive well-being in the face of losses during the last
quarter of our lives. These include planning carefully and well
ahead if we want to continue to work beyond the normal retirement age; seizing opportunities to play (that is, activities that
we are not obliged to do, that we don't have to do well, and that
can be changed if we wish); recognizing that our immune system can be influenced by how we cope with stress; monitoring
our mood state after losses and acting if necessary; and conducting a life review that may include thinking about our own
personal epic from beginning to end or identifying particular
themes that characterize our life.

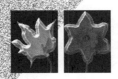

MYTH NINE: WISDOM REQUIRES BEING SMART AND ELDERLY

Until about twenty years ago, I was pretty certain that wisdom was a special gift, a built-in trait, unique to the highly intelligent and elderly. Only a few individuals possessed it. In my mind, I saw the wise old priests on a mountaintop staffing the temple at Delphi in ancient Greece, invested with special powers, answering unanswerable questions or solving knotty paradoxes brought by supplicants who had pilgrimaged hundreds of kilometers to hear their words. Only these venerable priests, the best and the brightest, could dispense wisdom.

In those years when I thought about wisdom I recalled words from Proverbs, "Happy are those who find wisdom, and those who get that understanding, for her income is better than silver, and the revenue better than gold. She is more precious than jewels, and nothing you desire can compare with her." This not unusual view of wisdom—superior to silver and gold, more precious than fine jewels—confirmed the perception that wise men and women have a rare gift of intelligence.

Wisdom, too, has become linked to older age. For instance, Roman statesman and orator Cicero wrote that "it is in old men that reason and good judgement are found, and had it not been for old men no state would have existed at all." The Old Testament book of Job contains the verse, "Wisdom is with the aged, and understanding in the length of days." Later, in the Wisdom of Solomon is the phrase, "Wisdom is the gray hair unto man." Even when we go back and read the Old Testament citations and find that the quotes are taken out of context, they remain embedded in our minds. Some of today's most influential thinkers about the life cycle believe that wisdom accumulates with age. Erik Erikson, the first American psychologist to extend developmental theory into older age, believed that wisdom is unique among the generally declining curves of our physical and intellectual capabilities as a power that actually can increase with age.

During the past decade, Paul Baltes and his colleagues at the Max Planck Institute for Human Development and Education in Berlin have been studying wisdom. They focused their efforts on distinguishing between wisdom based on knowledge only and that rooted in "excellent judgment and advice about important and uncertain matters of life." They believed that the highest wisdom-related skills, which they have called cognitive pragmatics, may well be associated with the last season of life. The Berlin scientists go on to describe wisdom in terms not so different from my vision of the Oracle of Delphi: "superior knowledge . . . with extraordinary scope, depth, and balance applicable to specific situations." Not surprisingly, they believe that "wisdom is very difficult to achieve," certainly not a quality that you or I, or most mortals, can aspire to.

◢ WISDOM: THE REALITY

At the Max Planck Institute, a test for wisdom was based on complex life dilemmas. The investigators scored the responses on the basis of how they thought wise people should answer them. Higher scores on the wisdom test were associated with responses that were neither black nor white, had a broader perspective, and were not judgmental.

Then they gave the test to sixteen people in Germany who were considered wise. These "wise men" ranged in age from 41 to 88, averaging about 67. Nearly half had been members of the German anti-Nazi resistance movement in World War II. Their responses were then compared with those of other older and younger adults who also took the test. Unfortunately, the results the Berlin investigators obtained conflicted with their model of wisdom. First, there were only small age effects; that is, not all older people outscored the younger adults on the wisdom test. Second, the wise men showed a greater range of scores on the wisdom test than the "normal" adults did. Although the average wise man outscored the typical older and younger adults, as individuals they obtained some of the lowest scores on wisdom. For instance, among those volunteers 70 and beyond, the highest wisdom score was earned by an ordinary subject and the lowest by a wise man. Moreover, a quartet of 30-year-olds had higher wisdom rankings than three-quarters of the wise elders.

Hmmm . . . what do we make of this? Perhaps these scientists did not have a sufficiently powerful test of wisdom, and, as a result, the designated wise men did not stand out as expected on the instrument. Perhaps more questions, or different types of problems, would have allowed the wise men to distinguish themselves. It is also possible, of course, that the characteristics of wisdom are not unique to those rated as gifted, successful, moral, admired, and elderly. Perhaps, as the results of the Berlin study show, all of us possess qualities of wisdom, even the most ordinary—even the young.

My first inkling that something was amiss with this elite view of wisdom had actually come several years earlier from a comment made by my friend Carl. At the time, Carl was an 80-year-old physician whose remarkable career had recently been capped by the publication of his new book on eighteenth-century medicine. Afterward, he was asked by a literary magazine to reflect on his life. "Just share with us your accumulated wisdom," the editor had told him. "I don't have any wisdom," he lamented to me. "Why do people think that just because you're old you have any special wisdom." This was from a highly intelligent man whose distinguished career included numerous books, creation of a new school of thinking about the mind-body connection, a professorship at a major New York teaching hospital, and, lately, supervision of new generations of mental health professionals. Why, then, didn't Carl think he was wise?

■ CHARACTERISTICS OF WISDOM

Carl's problem was that he shared my "Oracle of Delphi" view of wisdom. Although he had reason to believe he was competent because of his knowledge, judgment, and other assorted gifts and achievements, he did not think he was any smarter than most of his students. Therefore, in his own eyes, he didn't possess any particular "wisdom." This restricted view of wisdom overlooked the very qualities that made him truly wise—his modesty, kindness, dispassion, and self-control. In the past 2,500 years, these are the characteristics that have been most often mentioned in the same breath as wisdom.

Modesty

Like my friend Carl, most wise individuals don't think of themselves as possessing any special powers of wisdom. They are modest. And they will tell you that their modesty about their powers to understand the complex and uncertain matters of human experience is well deserved. The more they learn, the less they know for certain. It is not hard for them to relate to the lines from the eighteenth-century English poet William Cowper, "Knowledge is proud that he has learned so much; /wisdom is humble that he knows no more."

Lessons from my own experience confirm these sentiments. A quarter-century of counseling young people has taught me that there are many individuals that will be impervious to my best efforts to help them. A month after writing a paper setting down the precise steps for treating students with performance anxiety, the method failed with the next two undergraduates I saw. Teaching has always been an activity I have loved, partly because I imagined I was good at it. But new generations of students have begun to pick my ideas apart and let me know that they found my methods of instruction leaving something to be desired.

The same scenarios have played out in other parts of my life. From these experiences, I have discovered just how fragile my self-confidence is, how quickly it can dissolve into uncertainty, panic, and despair. I can't honestly say that I have enjoyed the pain associated with the deflation of my young adult arrogance, by the failure of some of my best notions, by the recognition that others close to me have had ideas better than mine, or from the feedback that what I was doing was not working. Neither have I liked confronting the fact that I sometimes fail at just those things that I think I am best at. But, as the years have passed, humility has gradually filled the void left by my eroding certainty. Maybe that humility is where we all begin to find wisdom.

I hasten to add that there has been some useful learning in these humility-inducing experiences: My theories about the treatment of performance anxiety have broadened since the two failures, and I am better at it now, although not nearly as good as I once thought I was. But more than this, my hard-won humility has caused me to be more comfortable with uncertainty, with not knowing as much as I would like to know, but with being able to soldier on anyway. Moreover, I am more open to new ideas, more accepting of failure, and slower to judge. I have learned that with me truth accumulates and bad ideas don't replicate.

Humility also enables me to feel more comfortable seeking the counsel of those considerably junior to me. In response to some of the negative feedback I was getting from my class about relying too much on a lecture format, I sought the advice of a 28-year-old multimedia specialist. My lectures are now augmented by graphs, charts, pictures, and written material beamed onto the screen from my laptop and augmented by CD-ROM.

Another young colleague opened my intellectual horizons to the Chinese philosopher Lao Tsu. The wisdom of Lao Tsu has long been an influential part of China's philosophical tradition. A recent publication, *The New Lao Tsu*, provides a remarkably clear English interpretation of this ancient wisdom. I was comforted to find that modesty is often mentioned in the same sentence as wisdom. Lao Tsu captures the power of humility in these lines: "This is why the highest condition/of understanding/ Is deep humility." The threat of modesty to those invested in the status quo is suggested by this quote: "The greatest strength/ arises from humility." And this one: "Practice humility to obtain greatness."

Humility, perplexity, and modesty are not weaknesses. Considerable strength lies in being uncertain about the nature of truth. The similarity between *The New Lao Tsu* and the thoughts of Socrates, who lived about the same time half a world away is striking. Socrates has been said to be the Western world's greatest philosopher. Yet Socrates did not believe he was a wise man. In fact, he often said he was more perplexed about the nature of truth than were the young people who were his students. Ironically, it was this admission of confusion about the nature of truth that caused his enemies to bring him to trial, and to require him to drink the hemlock.

A contemporary example of the strength of humility can be found at every AA meeting. The first step to sobriety for alcoholics is to admit their powerlessness over their urge to drink. The power of this humility has enabled two million individuals to give up their addiction to alcohol. Think about the alcoholic's public declaration that he is powerless to control his drinking and therefore must abstain entirely. Contrast the tensile strength of this humble admission with the attitude of the swaggering drunk who slurs that, sure, he drinks, but he can control it any time he wants to.

Kindness

Think about the wise people you have known. Have any of them been disagreeable and mean-spirited? Probably not. When we imagine someone with wisdom, we almost always picture a person who is benign, often kind. This picture of someone who is wise has remained constant for at least 2,500 years.

Nearly 500 years before the birth of Christ, the writings of Buddha made a special place for kindness in the pantheon of qualities associated with wisdom. Buddha, whose given name was Siddhattha Gotama, lived in what is now Nepal from 563 to 483 BCE. Buddha was born into a family of great wealth. His father tried to shelter him from worldly pain and lavished great luxury upon him. In his twenty-ninth year, while riding in the royal park, he saw four men who were to change his life: an old man, a sick man, a dead man, and a beggar. In a flash of insight, he saw that no matter how luxurious his life, there was unavoidable suffering in the world and, in the end, certain death. Depressed by this insight and unable to reconcile this reality with his experience as a pampered and protected young man, he renounced his sumptuous life. Buddha became a teacher and philosopher, founding a religious tradition that has influenced tens of millions of adherents in Japan, China, Southeast Asia, and, more recently, the West.

High on Buddha's list of the ten duties of a wise leader are kindness and gentleness. In other writings, he is more specific about the behaviors that typify someone who is wise, including abstaining from harsh and abusive language, backbiting and gossiping, and telling lies. Buddha set a high standard for those of us who aspire to being kind. The eighteenth-century French philosopher Jean-Jacques Rousseau made the connection between kindness and wisdom when he wrote, "What wisdom can you find that is greater than kindness?" A century later, the extraordinary German writer Friedrich Nietzsche said, "The growth of wisdom may be gauged exactly by the diminution of ill-temper."

For the last three decades, social scientists have been searching for a more precise definition of wisdom. For the most part, their approach has consisted of asking people what traits they thought wise people might possess. Many of the words used to describe wise people are traits of kindness. Subjects in a study at Yale described wisdom as having attributes of "concern for others." Research in California found that words used to describe wise individuals were often not intellectual: "gentle," "compassionate," "empathic," "nonjudgmental," and "having a sense of humor." These characteristics have more in common with qualities of the heart than of the head.

Dispassion

Concord philosopher Henry David Thoreau once wrote, "it is characteristic of wisdom not to do desperate things." In many ways this line captures the essential aspects of dispassion: calmness and the freedom from passion. An additional facet is maintaining a psychological distance from those seeking the advice of the wise. The dispassion of wisdom reminds me of the emotional distance that the very best teachers, physicians, priests, rabbis, and ministers are able to maintain in their work with the troubled and sick. If they are too close to the distressed and afflicted, they will be unable to assess the nature of someone's difficulties and act appropriately to remedy it.

This quality is not limited to academics and professionals. Others I have known exhibit this same dispassion. Kenny, a life-long friend of my father, ran a dealership that sold Dodge pickups to generations of residents in a small southwestern Missouri town. He continually refused to take over a larger dealership in Springfield. "Why do I want all that aggravation?" he said. "I have everything I want here." Besides, he was needed by men in that small community who met every morning in a coffee shop at about 5:30 AM. There Kenny listened patiently to the marital, financial, and personal problems of his friends, never condemning, always gentle, never expressing much emotion. Yet you could feel his presence and warmth. The detachment with which he could listen to the personal dramas of others would have been the envy of any mental health specialist.

And there was John, the young professor who taught me freshman English. When I began his class in September, I stuttered badly. Years of working on this problem had met with no success. The class required us to read the Greats and discuss their ideas. Every day was terrifying for me because I had trouble articulating what I wanted to say. The professor never entered into my struggles with stuttering. Instead, John stood apart, quietly encouraging me to share my thoughts with others in the class, however halting and inept the words must have seemed. He usually found something in what I said that he could agree with. By the end of the term, my stuttering problem of more than a decade was hardly noticeable. Thank you, John.

Both of these men shared a remarkable calmness in the face of the tribulations of others and perhaps their own as well. Somehow they have developed the ability to be slightly detached in the presence of pleasure or pain, theirs or yours. In good times, I noticed that they are usually not quite as happy as I was, seemingly acutely aware of the reversal of fortune that hovers over many happy occasions. They also seemed to know that bad times, no matter how nasty, pass. They did not rail against the fates or tragedies that befell them, but bore them silently or stoically. They intuited that pain passes more quickly if not resisted.

Self Control

When I think of someone who is wise, the picture of a Buddhist monk fills my mind. There he stands, in saffron robe and shaved head, with a look of remarkable serenity. He is the picture of self-control, a primary characteristic of wisdom. In fact, present-day Buddhist monks are the direct descendants of Buddha. Buddha thought that wise individuals should have patience, forbearance, and tolerance. They should be able to remain calm in the face of hardships, difficulties, and even insults. Self-control and mastery of our own temper are key elements of wisdom. To quote from the writings of Buddha, "The wise are controlled in deed, controlled in words, controlled in thoughts, verily, they are fully controlled."

That self-control is not easily accomplished is seen in his statement that the "senses are mastered like horses well under the charioteer's control, he who is purged of pride, free of passions." This comment is reminiscent of Freud's idea that the ego, or our capacity for self-control, sits astride a person's id, or impulse life, much like a rider on horseback. For both, the most admirable of the conquerors is the one who conquers himself.

As someone who spends most of his week trying to help students and others in crisis, I know how difficult it is to restrain my impulse to "rescue" these troubled youth by guided insight and action. Experience has taught me that often what they need is a nonjudgmental, dispassionate ear, a person who will listen and resist spoiling their thinking process with advice. Nowadays, I am more often pleased with what I could say, but do not. There are moments in my counseling of others when I think of myself as having much in common with the ancient shamans, whose fate it was to absorb the malevolent spirits of the troubled. Osmosing their demons seems to elevate the moods of many and restore the sanity of some. I may feel a little worse, but not as bad as they do, for I have developed some immunity to these virulent strains through long exposure.

Pathways to Wisdom

Earlier I described the studies of wisdom carried out by Paul Baltes and his colleagues at the Max Planck Institute in Berlin. As part of their efforts to understand what goes into the creation of wisdom, they speculated that wise individuals have "participated in favorable, wisdom-prone circumstances." It is not just age, they thought, but certain types of life experiences that matter. They did not, however, mention what these "wisdom-prone circumstances" might be. I had a firsthand experience with one of these "wisdom-prone circumstances" several years ago.

Suffering

When I was 35, I remember celebrating the holidays with my family and feeling exceptionally satisfied with my life. Happily married, with adoring children, I headed a psychology service for students, taught a major graduate course at Harvard, and presided over a thriving consulting practice. Life was sweet. I was on the fast track. Ten years later, my marriage was in trouble, I had alienated two of my closest friends, my children were avoiding me, and my wife contracted a serious chronic disease. If that were not enough, I had been maneuvered out of my administrative position by someone shiftier than I was, my beloved course was eliminated as a result of to budget cuts, and the neglected private practice was falling apart. Then, someone I was trying to help overdosed. Life was a nightmare.

Distraught and in disarray, I sought the counsel of George, a retired professor and a friend of mine. George listened calmly as I downloaded my woeful tale. Then he said, "You will find that all of the experiences in your life will be valuable to you at some point later on, most especially the worst ones." Maybe because I was expecting to be supported and reassured by this wise man that I was still a worthwhile person, or to be given direction as to how to rediscover the happiness of a decade earlier, or at least to be told how to find my way out of the terrible mess my life had become, George's comment smacked me with the force of a wet towel across the face. What he said seemed unsympathetic and not very helpful. I was looking for advice on how to reconstruct my life. But he was right. In the nearly two decades since then, I have discovered that George's comments were right on target.

Suffering is not all downside. Suffering forces us to find ways to cope with adversity; it is a source of resilience. These reactions to the hard times in our lives become the cornerstones of our character. And suffering leads to experience from which we learn important things about ourselves and the world around us. My personal suffering has caused me to be far more empathic and compassionate with troubled patients and friends. I am far less judgmental about the "right" and "wrong" answers to questions my colleagues and I confront in our daily lives. As a fellow sufferer, I am a better friend, a better spouse, a better father, and a better grandfather.

If suffering is one source of wisdom, and suffering is an ordinary human experience, are there other ordinary events all of us ordinary people confront in our lives that are wellsprings of wisdom? Again, both ancient and modern thinkers have identified a list that can be condensed into those additional ordinary experiences that lie on the pathway toward wisdom: a life fully lived, self-knowledge, and learning from growing older.

A Life Fully Lived

Wisdom grows out of a life rich in experience and passion, as well as in suffering. "Surely, you can't be serious," you may think. "How do you go from passion to dispassion? How does a life lived to the fullest relate to modesty and self-control?"

Over two millennia earlier, Buddha set down the four Noble Truths. The first was that living involved suffering and pain. We have already covered that ground. The second of the four Noble Truths of Buddha is a thirst for living, for sensual pleasure, for achievement, for power, and for knowledge. The writings of Buddha acknowledge that these passions can lead to the dark side of human nature—greed, lust, economic inequality, and war. But these passions can be a source of good as well as bad, and can even represent a life force. Without these intense emotions, we do not experience life completely.

As these passions are reined in through experience or diminish naturally with age, they provide an emotional basis for being able to understand the passions of others. Buddha's belief that the passions of youth, diminished by age and controlled by experience, are fundamental to wisdom, echo in the words of twentieth-century Western writers such as the author of *Goodbye, Mr. Chips*, James Hilton: "Perhaps the exhaustion of passions is the beginning of wisdom." In a similar vein are these lines from Laurence Hope: "For this is Wisdom; to love, to live,/To take what Fate, or the Gods, may/give."

So, we have this paradoxical view about wisdom. On one hand, wise people we know share the quality of dispassion. On the other hand, it seems that a pathway to wisdom includes being driven, passionate, competitive, and possibly dangerous. As I was puzzling through this enigma, the often-quoted observations of Oliver Wendell Holmes, Jr. came to mind: "I think that as life is action and passion, it is required of man that he should share the passions and action of his time at the peril of being judged not to have lived."

I believe that he was talking about being a soldier in the Civil War and being shot at when he spoke these words. Still, it seems to me that most of the older individuals I have known who struck me as unusually wise were in fact passionate youths and adults. They fought in our wars, or fought against our wars; they pushed themselves hard in school or they pushed hard against those who were pushing them; they have lusted and loved, broken hearts and had their hearts broken. They competed for resources, power, and prestige as young adults. In their prime, they coveted and sometimes gained important, influential positions and recognition.

How do you go from that type of mentality to being a dispassionate wise old man or woman? Maybe it is because we experience a diminished lust for "getting and begetting," or because we learn that the costs and rewards of our passions often cancel each other out. I know that now, in my young-old years, I can comfortably lose a tennis match, play second fiddle on a committee, or brake at a yellow light rather than scream through the intersection as I would have done twenty years ago. It is not that winning or controlling these parts of my life aren't fun anymore, but I can savor the playing now, not just the winning. I enjoy participating with others, not just being the leader. I appreciate the commute and the commentary on NPR, rather than constantly checking the clock to be sure I will be on time for my 8 o'clock.

Coming to Know Yourself

Opinion is almost unanimous that self-knowledge is an essential source of wisdom. Inscribed on the temple at Delphi is one of history's most famous phrases: "Know thyself." In the East, the wisdom of Lao Tsu is conveyed in words nearly identical to the Delphic engraving:

> *Knowing others*
> *is understanding;*
> *Knowing self*
> *is wisdom.*

In one form or another, this same thought appears across cultures throughout history. Modern-day philosophers and psychologists point to the virtue of self-knowledge. Existentialist Søren Kierkegaard writes powerfully about the unexamined life not being worth living. And Freud, along with mental health professionals today, believed that self-knowledge is essential to being able to understand and assist others with their problems in living.

Self-knowledge is hard won. As someone who has trained to be a psychotherapist and to recognize my own blind spots, I find that I still occasionally react to client's troubles with statements that are more about me than about them. This self-scrutiny is uncomfortable and sometimes painful. If we listen carefully to what our family and close friends tell us about ourselves (use as a criterion what two people who know us describe as a particular trait), we may get other surprising, and not always pleasant, insights into our character.

This is not to say that wisdom requires that we energetically catalogue all of our weaknesses, warps, and foibles. Most, if not all of us, elect to live with being a techno-phob or a constant misplacer of things, with our addiction to chocolate or cigars, with the inner belief that we are far more talented than people give us credit for or that we are an impostor. We really don't want to know why we have these quirks or thoughts, and we have no plans to change.

A psychological thinker who has described this life-long journey to self-knowledge is Erik Erikson. He coined the term *identity crisis*. He was also interested in wisdom. He saw it as a unique adaptive strength of older age. He made the critical point that the emergence of wisdom as a late-blooming power depends on adequate psychological adjustment in the earlier portions of our lives. He asserted the formation of wisdom follows from successfully confronting particular developmental challenges associated with earlier age and moving on.

Successful transition through earlier periods of the life cycle prepares the individual for the final phase, where wisdom is the principal virtue to be developed. Erikson said that at every new stage of the life cycle we again confront and resolve those problems left over from earlier periods of our life. If in our youth we never really developed a sense of identity, this problem will resurface at this final phase of our lives. We may again face this problem, perhaps finally forming an idea of who we are and what our purpose has been in this life. Or we may have to live with the sense of not knowing.

We may also have skated past other developmental tasks, never honestly looking them in the eye, and so never making the adjustments required for a reasonably normal life. I have known many men who sacrificed their marriage, the love of their children, and the affection of friends for satisfactions garnered from their work. When they retire, or are sacked, or come out on the wrong end of a merger, when they finally come home looking for support and understanding, their spouses are packing their bags, ready to leave. Their children are distant and alienated; friends from their 30s and 40s have evaporated. Small wonder there are so many lonely, desperately unhappy, older single men.

This problem is not confined solely to males. The same phenomenon occurs to women who have made the same choices, although most female workaholics have struggled harder than their male counterparts to maintain close friendships. There also are those women who have sacrificed "everything" for their families, excluding from their lives the pleasures derived from work, friendships, and playful activities. They find themselves with a huge void in their lives when their kids leave home and their spouses depart through death or divorce.

Sometimes old age brings with it the opportunity to develop caring, loving, and mutually satisfying relationships for the first time. Since his remarriage to a woman in his young-old generation, my long-time friend Steve's personality has undergone a metamorphosis. I knew him in high school and followed his success first as a biology teacher and then as a school superintendent. He had a solid, but cool, relationship with his wife. I never saw them touch each other after the wedding ceremony, although they must have because they eventually had two children. Then his wife died of cancer. Several years later, Steve met Tanya and something in him opened up. Now they hold hands, hug each other, and kiss publicly. Steve is now far more informal, funnier, and back to being the warm friend I remember from our teenage years.

Continuing to Learn While Growing Older

Just as self-knowledge does not automatically increase with advancing years, so too wisdom does not just accumulate naturally along with gray hair and wrinkles. Others have said this before. Nearly a half-century ago, the American writer Langston Hughes said, "Age has nothing to do with wisdom," a sentiment expressed by the great German writer Goethe two hundred years earlier. And more than two thousand years before that, the Roman playwright Plautus wrote that wisdom did not come from the passing of years but from character. They may overstate the case slightly, but the point is well made: More birthdays does not guarantee greater wisdom. It emanates from continuing to be open to experience, to learn from it, and to change in small ways as a result. Wisdom evolves from a life fully lived, enabling us to understand the passions of others, and from our own suffering, which provides a basis for judgment and intuition. Wisdom emerges from the self-knowledge that grows out of living with ourselves through the epochs of our life span.

While it is true that many wise people are older, it doesn't follow that all elders are wise. I am reminded of a senior fifth grade teacher I once met while consulting about a troubled boy in her class. The student had attention deficit disorder and couldn't sit still. He was difficult, but she was brutalizing him. When I asked her if she had tried some of the new behavioral techniques developed to help these youngsters, she snapped, "I've had thirty years of experience, young man!" Before I could think, I heard myself retorting, "Have you had thirty years of experience, or one year of experience thirty times?" Just as I was about to apologize for losing my professional cool, the teacher replied after a moment, and to my surprise, "That was an offensive remark, young man. But you just might have a point. Let me think about it." Later, the teacher told me she modified her instruction, using techniques for behavior reinforcement that enabled the boy to read and pay attention in class in spite of his attentional problem.

Wisdom accumulates as long as we can continue to learn while aging—about ourselves and about others, about the world around us. For example, I've learned, in the words of our Air Force unit's first sergeant, that some days you eat the bear, and some days the bear eats you, a surprising idea to someone four months out of Harvard and trained to be the diner and not the dinner. I've learned that when I am highly stressed, saying "yes" to requests to commit my future time and labor is far easier than saying "no," so I try to put off making these decisions until I can take a deep breath and think about what this request entails; that our good deeds are likely to be ignored, trivialized, or punished, so I had better feel good about going out of my way for others; that enemies I have made along the way have had far more negative influence on my life than my friendships have benefitted me, so I am cautious about saying things that may antagonize; that not every battle requires fighting or winning, so it is useful to learn when to hold and when to fold; that there is far more to be learned from failure than from success, so I try to muster the courage to look at what went wrong rather than automatically saying, "If I had it to do over again, I would do the same thing"; that truth is nearly always relative, so there are at least two sides to every story and more than one answer to most questions; that it is pretty certain that those qualities we most cherish in ourselves will sometimes fail us, and we will suffer terribly, but that the hellfire that melts butter also can harden steel.

I think that the wisest people are often those who are no longer highly competitive. It is hard to be calm, undriven, and detached at home or on the job while striving for success. When your world turns on making the green light or hitting the rotary just right, getting your daughter into a sixth grade honors math program or trying to motivate your son to prepare for his bar mitzvah two weeks from now, or making a sale or beating a rival to publication, the qualities of wisdom are not especially adaptive. This is why we often associate wisdom with getting older. These women and men are no longer striving to beat everyone else to the top.

As I write these words, it occurs to me that one of the wisest men in history was in his 30s when he was crucified: Jesus Christ. Buddha was 30 when he gave up his life of wealth and privilege to begin his life as a pauper; his actions eventually led to the creation of one of the most powerful religious traditions in history. Perhaps the message for us is that we can begin our search for wisdom early in our lives; we don't have to wait for the emergence of wrinkles and gray hair.

⚜ GETTING WISDOM: A JOURNEY MORE THAN A DESTINATION

Having now set down the characteristics of wisdom, I find myself thinking that these qualities are about as easy to develop as those required to follow the Golden Rule, the Ten Commandments, and the Boy Scout Oath. If I look at myself unblinkingly, I don't think I would score any better on these traits of wisdom than on any other scroll of ideal virtues. No one who has ever dared to try writing can be said to be dispassionate or, for that matter, modest. The fire that drives this author is fueled by an emotional intensity that propels me to write early in the morning and late at night, on weekends and holidays; it is rooted in the desire to challenge existing ideas that I view as incomplete or wrong, and state my own view of the truth. The same motives drive my teaching and public speaking. Not much dispassion in these activities. For me, modesty has been a quality far more impressed on my character by decades sprinkled with humbling experiences than a virtue actively sought.

Maybe kindness is a quality of mine that others might rate as above average. Certainly I think of myself as accepting and not mean-spirited. Fragmentary evidence around me doesn't contradict this self-perception. Panhandlers, evangelists, and lost tourists regularly seek me out in the street. But then I think of my behavior over the past week. On Saturday, I made a nasty crack to my spouse of forty years about her new hairdo and ignored my daughter's earnest efforts to help me with Christmas shopping. Yesterday I made an unnecessary critical remark to a young colleague who was trying her best to develop a form to help us keep track of what we do. It is only Tuesday and I'm already headed south on the kindness scale.

Self-control has never been my long suit either. Relative to the ideal, I am hopelessly low; I usually can be counted on to say what is on my mind, disagree publicly with ideas that hit me wrong, and make a joke that may or may not turn out to be amusing. As a clinician, my style is to work close to the troubled client, being less dispassionate and less standoffish. It is important to me that they overcome their problems, and they know it.

It bothers me when our efforts fail. It still does after thirty years. So, an objective ranking puts me well into the bottom of any absolute scale of modesty, kindness, dispassion, and self-control.

How about yourself? How would you rate yourself on modesty, kindness, dispassion, and self-control? How would your closest friends and family members judge you? Hopefully, you will rank much higher than I do—but probably several rungs short of your aspirations.

A difficulty with these qualities of wisdom is that many are not especially compatible with setting high standards for yourself at school or on the job, being competitive, and making sacrifices to get to where you want to go. Being successful in most organizations seems to require the antithesis of wisdom; promoting ourselves when the opportunity opens rather than being modest about our, probably modest, ideas and achievements; ignoring others in need of kindness because we don't have the time to hold out our hand; caring deeply about everything and everyone in our personal world instead of being dispassionate; and seizing opportunities instantly when they appear rather than being patient and controlled.

Whatever the reasons, most of us will fall short of fulfilling these standards of wisdom, or the Golden Rule, or the Ten Commandments, or the Boy Scout Oath. Does this mean that we have no hope of becoming wise? No, on the contrary, wisdom is a process of becoming rather than being, a journey rather than a destination. And people whom we think of as wise are not wise all the time by our criteria or theirs. They have days, maybe weeks, of falling short of the ideal. Their judgment too will not always be on target. People who have a lot of good ideas also have a lot of bad ones. But what may distinguish their lives individually is their willingness to keep making the effort. Wisdom, then, may be more like a batting average, where the best are successful less than half the time and the rest far less than that. Just as we venerate the .400 hitter in baseball, we pay homage to those individuals who may be twice as wise as we are, but who are still mortal.

Wisdom doesn't require a special intellectual gift, an Ivy League education, or even an advanced age. Certainly being smart and getting older help, but these are not requirements and are no guarantee. Most who have lived fully and have had the courage to examine their experiences and learn from them will find the qualities of wisdom—modesty, kindness, dispassion, and self-control—emerging in their behavior. This type of wisdom grows out of ordinary lives lived by ordinary people. Thus, wisdom, unlike IQ, is within the grasp of most, because it depends more on judgment coming from living fully than education, more on mastery of challenges and crises than on intellectual achievement, more on human understanding than on scientific knowledge. The majority of us possess a streak of wisdom within us to be nurtured.

★ RECAPPING

The idea that wisdom goes together with being smart and elderly is well established in our culture. The truth is that being highly intelligent and older are advantages, but wisdom requires neither. Tests of wisdom have discovered ordinary, young adults outscoring many selected wise men. Some of the wisest people in the Western and Eastern world were well short of 40 when they made their wisdom known to others. Qualities associated with wisdom include modesty, kindness, dispassion, and self-control. These are hard-won virtues emerging from suffering, a life passionately and fully lived, self-knowledge, and continuing to learn from experience while growing older. Many of us will fall well short of perfection on all or, perhaps, most of these virtues. The frequency with which we exhibit wise behaviors resembles the batting averages of major league players. The very best batters hit about .400; the rest of us are well short of this percentage. Thus wisdom is more of a process than an outcome. This definition of wisdom suggests that it grows out of the ordinary experience of ordinary people. Unlike intelligence, it is within the grasp of the majority of us because it depends more on learning from life experiences than on ability or being elderly.

10

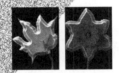

SUMMING UP:
GUIDELINES FOR OPTIMAL AGING

For our society to function optimally in the new millennium, the contributions of its robust elders, most especially the aging baby boomers, will be required. Because the boomers are followed by the baby bust generation—those born between 1965 and 1977—the US economy will need active workers who are in the last quarter of their lives. Active oldsters will have greater incentive to continue to work as the age at which social security benefits can be collected steadily creeps toward 70.

A vigorous economy also rests on our ability to contain the medical costs of caring for those in the last season of their lives. Otherwise, the portion of the budget allocated for elder health care will continue to grow, consuming resources that should be channeled to other needs such as childcare, education, and scientific research. Progress in containing health care costs has been made through better medical management and by decreasing the percentage of older American citizens unable to care for themselves due to ill health. This latter figure has dropped 15 percent in just over a decade. These advances are due to the medical discoveries of the 1970s and 1980s—less smoking, better diets, exercise, more effective medicines for heart attack victims, transplants and surgery to restore vision, vigor, and locomotion. Much more is known today about what each of us can do to age optimally, and more discoveries are on the way.

The quality of the fourth quarter of our lives is as much something we create for ourselves as it is determined by forces beyond our control. It is now clear that certain attitudes and actions we practice will raise the probability of aging optimally. Here I sit, then, ballpoint in hand, pretty well up to date on what modern science has to say about optimal aging. What advice do I have for you and yours, for my children and my grandchildren, about how we might maximize our potential in the last quarter of our lives? Here is what I believe to be true.

Exercise Regularly

If I could make only one suggestion to my children and grandchildren about optimal aging, it would be this: Get regular exercise. Exercise will add years to your life and improve the quality of those additional years. Exercise has been found to be correlated with better cardiovascular functioning, which itself is associated with a fuller, longer life. People who exercise have better blood flow to their brains, a finding that probably explains why aerobic and anaerobic training result in quicker processing speed, better memory, and clearer reasoning. Physical conditioning also enhances immune system operations, thereby making us less susceptible to disease and able to recover faster from illness. And it is positively associated with lower tension levels, improved mood, and better self-concept.

Starting early is an advantage, of course. But it is almost never too late. Research results from the East and West, North and South, all show that individuals in the fourth quarter of their life can improve their physical abilities remarkably. Elderly volunteers—ages 70 to 98—who engaged in strength training more than doubled their muscle strength; and their walking speed increased almost 50 percent.

The jury is still out on how much exercise is needed to produce benefits. Some argue that frequent heavy workouts are necessary—as in serious sweating four times a week—before we can expect to realize significant gains. Others have found that regular moderate aerobic, or even anaerobic training, yields the same positive results. Our own studies of the mental functioning of older physicians yielded an inverted U-shaped curve, showing that the best-functioning physicians engaged in moderate exercise whereas lower scorers were either engaged in vigorous workouts or none at all. Furthermore, there is individual variation in how much exercise is required to produce results. My guess is that this variation is related to how physically fit we are to begin with: Those of us in the best shape may require more strenuous exercise to reap benefits, whereas others who are less fit at the start may need only a moderate workout.

Few of us will escape the inevitable medical conditions and diseases that accompany growing older. If the bad news is that health problems are unavoidable, surely the good news is that the best preventive measure we can take is within our control. It is regular exercise.

Be Open to Diverse Experiences

Bigger brain cells are associated with greater engagement in different kinds of experiences. Studies of the brains of laboratory animals and humans have found that neurons grow by dendritic branching, a process promoted by diverse activities.

In Chapter 6 we heard the story of Betty Friedan's Outward Bound experience and the Elderhostel experiences of the "Professors Boring." Friedan writes about how much her life has been enriched by the challenges of the Outward Bound program; and the two professors were clearly rejuvenated by their Elderhostel studies in Italy and Greece. On the whole, Elderhostelers, presumably taking courses to enrich their lives, tend to be brighter, more energetic, and better able to cope with stress than the average person in their age group. Our own studies with physicians discovered that even a simple index of diversity distinguished the higher functioning older physicians: The elite physicians read for challenge as well as for pleasure more often than the physicians with average scores did. The higher scorers also spiced their lives with more frequent contact with the younger generations—students, children, and grandchildren.

A person who has been thinking longest about the factors that contribute to optimal aging is K. Warner Schaie, the director of the famous Seattle Longitudinal Study. He and his coworkers isolated factors that they believe are correlated with maintaining high levels of mental vigor well into later life. They identified many variables that have to do with being open to new and stimulating experiences. An example is pursuing challenging academic programs and working at occupations that require complex thinking. Another illustration is pursuing avocational activities that expand horizons, such as travel to unfamiliar countries.

When I think of these findings, I remember my friend Harry, in Houston. A man of my young-old years, he runs several fast-food franchises. Last year his wife, Charlotte, told him that they were getting too set in their ways. They needed to do something challenging. The next thing Harry knew, they were trekking in Tibet with Sherpa guides. Harry later described to me how he spent Christmas Eve of that year, shivering in his sleeping bag at 12,000 feet in a tent secured to a mountainside by pitons. "I guess what doesn't kill you, helps you," he commented on his return. But he went on to say that it has been a long time since he felt any better than he does now. Although some of us might think that Harry and Charlotte went a little overboard in their quest for excitement, it certainly makes intuitive and scientific sense that a little stress opens our senses and our minds.

"So if my idea of a great vacation is to play golf every day at Hilton Head," my son asks, "does that mean my brain cells will shrink?" Not necessarily. But what is probable is that doing something over and over again doesn't do much to expand our mental capacities. The people who are not doing much to keep their minds vital are those for whom every day follows the same pattern; they work at the same repetitive jobs and do exactly the same things every weekend, go to the same places for vacation, read the same books, watch the same movies and TV shows in an unbroken line.

But, if our work happens to provide us with all the stimulating challenges we can handle in a week, and if our family and friendship networks overflow, we don't need our playtime to challenge us also. We have all the enrichment needed to encourage those dendrites to branch. Sometimes the pleasant repetition of swinging a golf club and walking after the ball on a beautiful green fairway provides the soothing restoration necessary to sustain our mental health.

Learn to Use a PC

The biggest regret I have had over the past decade is not learning to use the personal computer sooner. The reason: technophobia, or fear of unfamiliar machines of seeming incomprehensible complexity. I have paid a large price over the last ten years in fear of having my ignorance revealed, in a dependence on others for things I could and would have preferred to do myself, in being hamstrung by old inefficient ways of analysis and graphic design, and in isolating myself from new generations of researchers and clinicians who are more up to speed in the PC world.

Having learned the rudiments of computer operations, I can now word process documents (such as this book), make graphs and charts for my classes and lectures (which can be beamed directly on to the screen from my laptop), coordinate from my office an international conference by using e-mail and the facsimile capability of my computer, and update myself on a particular topic through the Harvard and other library systems. If I am puzzled about a particular problem a patient of mine has, such as a 72-year-old with ringing in the ears, and there is not much mention of it in recent professional literature, a few keystrokes bring up 262 references on tinnitus from the Internet.

My personal life is eased by being able to find the best price for a new Volvo, to buy books on-line at a huge discount, to make reservations for a flight to Seattle and hotel accommodations there, to obtain a map showing the best route to Syracuse, or to shop for groceries that will be deposited on my back porch tomorrow afternoon. And I am merely a weekend sailor in these waters. There remain a number of icons on the main menu that I have not yet explored.

The computer has unique potential to enhance the quality of living for those of us in the last seasons of our lives, especially those who have problems getting around. The PC opens opportunities for social interactions with loved ones and new ones. Numerous grandparents today regularly communicate with grandchildren, family members, and other friends through e-mail. And seniors meet other seniors through on-line services such as SeniorNet. The sharing of experiences, feelings, and thoughts in these virtual relationships is often far greater than what happens when these same people meet in the flesh. Plus, a great advantage of an electronic relationship is that you don't have to synchronize your communications with each other. You can communicate when you are at your best; others can read your message at their leisure and get back to you when they are in the mood.

I hear the opportunities for virtual play are breathtaking—although, frankly, I haven't done much with these opportunities. Not only are there simple (solitaire) and complex games (such as new versions of games resembling Dungeons and Dragons), there are exotic trips to be taken, fantasies to be indulged, and personalities to be taken on. And the computer is ready to play whenever you are.

Our children and grandchildren above the age of 5 are already comfortable with the PC, so we don't have to worry about them. They will carry these skills into their later years, and the quality of their lives will be better for it. It is the 60+ crowd that needs encouragement. We need to overcome our fears, our inertia, or whatever else it is that holds us back, so that we can enrich our lives through this remarkable invention.

Develop Several Ways of Coping with Stress

A few years ago I was part of a panel to help students who are under stress. It was final exam time at Harvard, and the undergraduates were complaining about the unbearable pressure they were under. When it was my turn to talk about the value of learning ways to cope with tension, I commented that this would probably not be the most stressful period of their lives. An avalanche of hisses (the Harvard equivalent of booing) tumbled down upon me. What these students didn't want to hear is that the years beyond college are going to be peppered with challenges that will make final exam pressure seem trivial, put the trauma of a romantic breakup or not getting into medical school into the proper perspective of being a bump in the road, not the end of it.

Those of us who have returned to our twenty-fifth or fiftieth college reunions have something to say to those youngsters about what is out there to be faced. We know, for example, that some injuries are self-inflicted, but other pain, undeserved, heaps upon us. We know that we may be visited by those very things we fear the most and will suffer terribly. And we know, having lived more than half our days on Earth, that there is much more to be endured in life than achieved. In the words of Rabbi Harold Kushner, "Bad things happen to good people." So be ready. Being ready means inventorying the ways you cope with stress. When you look at how you are coping, keep in mind these two principles: More is better; and be sure your ways of coping don't create additional problems.

Optimal agers I have known have lots of ways of managing the effects of unpleasant events. There is my old friend Geoff, who has had more than his share of demons to battle. He has kept himself reasonably normal into his eighth decade by his born-again Christian faith, by working out regularly, by spending part of every week with the grandchildren who live nearby, and by lecturing to students in college Christian fellowships. No doubt his religious faith, developed in his undergraduate days, regularly tested and renewed, has sustained him. So, too, has his exercise program gotten him through some difficult times, as has the comforting presence of family members and the stimulation of young people.

Being a practicing believer and exerciser, having good relationships with loved ones, and working with young people are stress-eaters. But lots of other ways of managing stress work just as well. Appreciating the arts or performing them lifts the spirits when things are bad. My beloved spouse loves pounding out Wagner on the piano when things have not gone her way. Others find solace in long, quiet walks or in romantic novels. Gardening or doing almost anything with my hands relieves my tension. The more ways we have to deal with stress, the better.

Beware that the ways you use to reduce pressure don't become a problem in themselves. In my childhood, I saw grown-ups meet their challenges with the assistance of cigarettes and alcohol. My generation tried them, but they didn't work for us because we found that the costs assessed against physical and mental health far outweighed the benefits. Scan your stress reduction measures. Are you using emotion-focused ways of coping with unpleasant feelings rather than correctly addressing the problems creating the distress? Are you praying for divine intervention to relieve your fears rather than helping yourself? Are you jogging to avoid feeling down rather than engaging the reasons you are moody and listless? Do you pop tranquilizers or antidepressants instead of addressing the source of these tensions? Do you feel better by putting unpleasant realities out of your mind—a lump here, a funny colored splotch there, that persistent cough—instead of getting a medical checkup? Be aware that every way we have of making ourselves feel better has a downside, such as ignoring a physical problem that can be remedied. As we grow older, sometimes the best we can do is practice suppression, putting bad feelings out of our mind so that we can enjoy other parts of our lives. But, take stock. Don't overuse emotion-focused coping strategies that preclude actions to address the source of our distress.

Gender Differences Widen, Not Narrow, with Age

A half-century ago, the average female life expectancy in the United States was about 70, whereas her male counterpart could count on about 65 birthdays. In other words, there was about a five-year difference in life span. In 2000, the average baby girl will live to 80; and the projected life expectancy of a male newborn will be 73. You do the math. This is a seven-year gap. In other words, the gender difference in life expectancy has grown about 40 percent in the past fifty years.

This change may be a numerical symbol of the differences between females and males that widen with age. In previous chapters we discovered, for instance, that older women are generally in better physical shape than men in their young-old years, as judged by the effects of aerobic training on cardio-vascular status. We also learned that the correlation between the size of social networks and health shows that females can remain in good health with fewer intimates than males can, perhaps because a female's friends are closer. Older men don't fare very well on their own because of fewer close friends. To age optimally, older men need to create larger social networks. Start now.

Striking, too, are the personality changes accompanying aging; again, the sexes seem to be moving in opposite directions. Men are likely to become milder and less aggressive with age, less determined to be independent. Women, however, grow increasingly independent, adventuresome, assertive, and more comfortable with overt expressions of anger as the years pass.

It is interesting to note how blind people in our culture are to these growing differences. I found evidence of this subtle stereotyping at the card section of a local supermarket. I was looking for an anniversary card for friends who have been married for thirty years. As I picked through the cards, I was struck by how little difference existed between the males and females portrayed, especially on the cards for the twenty-fifth anniversary and beyond. The sexes were depicted as two bunnies, two mice, two red foxes, two turtles, and two chipmunks. The gender was displayed only by a bow between the ears here, a bow tie there, or pants and a dress. Several cards made no effort at all to identify the sex, just two turtles, butterflies, kittens, or teddy bears. Is it possible that all elders look alike to the artists creating anniversary cards?

We ignore these growing differences at our peril. At the Center on Aging in Los Angeles, research on older couples found that the marriage suffers when the freshly retired husband suddenly intrudes upon the wife's domain. There he is with nothing to do, energetic and restless, wanting to do something useful. So he gives his spouse a lot of advice about how to reorganize the spices, vacuum more efficiently, and run the dishwasher with greater economy. Before long, the wife retaliates and things get nasty. There is much truth in, "I married him for better or worse, but not for lunch."

You retired husbands had better be ready for your wife of forty years to want to be rid of you for portions of the day so that she can get on with her life independently. This behavior can be confusing to the formerly busy man whose spouse used to complain that he spent all his time working and never had any time for her. Older men, especially those who are retiring, need to find something to do away from the woman's domain, out of the house, so that harmony can be maintained.

There are two other gender-based challenges for older women and men. The first derives from the fact that females as a group are likely to be in better physical shape than their male counterparts; therefore they may be more adventuresome. Not being in shape embarrassed my friend Noah after he retired from Harvard. I ran into Noah and his wife, Rachel, at a bas mitzvah. I noticed that Noah was walking with a cane and limping. He told me the story. Shortly after he gave up working full time, Rachel suggested they take a Elderhostel program in New Mexico. It was an archeological survey. Noah described the average day: "What we did was line up thirty feet apart and walk across the foothills looking for pottery chards, arrow heads, or any other evidence of early inhabitancy. If someone spotted a cave forty or fifty feet above the ground, we had to climb up and look. We began at 5:30 AM and stopped when the temperature hit 100 degrees, which was about noon." Popping two ibuprofen, he added, "She wants to go back next year." As soon as he recovers, Noah said he was getting a membership at Gold's gym. The moral for you men fresh from retirement with a spouse of your generation: hit those weights, get on the stairmaster; otherwise you won't be able to keep up with her.

Greater longevity for women is not all good news. The fitness of the young-old females can give way to greater physical problems later on. The average mother and grandmother of today's young adults can expect to spend three years of the last season of her life in poor physical health. Of course, it may be that this generation of adult women will be able to decrease the number of dysfunctional years by means of better nutrition, exercise, and hormone replacement therapy. And, no doubt, more discoveries are on the way.

Retirement Is Overrated

Among those I know, especially the young-oldsters who liked their work, retirement is not welcome. In Chapter 8, we reviewed a study of nearly 13,000 older workers and found that most of them said they would like to throttle down gradually rather than leave the workforce all together. Most believed, however, that it was impossible because no part-time opportunities existed where they were employed.

These statistics find regular confirmation in the 60- to 75-year-olds who have crossed my path. The most capable of the 70-year-olds we tested in the MicroCog study, for example, did not go gently into the sunset of their careers. Many were reluctant to give up their work or positions of leadership and responsibility. Consider my insurance executive neighbor, Shelley, who took his company's buyout offer eighteen months ago. For the next half-year, he and his wife, Laura, traveled and visited friends and family and started to breed Jack Russells. About six months ago, I ran into Shelley at a neighborhood get together. He seemed uncharacteristically irritable and withdrawn. Laura whispered to my spouse that Shelley couldn't find anything to do and she was worried about him. A dozen Saturdays later, I met Shelley at the dump. He engaged me in conversation with his usual animated spirit and humor. Before I could comment on the change, he handed me a business card. He was now the general manager of a small venture capital company. "I'm having the time of my life," Shelley grinned. "After six months, I had all the retirement I could handle. I needed something useful to do." Laura has passed the word around the neighborhood that, contrary to allegations, she did not call a headhunter to find work for her husband.

Like Shelley, many individuals discover that, after six to twelve months of not working, the batteries are recharged and they are ready to go again. Sadly, Shelley's success in finding a challenging job is unusual. The initial work experiences of Tom and Gail in Chapter 8 trace a far more predictable path. If you think you will want to continue to work after the usual retirement age, examine your skills well before you are eligible for your first social security check. Look at the want ads and imagine yourself applying for job openings in your occupation. Do you qualify? Do you need serious retraining? Even then, what would your chances be? Then ask yourself: "When was the last time a headhunter called?" People with technical skills, those who can teach or doctor, keep books or complete someone else's income tax form, fix computers or VCRs, plumb or wire or lay bricks, usually can find all the work they want at 60+. Many retirees open their own small businesses or franchises. Even though they work long hours, they have control over their lives. Consulting works, too, especially if you have a niche. Three university administrators I have met in the last decade have done well with their specialties: one is an expert on how to rehabilitate old science buildings; a second is a whiz at putting on special occasion functions for the grandees; a third sold his skills as a benefits and compensation expert to educational institutions.

Be careful about tying too much of your self-esteem to what you do, especially if you are very good at it, and especially if you will have a brief shelf life. I am thinking of professional athletes and models and fighter pilots, or others who, because of their unique attributes, spend a few years in the spotlight. Many do not retire gracefully from being the center of attention or from doing what they love, because they know that nothing else they will ever do will bring the same challenge, the adrenaline rush, and the pleasure that comes from sinking a three with someone hanging all over you, from swinging down the runway garbed in this spring's latest, or from landing a modern jet at night on an aircraft carrier deck.

It is not surprising to me that the best coaches were not themselves great athletes. Sitting on the bench, even in the big leagues, brings home the message that they had better start to think about a career when their playing days are over, which could be tomorrow. So they pay attention, begin to focus on the art of coaching, look for off-season jobs at sports camps, and start to make their interests known. They step easily into work when their athletic careers end. I believe the same process occurs with pianists, actors, and other artists who become gifted teachers. This doesn't mean that great performers should give up. Some have been able to reinvent themselves as motivational speakers, announcers, PR executives, and small business owners. But they all started early so that they were ready when the spotlight moved elsewhere.

There are other ways of feeling useful besides being paid for it. Volunteer work satisfies many. In Chapter 1, I described the RV gypsies who work for Habitat for Humanity. Then there is grandparenting, another enterprise that enables us to feel competent and useful. Grandmothers have always been recognized for their valuable role in nurturing the next generation, but grandfathers are also important. The most significant man in my wife's life was her grandfather, who taught her to ski and to skate, and instilled a love of gardening. When he was very old, he planted two trees. I bet he knew that they would be here after he was long gone and that when his beloved granddaughter looked at them, she would think fondly of him. And she does.

Cultivate Your Reserve Capacities

During last year's graduation at Harvard, I invited my old friend and senior consultant Ben to join us for a celebratory lunch for this year's trainees at the faculty club. Now the faculty club is about a half-mile from my office. Ben has had two heart attacks and metastatic cancer. When I last saw him six months ago, he had had trouble walking up a flight of stairs without stopping. So I volunteered to drive over to the faculty club. "No," he insisted, "I'll walk." And walk we did. Over and back, keeping up with the pace of the young trainees. Afterward I commented that his walking over there and back was quite a contrast to a year ago. Before I could ask, he said, "It's my new rowing machine." After last year's difficulty, Ben made up his mind to improve his cardiovascular fitness. Never an athlete, he invested in a personal trainer and exercise equipment. "The first week I

could only row two minutes at dead slow, but now I'm up to
twenty minutes at a pretty good clip," smiled Ben. "My days
may be measured," he smiled, "but I'm going to live every one to
the hilt."

Ben's story illustrates the fact that each of us has reserve
capacity we can tap into even when we are old and sick, and the
grim reaper has us in his sights. Most of us can improve our
cardiovascular fitness very late in life. Like those old-old individuals at the Hebrew Rehabilitation Center for the Aged in
Boston, we can develop the muscles and the greater flexibility
that will enable us to walk or to climb stairs and get around far
more easily than before.

Reserve capacity is more obvious in the physical domain,
but it also exists in other parts of our lives. Take cognitive training. If we are willing to spend time practicing, it works for
nearly everyone, everywhere, even those in the last season of
life. Many different methods yield positive results. For example,
there is the method of loci described in Chapter 6. That technique involves associating things to be recalled with a room in
your house or familiar landmarks where you live. It works for
me. You may find your recall is improved by concentrating a
few moments longer when you meet new people. These extra
moments of effort enable you to be sure that you hear the
names and that they have sunk in. You also can use clustering
when you have a number of errands to do, putting items into
groups for easier retrieval later. At malls and airport parking
lots, you stop at the door from which you will be exiting and
look at where your car is parked. Or if you're not in the mood
for that, just write down the location. Then there are electronic
memory boosters, which many of my friends use.

In the last season of our lives, it seems that every passing
year involves giving up the things we used to enjoy. Eyesight
dims, hearing weakens, joints give out, dread diseases loom.
How is it possible to think about developing reserve capacity
under these conditions? The answer is to employ a strategy that
enables us to live our lives to the fullest while recognizing the
reality of growing limitations. An example is selection, optimization, and compensation, techniques described in Chapter 2.

Remember the example of Arthur Rubenstein. Although aging was taking its toll, he was able to continue his distinguished solo career by careful selection (playing a more limited repertoire), optimization (practicing harder), and compensation (making up-tempo sections seem faster by playing the preceding passage more slowly).

The rest of us can get the most out of our later years be using similar techniques. Selection means conserving our available energy by doing fewer things; for example, we can move to a kinder climate so that we don't have to shovel snow; or we cn move to a retirement home, where someone else can care for the lawn, or an assisted-living facility, where we can get the help we need so that we can spend our available energies doing things and being with people we care about most. Optimization involves allocating our remaining energy to the maintenance of those activities we have selected. For you, it may be developing your interest in the personal computer. So you take classes, check books out of the library on word processing, e-mail, and the Internet, and seek out others with similar passions. Me, I focus on improving my doubles tennis game, which I have noted that people well into the last season of their lives still play. So I take lessons, read books on strategies, and obsess about how tightly my racket should be strung. Compensation involves correcting physical weaknesses (hearing aids, cataract surgery, new man-made joints), using external aids such as wheelchairs and electric scooters so that we can remain in contact with those we care most about, and asking for assistance in other areas of our lives so that we can be as independent as possible.

I recognize that a number of my older relatives and friends—and perhaps elders that you know—have not followed many of these guidelines for optimal aging, yet they are doing pretty well. The reason is that these suggestions fall far short of exhausting all the factors that contribute to maximizing the quality of the last quarter of our lives. And, of course, a huge amount of individual variation exists with respect to what each of us needs to live fully.

Nevertheless, we have within us the potential to create a portion of the environment in which we will live out our last years. Each of these points raises the probability that you and I, our children, and our grandchildren will age optimally. There are no guarantees that practicing these actions and attitudes will result in your optimal aging or mine. Bad things happen even to the industrious and the faithful. But what is pretty certain is that the failure to take these guidelines seriously will create a last quarter of life in which optimal aging is unlikely. We may not be successful at everything we try, but the odds are overwhelming that we'll be 100 percent unsuccessful at those things we never attempt.

NOTES

Introduction

PAGE 3

On the basis of tests of hundreds of older physicians and others in late life D. H. Powell, *Profiles in Cognitive Aging* (Cambridge, MA: Harvard University Press, 1994), pp. 177–183.

Satchel Paige Several versions of this quote have been reported. The wording in this quote comes from Thomas Boswell, In the Changing Domain of Sports, The Impossible Has Become Routine, *The Washington Post*, May 11, 1986.

the difference between chronological and functional age An excellent description of the differences as well as the difficulty in measuring functional age is contained in L. Hayflick, *How and Why We Age* (New York: Ballantine, 1994), pp. 11–18.

PAGE 6

the difference between a 6-volt and a 12-volt battery This analogy illustrates what has come to be called the rectangular model of optimal aging in gerontology. All of us in this field are grateful to the work of English psychologist Patrick Rabbit, who first described this enormously useful concept. See P. Rabbit, Applied cognitive gerontology: Some problems, methodology, and data, *Applied Cognitive Psychology*, (1990) 4, 229–246.

PAGE 7

to develop MicroCog Powell, *Profiles in Cognitive Aging*, pp. 177–179.

those in the eighth decade of their lives Ibid., p. 79.

Benton's research team A. L. Benton, P. Eslinger, and A. R. Damasio, Normative observations on neuropsychological test performance in old age, *Journal of Clinical Psychology*, (1981) 3, 33–42.

PAGE 8

Hebrew Rehabilitation Center for the Aged M. Fiatarone, E. Marx, N. Ryan, C. Merideth, L. Lipsitz, and W. Evans, High-intensity strength training in nonagenarians, *Journal of the American Medical Association*, (1990) 263, 3029–3034.

Behavioral scientists in all time zones For example, a team of gerontological specialists at Pennsylvania State University demonstrated that the mental powers of older individuals can be refreshed by training. These researchers, K. Warner Schaie and Sherry Willis, and their students have published scores of papers and several books on cognitive training. For example, see S. L. Willis, Improvement with cognitive training: Which old dogs learn new tricks? in L. W. Poon, D. C. Reuben, and B. A. Wilson (Eds.), *Everyday Cognition in Adulthood and Later Life* (New York: Cambridge University Press, 1989), pp. 545–569.

Gerontologists examined differences in improvement Willis, Improvement with cognitive training, pp. 545–569. Schaie and Willis found that simple retesting mediated the fourteen-year average decline for the younger (67) and middle (74) age cohorts for the 81-year-olds. Cognitive training resulted in remediation of the average decline to seven years earlier, an improvement that occurred in both spatial orientation and inductive reasoning. It was thought that the older groups needed a longer and more structured cognitive training approach.

PAGE 9

Eubie Blake Cited in Sayings of the Week, *The Observer*, February 13, 1993.

A 1997 report by the National Academy of Sciences K. G. Manton, L. Corder, and E. Stallard, Chronic disability trends in elderly United States populations: 1982–1994, *Proceedings of the National Academy of Sciences USA* (1997) *94*, 2593–2598.

Chapter 1

PAGE 18

"Aging is such a dismal, boring subject." An especially depressing view of older age is contained in Simone de Beauvoir's *The Coming of Age* (New York: NY: Warner Paperback Books, 1970).

a new cognitive test D. H. Powell, *Profiles in Cognitive Aging* (Cambridge, MA: Harvard University Press, 1994).

better-educated individuals tend to lose their mental powers more rapidly This observation was first made by investigators with the Seattle Longitudinal Study and later confirmed by research on the East Coast and the South. See K. W. Schaie, The optimization of cognitive functioning in old age: predictions based on cohort-sequential and longitudinal data. In P. B. Baltes and M. M. Baltes (Eds.), *Successful Aging: Perspectives from the Behavioral Sciences* (New York: Cambridge University Press, 1990), pp. 94–117. Also M. S. Albert, K. Jones, C. R. Savage, L. Berkman, T. Seeman, D. Boazer, and J. W. Rowe, Predictors of cognitive change in older persons: MacArthur studies of successful aging, *Psychology and Aging* (1995) 10, 578–589.

PAGE 20

America is graying All the population statistics cited in this paragraph are drawn from US Bureau of the Census, *Statistical Abstract of the United States: 1995* (115th ed.) (Washington, DC: US Government Printing Office, 1995).

These projections probably underestimate the actual growth in the post-65 group In 1972 the projected population of those 65 and over for 1990 was 27,110,000. The actual numbers were 31,078,000. These data were drawn from the *Statistical Abstract of the United States: 1972*, US Bureau of Census, Current Population Reports (Washington, DC: US Government Printing Office, 1972). The 1990 data were drawn from US Bureau of Census, Current Population Reports (Washington, DC: US Government Printing Office, 1992).

not a uniquely American phenomenon For a population projections for East Asia and the United States, see L. Martin, Population and aging policies in East Asia and the United States, *Science* (1991) *251*, 527–531. For projections for the People's Republic of China, see Z. Wu, The psychology of aging in China, *World Psychology* (1996) *2*, 71–86. For other projections, see R. A. Butatao et al., *World Population Projections: Short and Long Term Estimates* (Baltimore, MD: Johns Hopkins University Press, 1990).

Page 21

three new professional journals These new professional journals were *Aging and Cognition*, *Mental Health and Aging*, and *Journal of Aging and Identity*.

most rapidly expanding divisions of the American Psychological Association A phone call to the American Psychological Association in Washington, DC on October 28, 1995, yielded the following data comparing the memberships in the APA in 1985 and 1994. During this period, the total membership grew from 62,547 to 80,810, an increase of about 29 percent; membership in the Aging Division grew 53.7 percent (from 1,049 to 1,612); and the Neuropsychology Division expanded 102 percent (from 1,785 to 3,605).

Page 22

exploits of Helen Klein Delta Airlines *Sky Magazine*, September 1995, pp. 18–20.

Senior Olympic Games in Osaka, Japan J. Foreman, Oldest Athletes Get Closer Look, *The Boston Globe*, June 28, 1993, p. 37, Health and Sciences Section.

the best US time for running ten kilometers Data on distance running came from a personal communication from Ryan Lamppa, US Track and Field: Roadrunners Information Center, Santa Barbara, CA. (805) 683-5868. October 11, 1995.

Page 23

organizations that employ us require This idea was stimulated by the following passage from Schiller: "Eternally fettered only to a single little fragment of the whole, man fashions himself only as a fragment; ever hearing only the monotonous whirl of the wheel which he turns, he never displays the full harmony of his being, and, instead of coining the humanity that lies in his nature, he is content with a mere impression of his occupation, his science." From J. C. F. von Schiller, *The Aesthetic Letters* (Boston, MA: Charles C. Little and James Brown, 1845), p. 22.

Tom Sawyer M. Twain, *The Adventures of Tom Sawyer* (New York: Nelson Doubleday, 1876), p. 7.

Page 24

"RV gypsies" Personal communication from Kandace Tornquist, Executive Director, Habitat for Humanity, Austin, TX, September 27, 1996.

Congress has passed a law banning age-based mandatory retirement Public Law 99-592.

Page 25

grounding of Bob Hoover A somewhat biased—but, my sources tell me, accurate—description of the FAA's grounding of Bob Hoover on the basis of neuropsychological tests was written by his attorney, F. Lee Bailey. See F. L. Bailey, Hoover vs the FAA. *Flying*, May 1994, pp. 58–76.

Page 26

Scientific studies recommended The studies influencing public safety officers were conducted by F. J. Landy et al., *Alternatives to Chronological Age in Determining Standards of Suitability for Public Safety Jobs* (University Park, PA: Center for Applied Behavioral Science, Pennsylvania State University, 1992). The study on tenured faculty was conducted by P. B. Hammond and

H. B. Morgan, *Ending Mandatory Retirement for Tenured Faculty: The Consequences for Higher Education* (Washington, DC: National Academy Press, 1991).

PAGE 27

older members of the Cornell physics department These examples of what college universities in the United States are doing to induce senior faculty to retire are taken from D. K. Wagner, An Aging Faculty Poses a Challenge for Colleges, *Chronicle of Higher Education*, August 8, 1997, pp. A10–A11.

fewer young people are entering the workforce today L. R. Offerman and M. K. Gowing, Organizations of the future: changes and challenges, *American Psychologist* (1990) *45*, 95–108.

PAGE 28

the average US worker closer to 40 than 30 These data are based on a middle-level projection for population growth. See H. N. Fullerton, Outlook 2000: new labor force projections, spanning 1988 to 2000, *Monthly Labor Review* (1989) *112*, 3–12.

average age of first retirement continues to decline Fullerton, Outlook 2000: new labor force projections.

PAGE 29

the proportion of retirees 55+ who have started working again These calculations are based on transitions per unit cohort at age 55 for 1980 and 1972. As an example, there were .366 returns to work among women in 1972 and .582 in 1980. See M. D. Hayward, W. R. Grady, and S. D. McLaughlin, The retirement process among older women in the United States: changes in the 1970's, *Research on Aging* (1988) *10*, 358–382. See also M. D. Hayward, E. R. Grady, and S. D. McLaughlin, Changes in the retirement process among older men in the United States: 1972–1980, *Demography* (1988) *25*, 371–386.

about two times a worker's annual salary I have been unable to uncover a specific reference citing empirical data to support this estimate. This approximation comes from discussions with two veteran directors of human resources. They are Daniel Cantor, former Human Resources Director at Harvard University, and Robert Burke, Director of Human Resources for the Putnam Companies. Independently, they arrived at the figure of twice an annual salary for executive level employees this way: search costs, 50 percent of the executive's compensation; lost productivity, about 100 percent; and training, 50 percent. This figure does not include efforts to improve the individual's performance before leaving and the adverse impacts on coworkers in the case of involuntary termination. It also does not include the cost to the organization of the lost productivity occurring when a valued employee departs during the period it takes to replace that individual.

Chapter 2

PAGE 34

science has thoroughly exploded The first article that drew my attention to the subject of variability within an age group was written by J. W. Rowe and R. L. Kahn, Human aging: usual and successful, *Science* (1987) *237*, 143–149.

PAGE 35

older physicians had far greater variability These data are summarized in D. H. Powell, *Profiles in Cognitive Aging* (Cambridge, MA: Harvard University Press, 1994), pp. 12–14, 42–45. Others have discovered the same thing. Two psychologists examined nearly 200 studies of aging—biological, cognitive, social, and psychological. In more than three-quarters of the reports, the variability of the age-group scores grew with age. See E. A. Nelson and D. Dannefer, Age heterogeneity: fact or fiction? The state of diversity in gerontological research, *The Gerontologist* (1992) *32*, 17–23.

A number of older individuals continue to function as well as individuals in their prime Consider, for instance, the test scores of our physician subjects above the age of 70. If we apply ordinary standards for normal cognitive aging, what proportions of those 70 to 74 would measure up? Ordinary standards for normal cognitive aging are a total score on MicroCog in the top 99 percent of physicians 45 to 64, with no more than one component score below the fifteenth percentile; 57.1 percent of the physicians tested met these criteria. The criteria for optimal cognitive aging is a score at or above the mean score for those 45 to 64 on MicroCog, with no component score below the fifteenth percentile; 20.4 percent of physicians in our sample met this criterion. It should be noted, however, that the growing variance in the older age groups is caused largely by a consistent lowering of the scores of a significant proportion of each census decade below that of the next younger sample. Among the physicians and normal volunteers 70 to 74, about 3.1 and 13.5 percent, respectively, had scores on MicroCog suggesting the possibility of cognitive impairment. At 75 to 79, the proportions in each group were 12 and 23.4 percent, respectively. See D. H. Powell, *Profiles in Cognitive Aging* (Cambridge, MA: Harvard University Press, 1994), p. 166.

Helen Klein Delta Airlines, *Sky Magazine*, September 1995, pp. 18–20.

PAGE 36

the saga of Captain Alfred C. Haynes This remarkable story is told in A. C. Haynes, *Flight Safety Foundation: Accident Prevention* (June 1991) *48*, 1–10.

PAGE 38

Swedish scientists tested 80-year-old identical twins G. E. McClearn, B. Johansson, S. Berg, N. L. Pedersen, F. Ahern, S. A. Petrill, and R. Plomin, Substantial genetic influence on cognitive abilities in twins eighty or more years old, *Science* (1997) *276*, 1560–1563.

dozens of twin studies See, for example, H. M. Chipuer, M. J. Rovine, and R. Plomin, LISREL modeling: genetic and environmental influences on I.Q. revisited, *Intelligence* (1990) *14*, 11–29. Also see J. C. Loehlin, Partitioning environmental and genetic contributions to behavioral development, *American Psychologist* (1989) *44*, 1285–1292.

doctoral dissertation of Susan Anderson S. L. Anderson, *Maintaining Cognitive Vigor in Later Years: The Contribution of Non-genetic Factors*. Unpublished doctoral dissertation, Boston University, Boston, MA, 1992.

PAGE 39

Ageism Negative stereotypes about older people, the vulnerability of elders to internalization of these beliefs, and activities to engage in to rebut these portrayals are contained in E. H. Erikson, J. M. Erikson, and H. Q. Kivnik, *Vital Involvement in Old Age* (New York: Norton, 1986), pp. 301–305.

PAGE 40

for over three decades Laws against discrimination on the basis of race, gender, and age have come on-line gradually, beginning with the Age Discrimination in Employment Act of 1967.

PAGE 43

for many, a gnawing sense of foreboding and apprehension This list of anxieties was inspired by, but not exactly reproduced from, the writings of my friend and colleague Peter J. Gomes, Plummer Professor of Christian Morals and Preacher to Harvard University. See P. J. Gomes, *The Good Book: Reading with the Mind and Heart* (New York: W. H. Morrow, 1997), pp. 203–204.

Over a half-century ago, a psychologist reported results K. Sward, Age and mental ability, *American Journal of Psychology* (1945) *58*, 443–449.

PAGE 44

anxiety is a frequently and strongly felt emotion These data are based on a structured interview used to collect information about symptoms on which the diagnosis of depression or anxiety is based. Subjects ranged in age from 18 to 65+ and were interviewed in Baltimore, MD; Durham, NC; New Haven, CT; and St. Louis, MO. Anxiety disorders were reported in about 7.8 percent of those 65+. This value can be compared to about 2.1 percent reporting signs of an affective disorder. See M. Gatz and M. A. Smyer, The mental health of older adults in the 1990s, *American Psychologist* (1992) *47*, 741–751.

describe two ways of lowering tensions associated with stress Their many writings on this topic include S. Folkman and R. S. Lazarus, Coping as a mediator of emotion, *Journal of Personality and Social Psychology* (1988) *54*, 466–475.

PAGE 46

middle-aged midwesterners A. DeLongis, S. Folkman, and R. S. Lazarus, The impact of daily stress on health and mood: psychological and social resources as mediators, *Journal of Personality and Social Psychology* (1988) *54*, 486–495.

A report from Pittsburgh W. J. Doyle, D. P. Skoner, B. S. Rabin, and J. N. Gwaltney, Jr., Social ties and susceptibility to the common cold, *Journal of the American Medical Association* (1997) *277*, 1940–1944.

PAGE 47

Among the Harvard graduates Psychiatrist George Vaillant has published a great deal on this topic. See, for example, G. E. Vaillant and C. O. Vaillant, Natural history of male psychological health, XII. A 45-year study of predictors of successful aging at 65, *American Journal of Psychiatry* (1990) *147*, 31–37.

as long as they are available emotionally Experts in this area differentiate between emotional support and instrumental support. A study carried out with subjects from three Eastern communities found that emotional support was more highly correlated with physical health than was instrumental support. See T. E. Seeman, L. F. Berkman, P. A. Chàrpentier, D. G. Blazer, M. S. Albert, and M. E. Tinetti, Behavioral and psychosocial predictors of physical performance: MacArthur studies of successful aging, *Journal of Gerontology: Medical Sciences* (1995) *50A*, M177–M183.

how younger and older adults cope with stress Folkman and Lazarus, Coping as a mediator of emotion.

differences exist, too, in how individuals react L. K. George and I. C. Siegler, Stress and coping in later life, *Educational Horizons* (1982) *60*, 147–154. Also see DeLongis, Folkman, and Lazarus, The impact of daily stress on health and mood.

PAGE 48

selection, optimization, and compensation P. B. Baltes, On the incomplete architecture of human ontogeny: selection, optimization, and compensation as a foundation of development theory, *American Psychologist* (1997) *52*, 366–380. Originally this concept was called selective optimization with compensation. See P. B. Baltes and M. M. Baltes, Psychological perspectives on successful aging: the model of selective optimization with compensation. In P. B. Baltes and M. M. Baltes (Eds.), *Successful Aging: Perspectives from the Behavioral Sciences* (New York: Cambridge University Press, 1990), pp. 1–34.

An ophthalmologist in Boston Charles L. Schepens is known as the father of modern retinal surgery. At 84, he no longer does eye surgery, but he consults with other eye doctors and their patients two days a week, lectures extensively, and is presently updating his classic text on diseases of the eye.

Chapter 3

PAGE 53

An excellent book on neuropsychological evaluation M. D. Lezak, *Neuropsychological assessment*, 3rd ed. (New York: Oxford University Press, 1995), pp. 170–276.

PAGE 54

I don't recall ever hearing any supervisors or senior colleagues In fact, a small literature exists on recovery from brain trauma. See, for example, A. Kertesz, Recovery and treatment. In K. M. Heilman and E. Valenstein (Eds.), *Clinical Neuropsychology*, 2nd ed. (New York: Oxford University Press, 1985), pp. 481–505.

PAGE 56

review in the *Journal of the American Medical Association* J. Francis, Review of *Profiles in Cognitive Aging*. In *Journal of the American Medical Association* (1996) *274*, 1402–1403.

"troublesome conclusion." This quote is drawn from a review by K. E. Cherry, *Contemporary Psychology* (1996) *41*, 342–344.

the mental ability scores of most of the physicians D. H. Powell, Profiles in Cognitive Aging (Cambridge, MA: Harvard University Press, 1994), pp. 90–96.

PAGE 57

Testing at Long Island Jewish-Hillside Hospital A. E. Willner et al., Analogical reasoning and post-operative outcome: predictions for patients scheduled for open heart surgery, *Archives of General Psychiatry* (1976) *33*, 255–259. See also C. J. Rabiner and A. E. Willlner, Differential psychopathological and organic mental disorder at follow-up, five years after coronary bypass and cardiac valvular surgery. In H. Speidel and G. Rodewald (Eds.), *Psychic and Neurological Dysfunctions after Open-heart Surgery* (New York: Thieme Stratton, 1988), pp. 237–249. These studies were conducted more than a decade ago. Considerable improvements have been made in cardiac surgery today, so the risk of cognitive impairment associated with this type of surgery has diminished greatly.

the Mayo Clinic See J. F. Malec, R. J. Ivnik, and G. E. Smith, Neuropsychology in aging: a clinician's perspective. In R. W. Parks, R. F. Zec, and R. S. Wilson (Eds.), *Neuropsychology in Alzheimer's Disease and Other Dementias* (New York: Oxford University Press, 1994), pp. 81–111.

PAGE 59

research reported by others in Berkeley, CA, and Atlanta, GA In Berkeley, the research was carried out by D. Field, K. W. Shaie, and E. V. Leino, Continuity in intellectual functioning: the role of self-reported health, *Psychology and Aging* (1988) *3*, 385–392. In Atlanta, the research was reported by T. A. Salthouse, *Theoretical Perspectives of Cognitive Aging* (Hillsdale, NJ: Erlbaum, 1991), p. 66.

PAGE 61

in the Pacific Northwest C. Hertzog, K. W. Schaie, and K. Gribbin, Cardiovascular disease and changes in intellectual functioning from middle to old age, *Journal of Gerontology* (1978) *33*, 872–883.

at Duke University in North Carolina The Duke studies found significant differences between the no CVD and CVD groups on Performance but not Verbal IQ. Like our own results, the differences were small but statistically significant. See L. W. Thompson, C. Eisdorfer, and E. H. Estes, Cardiovascular disease and behavioral changes in the elderly. In E. Palmore (Ed.), *Normal Aging: Reports from the Duke Longitudinal Study, 1955–1969* (Durham, NC: Duke University Press, 1970), pp. 227–231. For a review of the studies carried out in the Pacific Northwest, see K. W. Schaie, The Seattle Longitudinal Studies: a 21-year exploration of psychometric intelligence in adulthood. In K. W. Schaie (Ed.), *Longitudinal Studies in Adulthood and Development* (New York: Guilford Press, 1983), pp. 64–135.

PAGE 62

in 1989, a medical task force S. S. Harris, C. J. Casparsen, G. H. DeFriese, and E. H. Estes, Jr., Physical activity counseling for healthy adults as a primary prevention intervention in the clinical setting: report for the US Preventive Services, *Journal of the American Medical Association* (1989) *261*, 3590–3598.

A Philadelphia researcher The Optimal Aging Program at the University of Pennsylvania Medical School in Philadelphia combines aerobic and anaerobic training for seniors 65 and older (several are in their 90s). See J. D. Posner, Optimal aging: the role of exercise, *Patient Care* (1992) *26*, 35–52.

Scientists conducting the Seattle Longitudinal Study See Hertzog, Schaie, and Gribbin, Cardiovascular disease and changes.

Framingham Study See M. E. Farmer, L. R. White, R. D. Abbott et al. Blood pressure and cognitive performance: the Framingham Study, *American Journal of Epidemiology* (1987) *126*, 1103–1114.

PAGE 63

when chronic high blood pressure is not treated? M. F. Elias, P. A. Wolf, R. B. D'Agostino, J. Cobb, and L. R. White, Untreated blood pressure level is inversely related to cognitive functioning: the Framingham Study, *American Journal of Epidemiology* (1993) *138*, 353–364.

Studies elsewhere M. F. Elias, M. A. Robins, N. R. Schultz, and T. W. Pierce, Is blood pressure an important variable in research on aging and neuropsychological test performance? *Journal of Gerontology: Psychological Sciences* (1990) *45*, 128–135. Also S. R. Waldstein, J. R. Jennings, C. M. Ryan, J. M. Polefrone, T. V. Fazzari, and S. V. Manuck, Hypertension and neuropsychological performance in men: interactive affects of age, *Health Psychology* (1996) *15*, 102–109.

PAGE 64

The differences on the same measures Elias et al., Is blood pressure and important variable?

high-quality **life expectancy** US Department of Health and Human Services, Public Health Service, *Healthy People 2000: National Health Promotion and Disease Prevention Objectives*, DHHS Publication number (PHS) 91-50212 (Washington, DC: US Government Printing Office, 1991), p. 55. In fact, only 22 percent of adults engage in thirty minutes of light to moderate physical exercise five or more times a week.

Baylor College of Medicine R. L. Rogers, J. S. Meyer, and K. F. Mortel, After reaching retirement age, physical activity sustains cerebral perfusion and cognition, *Journal of the American Geriatric Society* (1990) *38*, 123–128.

PAGE 65

research on over 1,000 volunteers M. S. Albert, K. Jones, C. R. Savage, L. Berkman, T. Seeman, D. Boazer, and J. W. Rowe, Predictors of cognitive change in older persons: MacArthur studies of successful aging, *Psychology and Aging* (1995) *10*, 578–589.

moderate aerobic or anaerobic training R. E. Dustman, R. O. Ruhling, E. M. Russell, D. E. Shearer, H. W. Bonekat, J. W. Shigoeka, J. S. Wood, and D. C. Bradford, Aerobic exercise training and improved neuropsychological function of older individuals, *Neurobiology of Aging* (1984) *5*, 35–42.

PAGE 66

One study T. Ogawa, R. J. Spina, W. H. Martin, Jr., W. M. Kohrt, K. D. Schechtman, J. O. Holloszy, and A. A. Ehsani, Affects of age, sex, and physical training on cardiovascular response to exercise, *Circulation* (1992) *86*, 26–35.

PAGE 67

psychologists at the University of Virginia C. A. Manning, J. L. Hall, and P. E. Gold, Glucose effects on memory and other neuropsychological tests in elderly humans, *Psychological Science* (1990) *1*, 307–311.

Chapter 4

PAGE 70

"benign senescent forgetfulness" V. A. Kral, Senescent forgetfulness: benign and malignant, *Journal of the Canadian Medical Association* (1962) *86*, 257–260.

Age-Associated Memory Impairment (AAMI) Memory problems have to be severe enough to place someone with AAMI in the bottom 15 percent of normal adults on tests of memory. For description, see T. Crook, Age-Associated-Memory-Impairment: Proposed diagnostic criteria in measures of clinical change—Report of the National Institute of Mental Health Work Group, *Developmental Neuropsychology* (1986) *2*, 261–276.

PAGE 71

the aptitude scores were lower with each advancing decade D. H. Powell, *Profiles in Cognitive Aging* (Cambridge, MA: Harvard University Press, 1994), pp. 68–89.

PAGE 72

the work of Timothy Salthouse T. A. Salthouse, *Theoretical Perspectives on Cognitive Aging* (Hillsdale, NJ: Erlbaum, 1991), pp. 48, 239, 279.

Tests of processing speed T. A. Salthouse, *Mechanisms of Age-Cognition Relations in Adulthood* (Hillsdale, NJ: Erlbaum, 1992), pp. 87–93.

PAGE 73

Scientists might assess working memory A. Baddeley, Working memory, *Science* (1992) *255*, 556–559.

my desktop As far as I know, the desktop analogy was first used by D. E. Broadbent, *Decision and Stress* (London: Academic Press, 1971), pp. 376–377.

Dual-task attention The dual-task illustration is imaginary. Examples of dual-task tests along with the useful meta-analysis of twenty-five studies showing strong age-related decrement is contained in A. A. Hartley, Attention. In F. I. M. Craik and T. A. Salthouse (Eds.), *The Handbook of Aging and Cognition* (Hillsdale, NJ: Erlbaum, 1992), pp. 3–49).

PAGE 75

spatial rotation tasks For an excellent discussion of gender differences in different types of visuospatial ability, see M. C. Linn and A. C. Petersen, Emergence in characterization of sex differences in spatial ability: a meta-analysis, *Child Development* (1985) *56*, 1479–1498.

males have evolved special skills in spatial abilities The speculation that the evolution of spatial ability comes from D. M. Buss, Psychological sex differences: origins through natural selection, *American Psychologist* (1995) *50*, 164–168.

PAGE 76

Age differences in processing speed T. A. Salthouse, Why adult age differences increase with task complexity, *Developmental Psychology* (1992) *28*, 905–919.

PAGE 79

25 percent of high school and college students fail exams For an excellent review of the impact of anxiety on test performance and cognitive behavioral approaches to helping this problem, see B. A. Barrios and C. C. Shigetomi, *Behavior Therapy* (1979) *10*, 492–522.

excessive worry and emotional upset A. C. Register, J. G. May, J. C. Beckham, and D. J. Gustafson, Stress inoculation and bibliotherapy in the treatment of test anxiety, *Journal of Counseling Psychology* (1991) *38*, 115–119.

problem-focused and emotion-focused coping techniques A description of these anxiety management techniques was presented in Chapter 2. See S. Folkman and R. S. Lazarus, Coping as a mediator of emotion, *Journal of Personality and Social Psychology* (1988) *54*, 466–475.

PAGE 80

Three out of four highly anxious individuals Estimates vary considerably, depending on the type of interventions and the outcome criteria. The most effective programs applied both problem-focused approaches (for example, instruction in organization and memory training) and emotional-focused strategies (such as relaxation training, systematic desensitization, and self-control techniques). See, for instance, S. Tobias, Anxiety research in educational psychology, *Journal of Educational Psychology* (1979) *71*, 573–582. Also see Barrios and Shigetomi, *Behavior Therapy*.

PAGE 81

A 1996 study Talking more than fifty minutes per month on a cellular phone while operating a vehicle was associated with a 5.59 increase in the probability of a traffic accident. See J. M. Violnati and J. R. Marshall Cellular phones and traffic accidents: an epidemiological study, *Accident Analysis and Prevention* (1996) *28*, 265–270.

oldsters have little tolerance for being interrupted For a summary of several studies of dichotic attention with interruption, see D. E. Broadbent, *Decision and Stress* (New York: Academic Press, 1971), pp. 207–211.

Chapter 5

PAGE 84

Keith Sward K. Sward, Age and mental ability in superior men, *American Journal of Psychology* (1945) *58*, 443–479.

nearly everyone who has looked carefully For instance, T. A. Salthouse, *Theoretical Perspectives on Cognitive Aging* (Hillsdale, NJ: Erlbaum, 1991), pp. 141–152.

PAGE 85

two occupational therapists in Colorado This interesting study older and younger women rated on both motor and processed skills. Motor skills include walking, reaching, bending as well as aligning, positioning, or stabilizing. The examples of processed skills are attending, noticing, searching, organizing, and sequencing. See A. E. Dickerson and A. E. Fisher, Age differences in functional performance, *American Journal of Occupational Therapy* (1993) *47*, 686–692.

an eminent gerontologist K. Warner Schaie is, by consensus, America's most eminent gerontologist and the director of the Seattle Longitudinal Study. See K. W. Schaie, The Seattle Longitudinal Studies of adult intelligence, *Current Directions in Psychological Science* (1993) *2*, 171–175.

Dozens of other quotations A lengthy list of quotations over the past half-century in support of the use-it-or-lose-it theory is contained in T. A. Salthouse and D. R. D. Mitchell, Effects of age: a naturally occurring experience on spatial visualization performance, *Developmental Psychology* (1990) *26*, 845–854.

PAGE 86

our own research with physicians D. H. Powell, *Profiles in Cognitive Aging* (Cambridge, MA: Harvard University Press, 1994).

older physicians who continued to work Ibid., pp. 107–111.

PAGE 87

The beneficial effects of an active retirement R. L. Rogers, J. S. Meyer, and K. F. Mortel, After reaching retirement age, physical activity sustains cerebral perfusion and cognition, *Journal of the American Geriatric Society* (1990) *38*, 123–128. An activity index was calculated for each of the three groups. The activities included regular participation and planned exercises, bicycling, sports, dancing, and aerobics, as well as social activities such as housework, gardening, and hobbies. There was no baseline difference between those high-activity retired subjects and those who were working. The major difference in activity level was between the sedentary retired individuals and the other two groups. It should also be noted that only cognitive testing after four years was recorded. We don't know whether the retired sedentary subjects were lower at baseline on cognitive tests.

PAGE 91

dual-task attention An example might be talking on the telephone while proofreading a letter. An excellent summary of these studies is contained in A. A. Hartley, Attention. In F. I. M. Craik and T. A. Salthouse (Eds.), *The Handbook of Aging and Cognition* (Hillsdale, NJ: Erlbaum, 1992), pp. 3–49.

PAGE 92

Psychologists at Duke University C. P. May, L. Hasher, and E. R. Stoltzfus, Optimal time of day and the magnitude of age differences and memory, *Psychological Science* (1993) *4*, 326–330. The problem the older subjects had with memory in the afternoon was the failure to inhibit incorrect answers. It also appears the difficulty that seniors may have with memory in the PM is caused by a diminished ability to shut out distracting irrelevant stimuli, thoughts, or information, thus crowding working memory. See also C. May and L. Hasher, *Circadian Arousal and Cognition,* presented at the annual meeting of the American Psychological Association, New York, NY, August 1995.

PAGE 93

spatial memory is an early casualty of the aging process Subjects who were tested four times over a twenty-eight-year period in the Seattle Longitudinal Study declined in spatial orientation prior to a downturn in other abilities. See K. W. Schaie, Individual differences in the rate of cognitive change in adulthood. In V. L. Bengtson and K. W. Schaie (Eds.), *The Course of Later Life: Research and Reflections* (New York: Springer, 1989), pp. 65–85. Many studies, including our own research, have yielded similar findings.

PAGE 94

method of loci This technique involves associating a list of things to be memorized with a fixed list of places (or loci). For a fuller description, see J. A. Yesavage and T. L. Rose, Semantic elaboration and method of loci: a new trip for older learners, *Experimental Aging Research* (1994) *16*, 155–160.

Chapter 6

PAGE 103

the BBC aired a program *BBC Radio 4*, File on 4: Age Discrimination, September 5, 1995.

PAGE 104

USA Today "Age-bias cases gush from fountain of youth culture," by Melanie Wells, March 18, 1997.

PAGE 105

Wall Street Journal This excellent feature was written by Jonathan Kaufman. See J. Kaufman, A middle manager, 54 and insecure, struggles to adapt to the times, *Wall Street Journal*, May 5, 1997, p. A1.

PAGE 106

Marian Diamond She has devoted much of her career to examining the importance of enriched environments on anatomical changes in the brain, especially increased cortical thickness due in part to dendritic branching. This work, along with reports of many other scientists, is summarized in M. C. Diamond, *Enriching Heredity: The Impact of the Environment on the Anatomy of the Brain* (New York: Free Press, 1988).

PAGE 107

brain cells actually decreased in size Ibid., pp. 156–157.

A research team in UCLA B. Jacobs and A. B. Scheibel, A quantitative dendritic analysis of Wernicke's area in humans. I. Lifespan changes, *Journal of Comparative Neurology* (1993) *327*, 83–96. See also B. Jacobs, M. Schall, and A. B. Scheibel, A quantitative dendritic analysis of Wernicke's area in humans. II. Gender, hemispheric, and environmental factors, *Journal of Comparative Neurology* (1993) *327*, 97–111. It should be recognized that the evidence for a higher level of cognitive functioning in the 79-year-old woman with the thicker cortex who was mentally and socially active is indirect. No mental ability tests were administered.

PAGE 108

James responded From W. James, *The Will to Believe: And Other Essays in Popular Philosophy* (New York: Longmans, Green & Co., 1896), pp. 257–258.

PAGE 110

The Elderhostel program These remarkable, short, low-cost educational programs are housed in over 1,900 schools and colleges worldwide. Personal communication from Boston Elderhostel Programs, 75 Federal Street, Boston, MA, November 14, 1995.

PAGE 111

Outward Bound program Outward Bound began in North America in the early 1960s as an outdoor exposure and skills development program for young people. Presently, there are over fifty schools and centers on five continents. Their March 1966 catalogue lists eighty-five programs for individuals age "99+": Winter backpacking in the Appalachians, sea kayaking in the Everglades, rock climbing in the West. Nearly all the programs teach outdoor camping and navigational skills, hiking and climbing techniques, how to cope with being lost and alone in the woods, and drownproofing. For several, the minimum age is 50. Catalogues can be obtained from Outward Bound, Route 9D, R2, Box 280, Garrison, NY 10524-9757.

In an amusing chapter She decided to go on this challenging wilderness survival trip even though her eyesight had deteriorated to the point that her eye doctor had recommended cataract surgery. She believed that both the challenge of Outward Bound and the later cataract surgery, which restored her eyesight, are components of the fountain of age, the title of her book. See B. Friedan, *The Fountain of Age* (New York: Simon and Schuster, 1993), especially pp. 301–328.

PAGE 112

"Are women more likely to risk or relish new ways to test themselves than men?" This quote is from Friedan, *The Fountain of Age*, p. 305.

the lives of older women and men from blue-collar backgrounds The subjects were interviewed over an approximately twelve-year period. They were 57 to 79 when last interviewed in 1980. See M. Fiske and D. A. Chiriboga, *Change and Continuity in Adult Life* (San Francisco: Jossey-Bass, 1990), pp. 265–277.

PAGE 113

Lerman's book She describes teaching various types of movement and dance to the elders in residential and nonresidential centers through the Dance Exchange. The photo, now quite famous, is taken from a series of pictures at the Roosevelt Center for Senior Citizens in Washington, DC. See L. Lerman, *Teaching Dance to Senior Adults* (Springfield, IL: Charles Thomas, 1984).

MicroCog The development of the test is described in D. H. Powell, *Profiles in Cognitive Aging* (Cambridge, MA: Harvard University Press, 1994).

PAGE 114

A Penn State professor The students were better at entering the correct labels, numbers, and words for both tasks than at doing the more difficult formatting and using the formulae for calculating profit and loss. See A. J. Garfein, K. W. Schaie, and S. L. Willis, Microcomputer proficiency in later-middle-aged and older adults: teaching old dogs new tricks, *Social Behavior* (1988) *3*, 131–148.

PAGE 116

method of loci Among the dozens of techniques to enhance memory for new people, this is one I have found particularly helpful. See G. H. Bower, Analysis of a mnemonic device, *American Scientist* (1970) *58*, 496–510.

PAGE 117

Sherry Willis and K. Warner Schaie They and their students have published scores of papers and several books on their works with the Seattle Longitudinal Study and other groups. The study with "stable" and "decline" subjects was conducted with spatial abilities. See S. L. Willis and K. W. Schaie, Gender differences and spatial ability in old age: longitudinal and intervention finding, *Sex Roles* (1988) *18*, 189–203. Similar findings have been reported with reasoning and other cognitive skills. For example, see S. L. Willis, Improvement with cognitive training: which old dogs learn new tricks? In L. W. Poon, D. L. Rubin, and B. A. Wilson (Eds.), *Everyday Cognition in Adulthood and Later Life* (New York: Cambridge University Press, 1989), pp. 545–569.

Those *not* targeted Among many who have discovered that ability not selected for training failed to improve are G. W. Rebok and L. J. Balcerak, Memory self-efficacy and performance difference in old and young adults: the effect of mnemonic training, *Journal of Developmental Psychology* (1989) *25*, 714–721.

Paul Baltes The Berlin researcher divided the volunteers into three groups—training, self-guided, and control. There were no significant differences in the two training groups on measures of fluid intelligence and vocabulary. See P. B. Baltes, D. Sowarka, and R. Kliegl, Cognitive training research on fluid intelligence in old age: what can older adults achieve by themselves? *Psychology and Aging* (1989) *4*, 217–221.

PAGE 118

training has not been tested in real life Although the results of cognitive training programs have been impressive, they are still in infancy. It has not yet been demonstrated that they positively influence intellectual functioning in real life. For a critique of these programs, see Powell, *Profiles in Cognitive Aging*, pp. 152–161.

At Scripps University J. W. Anderson, A. A. Hartley, R. Bye, K. D. Harber, and O. L. White, Cognitive training using self-discovery methods, *Educational Gerontology* (1986) *12*, 159–171.

programs that include relaxation components J. A. Yesavage, Relaxation and memory training in 39 elderly patients, *American Journal of Psychiatry* (1984) *141*, 778–781.

PAGE 119

use relaxation or meditation by themselves? C. N. Alexander, E. J. Langer, R. I. Newman, H. M. Chandler, and J. L. Davies, Transcendental meditation, mindfulness, and longevity: an experimental study with the elderly, *Journal of Personality and Social Psychology* (1989) *57*, 950–964.

Salt Lake City R. E. Dustman, R. O. Ruhling, E. M. Russell, D. E. Shearer, H. W. Bonekat, J. W. Shigeoka, J. S. Wood, and D. C. Bradford, Aerobic exercise training and improved neuropsychological function of older individuals, *Neurobiology of Aging* (1984) *5*, 35–42.

scientists in the Midwest D. Papalia, J. Blackburn, E. Davis, M. Dellmann, and P. Roberts, Training cognitive functioning in the elderly—inability to replicate findings, *International Journal of Aging and Human Development* (1981) *12*, 111–117.

In Alabama F. Scogin and J. L. Bienias, A three-year follow-up of older adult participants in a memory-skills training program, *Psychology and Aging* (1988) *3*, 334–337.

PAGE 120

Seattle Longitudinal Study K. W. Schaie, The course of adult intellectual development, *American Psychologist* (1994) *49*, 304–313.

A Swedish report This unique research was conducted by T. Karlsson, L. Bäckman, A. Herlitz, L. Nilsson, B. Winblad, and P. Österlind, Memory improvement at different stages of Alzheimer's disease, *Neuropsychologia* (1989) *27*, 737–742.

psychologists at the Max Planck Institute R. Kliegl, J. Smith, and P. B. Baltes, On the locus and process of magnification of age differences during mnemonic training, *Developmental Psychology* (1990) *26*, 894–904. See also R. Kliegl, J. Smith, and P. B. Baltes, Testing-the-limits and the study of adult age differences in cognitive plasticity of mnemonic skill, *Developmental Psychology* (1989) *25*, 247–256. The improvement occurred with older adults when the words were presented at slower rates of speed, for example, ten to twenty seconds per word. At more rapid rates of one to five seconds per word, the increase in improvement was much more modest.

Chapter 7

PAGE 123

a common negative belief about aging Eminent scholars have written that "the aged live in a contracting social world in which participation declines." See I. Rosow, Old people: their friends and neighbors, *American Behavioral Scientist* (1970) *14*, 59–69. And, that "the problem of loneliness among the aged is apparent to community workers, particularly public health nurses, visiting nurses, and home health aides." See I. M. Burnside, Symptomatic behaviors in the elderly. In J. E. Birren and R. B. Sloan (Eds.), *Handbook of Mental Health and Aging* (Englewood Cliffs, NJ: Prentice Hall, 1980), pp. 719–744.

tops the list of stressful events At the very top of the scale rating the relative stress of particular events is the death of a spouse. See T. H. Holmes and R. H. Rahe, The social readjustment rating scale, *Journal of Psychosomatic Research* (1967) *11*, 213–218.

PAGE 124

Long-term friends can be as dear E. H. Erikson, J. M. Erikson, and H. O. Kivnik, *Vital Involvement in Old Age* (New York: Norton, 1986), p. 125.

PAGE 125

resume a normal, if altered, lifestyle within two years S. Zisook and S. R. Schucter, Uncomplicated bereavement, *Journal of Clinical Psychiatry* (1993) *54*, 365–372.

Social activities change Bass and Bowman, The impact of an aged relative's death in the family. In K. F. Ferraro (Ed.), *Gerontology: Perspectives and Issues* (New York: Springer, 1990), pp. 333–356.

PAGE 126

Substantial gender differences are apparent A summary of the male-female differences among older Americans is contained in C. F. Longino, Jr., B. J. Soldo, and K. G. Manton, Demography of aging in the United States. In K. F. Ferraro (Ed.), *Gerontology: Perspectives and Issues* (New York: Springer, 1990), pp. 19–43.

about the only place older men hold an edge Bass and Bowman, The impact of an aged relative's death in the family. Also see Z. S. Blau, Social constraints on friendships in old age, *American Sociological Review* (1990) *26*, 429–439.

average number of close associations is about ten at all checkpoints from 30 to 75 It should be noted that estimates of the size of social networks vary widely, depending on the criteria used to define who is in the subjects' circle of friends. As an example, a survey of middle-aged, preretirement adults in the San Francisco area found the average to be 5.4. See M. F. Lowenthal, M. Thurnher, D. Chiriboga, and associates, *Four Stages of Life: A Comparative Study of Women and Men Facing Transitions* (San Francisco: Jossey-Bass,

1975). Another northern California investigation found that the number of people the subjects said they could count on was about nineteen for men and women 36 to 64 and about fourteen among those 65+. See C. S. Fischer and S. L. Phillips, Who is alone? Social characteristics of people with small networks. In L. A. Peplau and D. Perlman (Eds.), *Loneliness: A Sourcebook of Current Theory, Research and Therapy* (New York: Wiley, 1982).

Only one in ten older Americans This is a study conducted in Denmark, Great Britian, and the United States. The frequency of intergenerational contact was even greater in non-US countries. See E. Shanas, P. Townsend, D. Wedderburn, H. Friis, P. Milhaj, and J. Stehouwer, *Old People in Three Industrial Societies* (London: Routledge and Kegan Paul, 1968). p. 197.

These connections V. L. Bengston and K. D. Black, Intergenerational relations and continuities in socialization. In P. Baltes and K. W. Schaie (Eds.), *Life-span Developmental Psychology: Personality and Socialization* (New York: Academic Press, 1973), pp. 207–234.

Being alone and being lonely U. M. Staudinger, M. Marsiske, and P. B. Baltes, Resilience and reserve capacity in later adulthood: potentials and limits of development across the life span. In D. Cicchetti and D. Cohen (Eds.), *Developmental Psychopathology: Risk, Disorder, and Adaptation*, Vol. 2 (New York: Wiley, 1995), pp. 801–847.

People over 65 are alone about half of their waking hours A useful summary of the research on this topic is contained in L. A. Peplau and D. Perlman (Eds.), *Loneliness: A Sourcebook of Current Theory, Research and Therapy* (New York: Wiley, 1982). Especially of interest is the chapter by R. Larson, M. Csikczentmihalyi, and R. Graef, Time alone in a daily experience: loneliness or renewal? pp. 41–53.

PAGE 127

this condition is imposed upon us J. M. Maxwell, Standards for centers and clubs for older people. In G. J. Aldridge and J. Kaplan (Eds.), *Social Welfare of the Aging* (New York: Columbia University Press, 1962), pp. 97–111.

Approximately 12 percent of senior citizens M. Fiske and D. Chiriboga, *Change and Continuity in Adult Life* (San Francisco: Jossey-Bass, 1990), pp. 204–205.

PAGE 129

When I began working at Harvard My primary appointment is at the Harvard University Health Services. The gender ratio is more equal there than in the faculty.

PAGE 130

about one older person in eight Fiske and Chiriboga, *Change and Continuity in Adult Life, pp. 204–205.*

PAGE 131

MIT professor Sherry Turkle S. Turkle, *Life on the Screen: Identity in the Age of Internet* (New York, NY: Simon and Schuster, 1995).

SeniorNet (www.Seniornet.org) From the SeniorNet HomePage, August 2, 1996. SeniorNet is not the only on-line service for older people. America Online also offers AARP Online. CompuServe has the Retirement Living Forum and Prodigy offers The Seniors Online Bulletin Board.

PAGE 132

In 1996, about 30 percent of people age 55+ owned computers R. P. Adler, Older adults and computers. Report of a national survey (SeniorNet, 1996). This study was based on random telephone interviews with 700 older adults. Computer use is effected substantially by education. Only 7 percent of those with less than a high school education used a computer, whereas just over half (53 percent) of those with a college degree reported computer use.

Jim That's Jim Olson, quoted on the SeniorNet HomePage, August 2, 1996.

Marge met Dick on-line Story on SeniorNet HomePage, August 2, 1996.

PAGE 133

Stanford psychologists Research on the desire among older and younger people with limited time available to reduce novel or potentially unpleasant contacts with others has been carried out by Stanford psychologists Laura Carstensen and her colleagues. See, for example, L. L. Carstensen, Evidence for a life-span theory of socioemotional selectivity, *Current Directions of Psychological Science* (1995) *4*, 253–258.

PAGE 134

"bank account" model T. C. Antonucci, Attachment in adulthood and aging. In E. Palmore, E. W. Busse, G. L. Maddox, J. B. Nowlin, and I. C. Siegler (Eds.), *Normal Aging: Reports from the Duke Longitudinal Studies* (Durham, NC: Duke University Press, 1985), pp. 257–272.

Psychologists at Rutgers M. A. Diefenbach, H. Leventhal, and E. Leventhal, *Perceived Social Support and Illness Among Elderly Adults: Quality over Quantity.* Presented at the annual meeting of the American Psychological Society, Washington, DC, June 1995.

PAGE 135

Studies of mature adults A superb review of this and related topics on social aging and adjustment is contained in Staudinger, Marsiske, and Baltes, Resilience and reserve capacity in later adulthood.

correlation between the size of social networks and illness or death J. S. House, K. R. Landis, and D. Umberson, Social relationships and health, *Science* (1988) *241*, 540–544. Studies of the recovery from myocardial infraction have found that a larger proportion of females than males with fewer close relatives are still alive after six months. See L. P. Berkman, The role of social relationships in health promotion, *Psychosomatic Medicine* (1995) *57*, 244–254.

the relative risk of catching a cold S. Cohen, W. J. Doyle, D. P. Skoner, B. S. Rabin, and J. M. Gwaltney, Jr., Social ties and susceptibility to the common cold, *Journal of the American Medical Association* (1997) *277*, 1940–1944. The unique feature of this study was that it measured the number of different types of relationships—for example, spouse, parents, children, neighbors, workmates, schoolmates, and so forth. It was the diversity of relationships more than the actual number of relationships that mattered as to whether someone caught a cold or not.

six months after a heart attack, socially isolated people died twice as often Differences were far more dramatic for those 75 and older. Among this group, nearly 70 percent of the socially isolated individuals but only about 25 percent of those who had two or more social intimates died within six months. See L. P. Berkman, The role of social relationships in health promotion.

the male-female differences House, Landis, and Unberson, Social relationships and health.

PAGE 136

more rigorous standards W. J. Dickens and D. Perlman, Friendship over the life-cycle. In S. Duck and R. Gilmour (Eds.), *Personal Relationships. 2: Developing Personal Relationships* (New York: Academic Press, 1981), pp. 91–122.

Far more often, their friendships are multidimensional C. D. Ryff, Psychological well-being in adulthood life, *Current Directions in Psychological Science* (1995) *4*, 99–104.

PAGE 137

a pair of young Yale graduate students They were Ellen Langer, presently a professor of psychology at Harvard University, and Judith Rodin, now president of the University of Pennsylvania. Cited in E. Langer, *Mindfulness* (Boston, MA: Addison-Wesley, 1989). In the study, subjects also were asked to take control of their schedule in other ways.

PAGE 138

osteoporosis shortens us a quarter of an inch a year As it turns out, there is no precise reference on the average amount of height older people lose after age 60. The women I talked with in the nursing home that my mother lived in for a decade were convinced that that was an accurate estimate. Some indirect support for this assessment comes from two articles on osteoporosis. Both measured diminished bone mineral density in adult women. In one report of females from 30 to 80, bone density decreased in the lateral spine and in the hip area about 11.2 percent at age 50 and 44.3 percent at age 80. See M. E. Arlot, E. Sornay-Rendu, P. Garnero, B. Vey-Marty, and P. D. Delmas, Apparent pre- and postmenopausal bone loss evaluated by DXA at different skeletal sites in women: the OFELY cohort, *Journal of Bone and Mineral Research* (1997) *12*, 683–690. To some degree, how much bone mineral density is lost is a function of where the analysis is carried out. For example, another article reported that lateral spine bone mineral density measurements show about 1 percent decrease per year whereas femoral bone loss in older women was 0.721 percent per year. Bone loss in the hip area was about 1.39 percent a year. See S. L. Greenspan, L. Maitlad-Ramsey, and E. Meyers, Classification of osteoporosis in the elderly is dependent on site-specific analysis, *Calcified Tissue International* (1996) *58*, 409–414. Taking these data conservatively in aggregate, we might not disagree with those nursing home ladies' estimates. Presuming that the average 60-year-old woman is about sixty-four inches tall, it would not be hard to imagine her losing between a quarter and a half inch in stature per year. However, we also need to be aware of the tremendous variability in older groups and remind ourselves that hormone replacement therapy may dramatically improve these numbers.

selection, optimization, and compensation The most complete statement of this theory extending over the life cycle is continued in P. B. Baltes, On the incomplete architecture of human ontogeny: selection, optimization, and compensation as a foundation of developmental theory, *American Psychologist* (1997) *52*, 366–380. Also see P. B. Baltes and M. M. Baltes, Psychological perspectives on successful aging: the model of selective optimization with compensation. In P. B. Baltes and M. M. Baltes (Eds.), *Successful Aging: Perspectives from the Behavioral Sciences* (New York: Cambridge University Press, 1990), pp. 1–34.

PAGE 139

the overall quality of life for the 60- to 75-year-olds is far better today
P. B. Baltes, On the incomplete architecture of human ontogeny.

percentage doubles every five years L. Hayflick, *How and Why We Age* (New York: Ballantine, 1994), pp. 90–91.

Elders in Berlin from 70 to 103 Baltes, On the incomplete architecture of human ontogeny.

PAGE 140

A classic study of learned dependency The research was carried out by Margaret Baltes. See M. M. Baltes, Dependency and old age: gains and losses, *Current Directions in Psychological Science* (1995) *4*, 246–251.

Chapter 8

PAGE 144

the Duke Longitudinal Study R. H. Dovenmuele, J. B. Reckless, and G. Newman, Depressive reactions in the elderly. In E. Palmore, E. W. Busse, G. L. Maddox, J. B. Nowlin, and I. C. Siegler (Eds.), *Duke Longitudinal Studies of Normal Aging* (Durham, NC: Duke University Press, 1985), pp. 90–97. Others elsewhere have reported a similarly high incidence of depressive symptoms in the elderly. For example, B. Gurland, J. Copland, J. Kuriansky, M. Kelleher, E. L. Sharp, and L. L. Dean, *The Mind and Mood of Aging: Mental Health Problems of the Community Elderly in New York and London* (New York: Hayworth Press, 1983). The research from the Duke Longitudinal Study classified between 30 and 50 percent as being at least mildly depressed. A closer look at their rationale for diagnosing these individuals as depressed suggests that they may have been overly sensitive to this condition initially. For example, labeled as mildly depressed was anyone who reported symptoms of depression less than once every two weeks, was not disabled by the feelings, and had no suicidal thoughts. Later findings from this research and from larger, more diverse groups failed to support these conclusions.

the National Institutes of Health convened a Conference on Depression in Late Life National Institutes of Health, *Consensus Development Conference on the Diagnosis and Treatment of Depression in Late Life* (Washington, DC: National Institutes of Health, November 1991), pp. 3–23.

have a higher risk for suicide These statistics are based on 1994 data. That year there were 31,142 suicides in the United States. Of these, 6,008 occurred in the 65+ group; 4,719 were among older white males. Of these men, a large proportion were 85. See J. L. McIntosh, *1994 Official Suicide Statistics* (Washington, DC: American Association of Suicidology, 1996).

Health and emotional stability decline in many A comprehensive and balanced review of the results in this area is contained in D. M. Bass and K. Bowman, The impact of an aged relative's death in the family. In K. F. Ferraro (Ed.), *Gerontology: Perspectives and Issues* (New York: Springer, 1990), pp. 333–356.

PAGE 145

90 to 95 percent of those who have lost a spouse S. Zisook and S. R. Schucter, Uncomplicated bereavement, *Journal of Clinical Psychiatry* (1993) *54*, 365–372.

Cornell scientists G. F. Streib and P. W. E. Thompson, Personal and social adjustment in retirement. In W. Donahue and C. Tibbitts (Eds.), *New Frontiers of Aging* (Ann Arbor, MI: University of Michigan Press, 1957), pp. 180–197.

PAGE 146

results have been reproduced many times For instance, R. C. Atchley, The process of retirement: comparing women and men. In M. Szinovacz (Ed.), *Women's Retirement* (Beverly Hills, CA: Sage, 1982), pp. 153–168.

Several thousand volunteers M. Gatz and M. A. Smyer, The mental health system in older adults in the 1990's, *American Psychologist* (1992) *47*, 741–751.

comprehensive interviews A summary of these studies is contained in J. P. Newmann, Aging and depression, *Psychology of Aging* (1989) *4*, 150–165.

more recent reports D. Blazer, B. Burchett, C. Service, and L. K. George, The association between age and depression among the elderly: an epidemiologic exploration, *Journal of Gerontology: Medical Sciences* (1991) *46*, 210–215.

PAGE 147

not everyone over 65 is at the same risk for taking his or her own life McIntosh, *1994 Official Suicide Statistics*.

most people say they are very happy or pretty happy E. Diener and C. Diener, Most people are happy, *Psychological Science* (1996) *7*, 181–185.

Psychologists at the University of Illinois Diener and Diener, Most people are happy. Also see D. Lykken and A. Tellegen, Happiness is a stochastic phenomenon, *Psychological Science* (1996) *7*, 186–189.

It has been suggested D. G. Myers and E. Diener, Who is happy? *Psychological Science* (1995) *6*, 10–19.

PAGE 148

Research using over 2,000 subjects from the Minnesota studies of twins These investigations controlled for gender, SES, and marital status. The findings from the studies of younger twins (tested at age 20 and then at 30) yielded low test-retest correlation (.50), so heritability was difficult to assess. The test-retest correlations for the monozygotic twins raised apart were slightly higher (.52) than that for the monozygotic twins raised together (.44).

Three out of four men and women in their 50s would like to stop working gradually Over 12,000 women and men, 51 to 61, were interviewed as part of the Health and Retirement Study carried out by University of Michigan researchers. Seventy-three percent said they would choose to continue some work after the normal retirement age. Institute for Social Research, *The Health and Retirement Study* (Ann Arbor, MI: Institute for Social Research, 1993).

PAGE 149

Even though much has been written For example, M. M. Morrison, Work and retirement in the aging society, *Daedalus* (1986) *115*, 269–293.

less than one organization in ten For instance, B. Jacobson, *Young Programs for Older Workers: Case Studies and Progressive Personnel Policies* (New York: Von Nostrand Reinhold, 1980). Of 13,000 companies contacted, only 91 (7 percent) indicated that they did anything unusual for retirement age workers. A decade later, things had not changed much. Evidence documenting the small percentage of US organizations that offer innovative working opportunities for older employees is contained in H. L. Sterns, N. K. Matheson, and L. S. Schwartz, Work and retirement. In K. F. Ferraro (Ed.), *Gerontology: Perspectives and Issues* (New York: Springer, 1990), pp. 163–178.

About one person in six Institute for Social Research, *The Health and Retirement Study*.

PAGE 151

"freeway faculty" B. Daley, Colleges using freeway faculty to hold down costs, *The Boston Globe*, January 26, 1997.

Nationwide, about 43 percent of those who listed their jobs as college teaching In 1996, 42.6 percent of 940,191 people who listed their primary jobs as teaching in postsecondary education worked part time. See US Department of Education, National Center for Education Statistics, *Institutional Policies and Practices Regarding Faculty in Higher Education: Statistical Analysis Report* (Washington, DC: US Government Printing Office, November 1996).

PAGE 154

Carolyn Heilbrun C. G. Heilbrun, *The Last Gift of Time: Life Beyond Sixty* (New York: Dial Press, 1997), p. 39.

Engaging in playful activities can be a powerful antidepressant For example, L. R. Dangott and R. A. Kalish, *A Time to Enjoy: The Pleasures of Aging* (Englewood Cliffs, NJ: Prentice Hall, 1979).

PAGE 155

difference between work and play For a lengthy description of the differences between work and play, see D. H. Powell, *Understanding Human Adjustment: Normal Adaptation Through the Life Cycle* (Boston: Little, Brown, 1983). Chapters 1, 6, and 8 describe working and playing activities through the life cycle.

PAGE 156

the personal computer brings a galaxy of interesting playful opportunities S. Turkel, *Life on the Screen: Identity in the Age of the Internet* (New York: Simon and Schuster, 1995), p. 236.

PAGE 157

the strongest predictors of happiness In this study, self-rated health was the strongest correlate of self-rated life satisfaction. See E. Palmore and C. Luikart, Health and social factors related to life satisfaction, *Journal of Health and Social Behavior* (1972) *13*, 68–80.

psychological well-being Marital status and degree of clinically associated physical impairment were the strongest independent variables associated with psychological well-being as rated by psychological tests. See L. K. George, The impact of personality and social status upon activity and psychological well-being, *Journal of Gerontology* (1978) *33*, 840–847.

and absence of depression Subjects rated as depressed on the basis of psychiatric interviews had lower self-rated health ratings over a ten-year period than those rated as not depressed. See J. B. Nowlin, Depression and health. In E. B. Palmore (Ed.), *Normal Aging II* (Durham, NC: Duke University Press, 1974), pp. 168–172.

The job of the immune system A readable, succinct description of the immune system is contained in L. Hayflick, *How and Why We Age* (New York: Ballantine, 1994), pp. 153–155, 341–363. For those who are not immunologists but would like to know more about the immune system, I recommend the introductory textbook by Janis Kuby. See J. Kuby, *Immunology*, 3rd ed. (New York: W. H. Freeman, 1997).

The immune system also plays an important role S. F. Maier, L. R. Watkins, and M. Fleshner, Psychoneuroimmunology: the interface between behavior, brain, and immunity, *American Psychologist* (1994) *49*, 1004–1017.

a large number of oldsters continue to have robust immune systems One explanation for these findings is that those elderly subjects had inherited a strong immune system, which is why they remain healthy. See G. F. Solomon and D. Benton, Psychoneuroimmunologic aspects of aging. In R. Glaser and J. Kiecolt-Glaser (Eds.), *Handbook of Human Stress and Immunity* (San Diego: Academic Press, 1994), pp. 341–363.

PAGE 158

over 400 adult volunteers in Pittsburgh, PA These classic studies were conducted by Sheldon Cohen and his coworkers at Carnegie-Mellon University. See S. Cohen, Psychological stress, immunity, and upper respiratory infections, *Current Directions in Psychological Science* (1996) *5*, 86–90.

regular, moderate exercise is associated with improved mood C. Folkins and W. Sime, Physical fitness and mental health, *American Psychologist* (1981) *36*, 373–389.

older adults who work out at least twice a week Other measures of immune system function are also positively influenced by exercising, including total leukocyte counts and interleuken-1 levels. See G. F. Solomon and D. Benton, Psychoneuroimmunologic aspects of aging. In R. Glaser and J. Kiecolt-Glaser (Eds.), *Handbook*, pp. 341–363.

The ways they coped with this bad news F. I. Fawzy and N. W. Fawzy, Psychoeducational interventions and health outcomes. In R. Glaser and J. Kiecolt-Glaser (Eds.), *Handbook*, pp. 365–402.

PAGE 159

more often put themselves first S. E. Keller, S. C. Shiflett, S. J. Schleifer, and J. A. Bartlett, Stress, immunity, and health. In R. Glaser & J. Kiecolt-Glaser (Eds.), *Handbook*, pp. 217–244.

more social ties had fewer colds S. Cohen, W. J. Doyle, D. P. Skoner, B. S. Rabin, and J. M. Gwaltney, Jr., Social ties and susceptibility to the common cold, *Journal of the American Medical Association* (1997) *277*, 1940–1944.

longer rates of survival for cancer and HIV patients G. Ironson, M. Antoni, and S. Lutgendorf, Can psychological interventions affect immunity and survival? Present findings and suggested targets with a focus on cancer and human immunodeficiency virus, *Mind/Body Medicine* (1995) *1*, 85–110.

problem-focused coping and emotion-focused coping Investigations of the Duke Longitudinal Study found that the two most frequent coping responses were a direct action and intrapsychic palliative responses. See L. K. George and I. C. Siegler, Stress and coping in later life, *Educational Horizons* (1982) *16*, 147–154.

PAGE 160

confronting significant stresses of later adulthood These were 375 women and men from the Duke Longitudinal Study. The major stresses included a serious illness, widow(er)hood, the last child leaving home, retirement, and the spouse's retirement. See E. B. Palmore, W. P. Cleveland, Jr., J. E. Nowlin, D. Ramm, and I. C. Siegler, Stress and adaptation, *Journal of Gerontology* (1979) *34*, 841–851.

PAGE 161

certain actions help For example, P. M. Lewinsohn, R. F. Munoz, M. A. Youngren, and A. M. Zeiss, *Control Your Depression* (Englewood Cliffs, NJ: Prentice Hall, 1978).

Three-quarters of the people coping with a serious stressful event S. Zisook and S. R. Schuchter, Uncomplicated bereavement, *Journal of Clinical Psychiatry* (1993) *54*, 365–372. Those who continue to be depressed often have had a history of depression.

PAGE 162

A new class of antidepressant "smart drugs" called SSRIs SSRIs are frequently better tolerated than the tricyclic or other classes of antidepressants. For older people, they may be safer, too, because they exhibit fewer adverse drug interactions with medications being taken for physical problems. For an excellent review, see G. D. Tollefson, Selective serotonin reuptake inhibitors. In D. F. Schatzberg and C. B. Nemeroff (Eds.), *Textbook of Psychopharmacology* (Washington, DC: American Psychiatric Press, 1995), pp. 161–182.

PAGE 163

A-B-C model of faulty thinking A. Ellis, *The Essence of Rational Psychotherapy: A Comprehensive Approach to Treatment* (New York: Institute for Rational Living, 1970).

Aaron Beck Among his most influential writings have been A. T. Beck, A. J. Rush, B. A. Shaw, and G. Emery, *Cognitive Therapy of Depression* (New York: Guilford Press, 1979).

multimodal, or integrative, therapy For example, A. Lazarus, *The Practice of Multimodal Therapy* (New York: McGraw-Hill, 1981). And J. Norcross, Eclectic psychotherapy: introduction and overview. In J. Norcross (Ed.), *Handbook of Eclectic Psychotherapy* (New York: Bruner/Mazel, 1986), pp. 3–24.

PAGE 164

life review This section was inspired by E. H. Erikson, J. M. Erikson, and H. Q. Kivnik, *Vital Involvement in Old Age* (New York: Norton, 1986), pp. 129–193, 288–290. Another who has written about this process is C. P. M. Knipscheer, Temporal imbeddedness in aging within the multigenerational family: the case of grandparenting. In J. E. Birren and V. L. Bengston (Eds.), *Emergent Theories of Aging* (New York: Springer, 1988), pp. 426–446.

the whole picture from our beginning to the present R. Schultz and J. Heckhausen, A life span model of successful aging, *American Psychologist* (1996) *51*, 702–714.

PAGE 165

M-Marsel Mesulam M-M. Mesulam, Involutional and developmental implications of age-related neuronal changes: in search of an engram for wisdom, *Neurobiology of Aging* (1987) *8*, 581–583.

Chapter 9

PAGE 169

Proverbs Proverbs 3:13–15. *The Holy Bible*, New Revised Standard Version (New York: Oxford University Press, 1989).

Page 170

"it is in old men that reason and good judgement are found" Cicero was making the point that the losses associated with old age are compensated for by greater authority and respect. This observation was likely limited to the class of people he knew. See *Cicero. De Senectute. XIX*, trans. W. A. Falconer (Cambridge, MA: Harvard University Press, 1992), pp. 79–82.

"Wisdom is with the aged, and understanding in the length of days." Job 12:12. *The Holy Bible*. King James Version (Cleveland OH: World Publishing Company). This verse is out of context because the point Job is making is that wisdom does not come from getting old but from God: "with God are wisdom and might;" (Job 12:13).

"Wisdom is the gray hair unto man."   Wisdom of Solomon 4:9. Again, the quotation conveys a meaning quite different from the point being made, which is about unlawful sexual unions. Those who abstain, who follow the Lord's prohibition, will escape punishment. Although they may die young, their understanding and faithfulness to this prohibition is the equivalent of living to a ripe old age. See Wisdom of Solomon 4:1–9.

Erik Erikson   Among the numerous writings of Erikson that I have found useful are E. H. Erikson, Reflections on Dr. Borg's life cycle, *Daedalus* (1976) *105*, 1–18. The material on older age is drawn from E. H. Erikson, J. M. Erikson, and H. Q. Kivnick, *Vital Involvement in Old Age* (New York: Norton, 1986).

Paul Baltes and his colleagues at the Max Planck Institute   P. B. Baltes and U. M. Staudinger, The search for the psychology of wisdom, *Current Directions in Psychological Science* (1993) 2, 75–80.

a test for wisdom   The test asked subjects to think out loud about different life situations, such as, "A 15-year-old girl tells you that she wants to get married right away, what would you advise her to do?" An example of a response to the dilemma netting a low score on wisdom is a certain "yes" or "no": For example, "A 15-year-old girl wants to get married? No, no way. Marrying at that age would be utterly wrong. One has to tell the girl that marriage is not possible." An answer rated by these researchers as high on wisdom is, "Well, on the surface, this seems like an easy problem. On average, marriage for 15-year-olds is not a good thing. I guess many girls might think about it when they fall in love for the first time. And, then, there are situations where the average case does not fit. Perhaps, in this instance, special life circumstances are involved, such that the girl has a terminal illness. Or, this girl may not be from this country. Perhaps, she lives in another culture and historical period. Before I offer a final evaluation, I would need more information." Before giving the test to designated wise men, it was administered to older individuals they thought might posses wisdom, in this case older psychologists and other older and younger adults. They compared their scores on this wisdom test with those of older and younger adults. What they reported was that more of the older psychologists had higher wisdom scores. This percentage was much higher than that of younger and older adult groups. These results were in sharp contrast to the findings of the performance of these groups on standardized cognitive tests, where the young subjects scored higher than the older psychologists. This research is summarized in P. B. Baltes, The aging mind: potential and limits, *Gerontologist* (1993) 33, 580–594.

PAGE 172

William Cowper   W. Cowper, The Winter Walk at Noon, *The Task*, Book VI (London: John Sharpe, 1817), p. 155.

PAGE 173

The New Lao Tsu   Taken from R. Grigg, *The New Lao Tsu* (Boston: Charles E. Tuttle, 1995).

PAGE 174

the power of humility Ibid., pp. 44, 89.

two million individuals It is hard to obtain accurate numbers about those who participate in Alcoholic's Anonymous. The local AA office in Boston said, "We don't keep statistics." But a 1996 book describing the history of AA reported that the worldwide membership exceeds two million. See "J.," *A Simple Program: A Contemporary Translation of the Book "Alcoholic's Anonymous"* (New York: Hyperion, 1996).

Buddha Most of what I know about Buddha has been drawn from the remarkable book of Buddha's life and writings by Walpola Rahula. See W. Rahula, *What the Buddha Taught* (New York: Grove Press, 1959).

PAGE 175

kindness and gentleness Rahula, *What the Buddha Taught*, p. 85.

Jean-Jacques Rousseau J.-J. Rousseau, *Emile ou De L'Education*, Book II (Paris: Garnier Freres, 1964), p. 62.

Friedrich Nietzsche F. Nietzsche, *Der Wanderer und Sein Schatten* (Paris: Chemitz, Verlag von Ernst Schmeitzner, 1880), p. 180.

a study at Yale R. J. Sternberg, Implicit theories of intelligence, creativity, and wisdom, *Journal of Personality and Social Psychology* (1986) *49*, 607–627.

Research in California V. P. Clayton and J. E. Birren, The development of wisdom across the life span: a reexamination of an ancient topic. In P. B. Baltes and O. G. Brim (Eds.), *Life-span Development and Behavior* (New York: Academic Press, 1980), pp. 103–135.

Henry David Thoreau H. D. Thoreau, *Walden.* (New York: Bramhall House, 1951), p. 22.

PAGE 177

the reversal of fortune that hovers Psychoanalyst Roy Schafer has much to say about what he calls the "tragic vision," which has much in common with the notion of dispassion. See R. Schafer, The psychoanalytic vision of reality, *International Journal of Psychoanalysis* (1970) *51*, 279–296.

pain passes more quickly if not resisted Rahula, *What the Buddha Taught*, p. 96.

"The wise are controlled" Ibid., p. 132.

"senses are mastered" Ibid., p. 128.

PAGE 178

Freud's idea S. Freud, The ego and the id. II, *The Standard Edition of the Complete Works of Sigmund Freud*, Vol. XIX, trans. James Strachey (London: Hogarth Press, 1923). p. 25.

ancient shamans I am indebted to my friend and colleague, Dr. Irving Allen, for stimulating this insight.

Paul Baltes and his colleagues Baltes and Staudinger, The search for the psychology of wisdom.

PAGE 180

The second of the four Noble Truths Rahula, *What the Buddha Taught*, pp. 29–34.

James Hilton J. Hilton, *Lost Horizon* (New York: William Morrow & Company, 1936), p. 213.

Laurence Hope L. Hope, The Teak Forest, *Complete Love Lyrics* (New York: Dodd, Mead & Company, 1937), p. 17.

Oliver Wendell Holmes, Jr. O. W. Holmes, Jr., *Dead, Yet Living: An Address Delivered at Keene, N.H., Memorial Day, May 30, 1884* (Boston: Ginn, Heath, & Company, 1884), p. 5.

PAGE 181

"getting and begetting" Sir William Osler said it this way: "The natural man has only two primal passions, to get and beget." See W. Osler, *Science and Immortality* (New York: Arno Press, 1977), p. 10.

"Know thyself" Quoted by Plutarch in A Letter of Condolence to Appolonius. In *Plutarch. Moralia. II*, trans. F. C. Babbit, reprinted 1972 (Cambridge, MA: Harvard University Press), p. 183. Socrates expressed similar thoughts. See, for example, Plato, Apology. In *Five Dialogues*, trans. G. M. A. Grube (Indianapolis, IN: Hackett, 1981), p. 41.

wisdom of Lao Tsu Grigg, *The New Lao Tsu*, p. 103.

PAGE 182

Søren Kierkegaard Among his many works on this topic is S. Kierkegaard (1849), *The Sickness unto Death*, trans. Alastair Hannay (New York: Penguin, 1989). Kierkegaard writes here about sickness as being mental, as in despair. But he believes that this despair, as in unrelenting self-analysis, not the pessimistic hopelessness of clinical depression, is a necessary process in the formation of an enduring sense of self. He had in mind the relation of self to a Christian conception of god. In particular, he felt that the people who most needed to go through a painful self-examination were those who professed a Christian belief but whose manifest behavior failed to live up to these standards.

Freud Freud discusses the need for self-understanding from the vantage point of the practicing psychoanalyst, who must guard against what Freud and others have described as countertransference. See, for example, S. Freud, The future prospects of psycho-analytic therapy, *The Standard Edition of the Complete Works of Sigmund Freud. XI*, trans. James Strachey (London: Hogarth Press, 1910), pp. 141–151. Also on the some topic, S. Freud, Recommendations to physicians practising psycho-analysis, *Standard Edition. XII*, pp. 111–120.

Erik Erikson E. H. Erikson, Reflections on Dr. Borg's life cycle; and Erikson, Erikson, and Kivnick, *Vital Involvement in Old Age*.

PAGE 184

Langston Hughes L. Hughes, *Simple Speaks His Mind* (New York: Simon and Schuster, 1950), p. 95.

Goethe The exact quotation is "Old we grow, indeed, but who grows wise?" From J. W. von Goethe, *Faust. II. ii*, trans. Charles Passage (Indianapolis, IN: Bobbs-Merrill, 1965), p. 267.

Plautus The exact quote is "Not by years but by character is wisdom aquired." See Plautus, The three-bob day, *Plautus. II. 2*, trans. Paul Nixon (Cambridge, MA: Harvard University Press), p. 133.

Chapter 10

PAGE 189

the baby bust generation L. R. Offerman and M. K. Gowing, Organizations of the future: changes and challenges, *American Psychologist* (1990) *45*, 95–108.

the portion of the budget allocated for elder health care In 1996, the Medicare and Medicaid outlays were $263.3 billion or 16.9 percent of the budget. In the year 2000, Medicare and Medicaid costs are expected to be 23 percent of the budget. See Office of Management and Budget, *The Budget of the United States Government: Fiscal Year 1998* (Washington, DC: US Government Printing Office, February 1997), p. 303.

PAGE 190

The quality of the fourth quarter of our lives This thought is drawn from the article by Paul Baltes. See P. B. Baltes, On the incomplete architecture of human ontogeny: selection, optimization, and compensation as a foundation of developmental theory, *American Psychologist* (1997) *52*, 366–380.

better cardiovascular functioning R. S. Paffenbarger, Jr., R. T. Hyde, A. L. Wing, and C. Hsieh, Physical activity, all-cause mortality, and longevity of college alumni, *New England Journal of Medicine* (1986) *314*, 605–613. For a more balanced view of the value of exercise, also see L. Hayflick, *How and Why We Age* (New York: Ballantine, 1994), pp. 277–283.

better blood flow to their brains R. L. Rogers, J. S. Meyer, and K. F. Mortel, After reaching retirement age, physical activity sustains cerebral perfusion and cognition, *Journal of the American Geriatric Society* (1990) *38*, 123–128.

aerobic and anaerobic training R. E. Dustman, R. O. Ruhling, E. M. Russell, D. E. Shearer, H. W. Bonekat, J. W. Shigoeka, J. S. Wood, and D. C. Bradford, Aerobic exercise training and improved neuropsychological function of older individuals, *Neurobiology of Aging* (1984) *5*, 35–42.

Physical conditioning also enhances immune system operations Measures of immune system function positively influenced by exercising include total leukocyte counts and interleuken-1 levels. See G. F. Solomon and D. Benton, Psychoneuroimmunologic aspects of aging. In R. Glaser and J. Kiecolt-Glaser (Eds.), *Handbook of Human Stress and Immunity* (San Diego: Academic Press, 1994), pp. 341–363.

lower tension levels, improved mood, and better self-concept C. Folkins and W. Sime, Physical fitness and mental health, *American Psychologist* (1981) *36*, 373–389.

PAGE 191

Elderly volunteers M. Fiatarone, E. Marx, N. Ryan, C. Meredith, L. Lipsitz, and W. Evans, High-intensity strength training in nonagenarians, *Journal of the American Medical Association* (1990) *263*, 3029–3034. The average improvement for knee extensor was 174 percent while in tandem gate speed improved 48 percent for the five subjects who completed assessments at the beginning and the end of the study.

Some argue that frequent heavy workouts M. S. Albert, K. Jones, C. R. Savage, L. Berkman, T. Seeman, D. Boazer, and J. W. Rowe, Predictors of cognitive change in older persons: MacArthur studies of successful aging, *Psychology and Aging* (1995) *10*, 578–589.

Others have found that regular moderate aerobic T. E. Seeman, L. F. Berkman, P. A. Chàrpentier, D. E. Blazer, M. S. Albert, and M. E. Tinetti, Behavioral and psychological predic-tors of physical performance: MacArthur studies of successful aging, *Journal of Gerontology: Medical Sciences* (1995) *50A*, M177–M183.

Our own studies D. H. Powell, *Profiles in Cognitive Aging* (Cambridge, MA: Harvard University Press, 1994), pp. 190–192.

Studies of the brains of laboratory animals M. C. Diamond, *Enriching Heredity: The Impact of the Environment on the Anatomy of the Brain* (New York: Free Press, 1988).

and humans B. Jacobs, M. Schall, and A. B. Scheibel, A quantitative dendritic analysis of Wernicke's area in humans. II. Gender, hemispheric, and environmental factors, *Journal of Comparative Neurology* (1993) *327*, 97–111.

Betty Friedan's Outward Bound experience B. Friedan, *The Fountain of Age* (New York: Simon and Schuster, 1993).

Elderhostelers M. J. Stones, L. Stones, and A. Kozma, Indicators of elite status in persons aged over 60 years: a study of Elderhostelers, *Social Indicators Research* (1987) *19*, 275–285. We have to be a little cautious in attributing causation to the Elderhostel experience itself. It could be that those signing up for these programs are brighter, more mentally stable, and fitter generally than those who do not.

PAGE 192

Our own studies with physicians Powell, *Profiles in Cognitive Aging*, pp. 190–192.

K. Warner Schaie K. W. Schaie, The Seattle Longitudinal Studies of adult intelligence, *Current Directions in Psychological Science* (1993) *2*, 171–175.

PAGE 194

SeniorNet This Web site can be accessed on Internet (www.SeniorNet.org).

opportunities for virtual play are breathtaking For instance, S. Turkle, *Life on the Screen: Identity in the Age of Internet* (New York: Simon and Schuster, 1995).

PAGE 196

more ways we have to deal with stress, the better F. I. Fawzy and N. W. Fawzy, Psychoeducational interventions and health outcomes. In R. Glaser and J. Kiecolt-Glaser (Eds.), *Handbook*, pp. 365–402. This observation has been made by others earlier. For instance, some have described two families of anxiety management techniques, problem-focused and emotion-focused coping. See S. Folkman and R. S. Lazarus, Coping as a mediator of emotion, *Journal of Personality and Social Psychology* (1988) *54*, 466–475. From the point of view of ego defenses, Vaillant has made a similar point. See G. E. Vaillant, *Adaptation to Life* (Boston: Little, Brown, 1977), pp. 276–277.

emotion-focused ways of coping Folkman and Lazarus, Coping as a mediator of emotion.

every way we have of making ourselves feel better has a downside D. H. Powell, *Understanding Human Adjustment: Normal Adaptation Through the Life Cycle* (Boston: Little, Brown, 1983), pp. 67–93.

A half-century ago *Vital Statistics of the United States*, Vol. 2, Mortality, 1988, Section 6, p. 13. Also see G. Spencer, *Projections of the Population of the United States by Age, Sex, and Race: 1988–2080* (Washington, DC: Bureau of the Census, 1989), Table B-5, p. 153.

PAGE 197

older women are generally in better physical shape than men T. Ogawa, R. J. Spina, W. H. Martin, Jr., W. M. Kohrt, K. D. Schechtman, J. O. Holloszy, and A. A. Ehsani, Affects of age, sex, and physical training on cardiovascular response to exercise, *Circulation* (1992) *86*, 26–35.

correlation between the size of social networks and health J. S. House, K. R. Landis, D. Umberson, Social relationships and health, *Science* (1988) *241*, 540–544. Studies of the recovery from myocardial infraction have found that a larger proportion of females than males with fewer close relationships are still alive after six months. See, for instance, L. F. Berkman, The role of social relationships in health promotion, *Psychosomatic Medicine* (1995) *57*, 244–254.

personality changes accompanying aging C. F. Longino, Jr., B. H. Soldo, and K. G. Manton, Demography of aging in the United States. In K. F. Ferraro (Ed.), *Gerontology: Perspectives and Issues* (New York: Springer, 1990), pp. 19–43.

the Center on Aging in Los Angeles R. A. Clay, Retiring poses different challenges for women, *APA Monitor*, December 1996.

PAGE 198

can expect to spend three years of the last season of her life E. M. Crimmins, M. D. Hayward, and Y. Saito, Differentials in active life expectancy in the older population of the United States, *Journal of Gerontology: Social Sciences* (1996) *51B*, S111–S120.

PAGE 199

a study of nearly 13,000 older workers Institute for Social Research, *The Health and Retirement Study* (Ann Arbor, MI: Institute for Social Research, 1993).

The most capable of the 70-year-olds D. H. Powell, *Profiles in Cognitive Aging*, pp. 190–192.

PAGE 202

Like those old-old individuals at the Hebrew Rehabilitation Center for the Aged Fiatarone et al., High-intensity strength training in nonagenarians.

method of loci J. A. Yesavage and T. L. Rose, Semantic elaboration and method of loci: a new trip for older learners, *Experimental Aging Research* (1994) *16*, 155–160.

selection, optimization, and compensation The most complete statement of this theory extending over the life cycle is contained in Baltes, On the incomplete architecture of human ontogeny. An earlier version of this model is P. B. Baltes and M. M. Baltes, Psychological perspectives on successful aging: the model of selective optimization with compensation. In P. B. Baltes and M. M. Baltes (Eds.), *Successful Aging: Perspectives from the Behavioral Sciences* (New York: Cambridge University Press, 1990), pp. 1–34.

Author Index

SUBJECT INDEX